BETWEEN POLITICS AND SCIENCE

The problems of delegation are fundamental to the relationship between politics and science. Politicians must be able to see, and scientists show, that research is conducted with integrity and productivity. In this book, David H. Guston combines political-economic, sociological, and historical insights to analyze the ways the integrity and productivity of research are negotiated in the United States. He shows how, after World War II, a "social contract for science" assumed integrity and productivity were the automatic products of unfettered scientific inquiry. Surveying four decades of controversies in science policy, Guston demonstrates how this assumption endured inquiries into the loyalty, the financial accountability, and the technological goals of scientists. But in the 1980s, as his rich empirical studies show, cases of misconduct in science and flagging economic performance broke the trust between politics and science. To reconstitute this trust and resolve the problems of delegation, scientists and nonscientists now collaborate in new "boundary organizations." Guston's focus on these boundary organizations reveals hidden layers of detail in the management of science policy and suggests that deft institutional design can create stable partnerships between politics and science.

David H. Guston is Assistant Professor of Public Policy in the Edward J. Bloustein School of Planning and Public Policy at Rutgers, The State University of New Jersey. He is also a faculty associate of the Belfer Center for Science and International Affairs at Harvard University's John F. Kennedy School of Government. Professor Guston coauthored *Informed Legislatures: Coping with Science in a Democracy* and coedited *The Fragile Contract: University Science and the Federal Government.* His articles have appeared in *Science and Public Policy, Social Studies of Science, Policy Studies Review, Policy Sciences,* and many other publications.

BETWEEN POLITICS AND SCIENCE

Assuring the Integrity and Productivity of Research

DAVID H. GUSTON
Rutgers, The State University of New Jersey

PUBLISHED BY THE PRESS SYNDICATE OF THE UNIVERSITY OF CAMBRIDGE
The Pitt Building, Trumpington Street, Cambridge, United Kingdom

CAMBRIDGE UNIVERSITY PRESS
The Edinburgh Building, Cambridge CB2 2RU, UK http://www.cup.cam.ac.uk
40 West 20th Street, New York, NY 10011-4211, USA http://www.cup.org
10 Stamford Road, Oakleigh, Melbourne 3166, Australia
Ruiz de Alarcón 13, 28014 Madrid, Spain

First published 2000

Printed in the United States of America

Typeface Sabon 10/12 pt. *System* DeskTopPro$_{/ux}$ [BV]

A catalog record for this book is available from the British Library.

Library of Congress Cataloging in Publication data
Guston, David H.
Between politics and science : assuring the integrity and productivity of research / David H. Guston.
p. cm.
Includes bibliographical references and index.
ISBN 0-521-65318-5
1. Science and state – United States. I. Title.
Q127.U6G87 1999
338.973'06 – dc21 99-12786
CIP

ISBN 0 521 65318 5 hardback

To my parents

Which is the cause, that the doctrine of Right and Wrong, is perpetually disputed, both by the Pen and the Sword: Whereas the doctrine of Lines, and Figures, is not so; because men care not, in that subject what be truth, as a thing that crosses no mans ambition, profit, or lust. For I doubt not, but if it had been a thing contrary to any mans right of dominion, That the three Angles of a Triangle should be equall to two Angles of a Square; *that doctrine should have been, if not disputed, yet by the burning of all books of Geometry, suppressed, as farre as he whom it concerned was able.* – Thomas Hobbes ([1651] 1983: 165–66, emphasis in the original).

Contents

Tables and Figures

Tables

Figures

Abbreviations

AAAS	American Association for the Advancement of Science
ADAMHA	Alcohol, Drug Abuse, and Mental Health Administration
AIDS	acquired immune deficiency syndrome
AK	Arkansas
AL	Alabama
APA	Administrative Procedures Act
CA	California
COSPUP	Committee on Science and Public Policy
CRADA	cooperative research and development agreement
CT	Connecticut
D	Democrat
DAB	Departmental Appeals Board
DHEW	Department of Health, Education, and Welfare
DNA	deoxyribonucleic acid
DOD	Department of Defense
FBI	Federal Bureau of Investigation
FCST	Federal Council for Science and Technology
FDA	Food and Drug Administration
FL	Florida
FLC	Federal Laboratory Consortium (for Technology Transfer)
FOIA	Freedom of Information Act
FSA	Federal Security Agency
FTTA	Federal Technology Transfer Act (of 1986)
FY	fiscal year

GA	Georgia
GAO	General Accounting Office
GPRA	Government Performance and Results Act (of 1993)
HHS	(Department of) Health and Human Services
HIV	human immunodeficiency virus
H.R.	House Resolution
HUAC	House Un-American Activities Committee
I	Independent
IA	Iowa
ILO	Institutional Liaison Office
IN	Indiana
IPA	institutional patent agreement
IRPOS	Interdisciplinary Research on Problems Relevant to Our Society
IRS	Internal Revenue Service
KS	Kansas
LA	Louisiana
MA	Massachusetts
ME	Maine
MIT	Massachusetts Institute of Technology
MN	Minnesota
MPO	misconduct policy officer
MT	Montana
MTA	materials transfer agreement
NAS	National Academy of Sciences
NASA	National Aeronautics and Space Administration
NATO	North Atlantic Treaty Organization
NC	North Carolina
NCI	National Cancer Institute
NHLBI	National Heart, Lung, and Blood Institute
NIH	National Institutes of Health
NSF	National Science Foundation
NTTA	National Technology Transfer Act (of 1995)
NV	Nevada
NY	New York

OH	Ohio
OIG	Office of Inspector General
OMAR	Office of Medical Applications of Research
ONR	Office of Naval Research
OPRR	Office of Protection from Research Risks
OR	Oregon
ORI	Office of Research Integrity
ORTA	Office of Research and Technology Applications
OSI	Office of Scientific Integrity
OSIR	Office of Scientific Integrity Review
OSRD	Office of Scientific Research and Development
OST	Office of Science and Technology
OSTP	Office of Science and Technology Policy
OTA	Office of Technology Assessment
OTT	Office of Technology Transfer
PA	Pennsylvania
PHS	Public Health Service
P.L.	Public Law
PMA	Pharmaceutical Manufacturers Association
R	Republican
R&D	research and development
RAC	Recombinant DNA Advisory Committee
RANN	Research Applied to National Needs
RI	Rhode Island
RIAP	Research Integrity Appeals Board
S.	Senate (bill)
TDC	Technology Development Coordinator
TMT	Technology Management Team
TRACES	Technology in Retrospect and Critical Events in Science
TUP	Technology Utilization Program
TX	Texas
WA	Washington (State)
WI	Wisconsin
WV	West Virginia

Preface

People often think of politics and science as entirely separate enterprises. Science is engaged in the high pursuit of truth, and politics is engaged in the baser pursuit of interests. Even for those to whom politics is a higher calling, pursuing justice or fairness, the distinction between these concepts and truth is an all too frequent and vexing occurrence. Moreover, justice and fairness are often impossible to define without reference to interests. Scientific truth, however, is often defined by its disinterestedness.

In this formulation, politics and science are clearly and precisely distinguished by the presence or absence of interests. Despite this demarcation, however, they remain in close proximity: the bright line between politics and science is a fine one.

Science policy perches uncomfortably on this fine, bright line. To one side is the rough and tumble, the horse trading and pork barreling, the colorful bustle of politics. To the other side is the ivory-towered, rational contemplation and methodical pursuit of truth. The traditional concern of science policy has been the transactions across this frontier. Policy for science involves the direction of funds and accountability from politics to science. Science in policy involves the provision of expertise from science to politics.[1] Its central problem in either case is the on-going struggle between the plausibly corrupting influence of politics as usual and the potentially unaccountable self-governance of an authoritative professional community. The history of science policy is often a history of the border skirmishes and rapprochements between the two parties.

Although science is a most intellectual of human pursuits, the scholarly coverage of this relationship between politics and science has often forgotten (or foresaken) the intellectual side of science policy and become lost in the particular battle for fiscal increments. Part of the goal of my discussion is to reinfuse science policy making with the understanding that budgets – while policies in and of themselves[2] – do not circumscribe all of policy, and that how we think about science, and about politics, is central to how we make policy for science.

To accomplish this goal, I want to examine that boundary between politics and science and, at least intellectually, expand it into a space that can be explored and explained. Does that liminal space have a structure and, if so, why is it structured in that way? How do we decide where politics and science – and therefore science policy – begin, and where they end? I find the opportunity for this study in areas of mutual interest to politics and science, the assurance of the integrity and productivity of research.

This book has many origins. One significant experience was my attendance at a NATO Advanced Studies Institute, "Managing Science in the Steady State," a decade ago. I gratefully acknowledge the travel grant I received from the National Science Foundation (NSF) to that meeting, for me a watershed, in northern Tuscany. A second experience was my work at the National Academy of Sciences for the Committee on Science, Engineering, and Public Policy on its study of scientific integrity. I owe many thanks to Larry McCray, Rosemary Chalk, Barry Gold, the panel members, and other friends and colleagues from that time.

This book began as my dissertation in the Department of Political Science at MIT. While working on the dissertation, I helped Ken Keniston and Sheila Widnall organize a faculty seminar at the MIT Program in Science, Technology, and Society, which eventually became *The Fragile Contract*. There are many ideas shared among the dissertation, that book, and this one.[3] Indeed, I remain indebted to all the people to whom I was indebted for the dissertation, particularly: from MIT, Gene Skolnikoff, Charlie Weiner, Charles Stewart, and Uday Mehta; and from the Belfer Center for Science and International Affairs at Harvard University's Kennedy School of Government (where I spent two happy years as a pre-doctoral and then post-doctoral student) Lewis M. Branscomb and Harvey Brooks. Parts of this book began as separate articles, and for commenting on drafts of those I thank Mark Brown, Bob Cook-Deegan, Steve Flank, Tom Gieryn, David Hart, Eric Kupferberg, Frank Laird, Richard Lehne, Kelly Moore, Arie Rip, Jeffrey Stine, and Stephen Turner, as well as the editors and anonymous referees who helped me improve these papers. Alex Holzman, Erin O'Toole, and others at Cambridge University Press labored generously on my behalf, and several anonymous referees of the manuscript helped me refine it.

Clinton Andrews, Bruce Bimber, Dietmar Braun, Michael Crow, and Jo-Ann Graziano read the complete manuscript and provided many helpful comments and observations. Dan Benson and Jorge Casimiro (the latter funded by a small grant from the Rutgers University Research Council) provided timely research assistance, and Laurie Santos and Mary Jean Lush dedicated administrative assistance.

Introduction: Making Space for Science Policy

> It is not that science did not deliver in so many ways over so many years, but rather that different times require different types of accountability.
> – Neal Lane, then director of the National Science Foundation (1997: 127).

In his important but now rarely read book, *The Scientific Estate*, political scientist Don K. Price (1965) devised an intellectual framework that sought to accommodate a free yet accountable science and a pluralistic and representative democracy. To resolve this thoroughly modern problem, Price found premodern inspiration. He drew on the medieval system of estates to organize what he called the "spectrum from truth to power."[1]

Four estates comprise Price's spectrum, and each is distinct in its pursuit of a defining function. The political estate pursues action and power, constrained by the forms of democratic governance. The scientific estate pursues knowledge and truth, constrained by the norms of scientific work. Between politics and science lie the administrative and professional estates, respectively. The administrative estate applies general or interdisciplinary knowledge according to public rules and laws, under the close oversight of the political estate. The professional estate applies specific or disciplinary knowledge according to private codes and norms, guided by the scientific estate.

One of Price's contributions in the formulation of the spectrum from truth to power is his interposing of the domains of administration and the professions between politics and science. By exploring this interposition, Price makes analytical space for science policy in an area that is neither pure knowledge nor pure action, but that has specific intellectual and practical foundations. A second contribution is his "twofold principle of freedom and responsibility" that governs relations among the estates:

> (1) the closer the estate is to the end of the spectrum that is concerned solely with truth, the more it is entitled to freedom and self-government; and (2) the closer it gets to the exercise of power, the less it is permitted to organize itself as a corporate entity, and the more it is required to submit to the test of political responsibility (Price 1981: 108).

This principle provides attractive normative guidance for a representative democracy like the United States, reliant on a pluralist conception of civil society and a vision of science as an independent but politically relevant – even sustaining – enterprise. A third contribution is his suggestion that, although conflict among the estates will occur, there will be no perpetual civil war among them, at least in the United States, because of its robust traditions of the sharing of power through constitutionalism and the division of sovereignty through pluralism and federalism.

But these contributions should not completely mask some of the shortcomings of Price's scheme. One could dispute, for example, the idea behind the spectrum that "truth" and "power" are completely separable concepts.[2] One could also criticize the vague differentiation between the descriptive and prescriptive aspects of the spectrum, which is somewhat characteristic of an analysis so focused on the functional roles of groups within society.

For the immediate purpose, however, there are specific shortcomings allied with each of the three contributions that must be addressed. First, although Price (1981: 106) acknowledges that the four estates "are by no means sharply distinguished from one another even in theory, but fall along a gradation or spectrum within our political system" and that advances in science itself often serve to reconfigure the functional boundaries between the estates, he focuses on the pursuits within each estate's boundaries and deals far too sparsely with the transactions across them. That is, although Price creates space for science policy between politics and science, he still relies too much on analytically and functionally imposed boundaries between estates. Second, each aspect of Price's twofold principle flows in only one direction. Although together they make for a reciprocal relation of sorts, it is possible that elements of freedom and responsibility flow in the directions opposite to the ones Price specifies. There may be mutual relations or dependencies between politics and science that Price does not account for. Third, Price's argument about the limits of conflict among the estates by tradition seems unsatisfactory because it does not suggest why those traditions need to be adhered to for the sake of politics and science. Some additional mechanism for stable engagement between politics and science needs to be described.

Price thereby leaves us with three problems: the problem of boundaries, the problem of mutuality, and the problem of stability. Combined, they suggest the role of science policy between politics and science may be larger and more complicated than Price contemplated. We therefore have to create still more intellectual space for science policy at this uncomfortable juncture between politics and science, contemplating not just the estates but the boundaries between them, not just the unilateral relations but the mutual ones, and not just tradition but other reasons for stability at these boundaries.

This space for science policy between politics and science is not historically unknown. In the 1880s, for example, a special commission of the U.S. Congress examined the newly burgeoning government research agencies with a neophyte's eye. After World War II, the United States had an important debate about the relation between government and science that had grown of wartime necessity, and about how that relation should be modified to continue in an appropriate fashion for peacetime. Vannevar Bush's duly famous volume, *Science: The Endless Frontier* ([1945] 1960), is the principal text of the postwar debate. John R. Steelman's less famous but similarly worthy *Science and Public Policy* (1947a-d) is another example.

The major changes in the postwar era, including the enormous growth at the National Institutes of Health in the 1950s and the creation of the National Aeronautics and Space Administration in 1959, were consistent with the future as charted by Bush and Steelman. On occasion, conflicts between politics and science broke the surface, such as the loyalty of federally funded researchers or the risks of genetic research. For the most part, however, until the late 1970s, science policy sailed smoothly on, steering by a polestar last sighted around 1950.

What has happened from the late 1970s through the 1990s is the primary subject of this book, and the occasion for my reexamination of the role of science policy. The 1980s, in particular, were a tumultuous time for science policy, as issues broke across the headlines of the popular press: SCANDALS IN ACADEMIC SCIENCE—MISCONDUCT BY PROMINENT RESEARCHERS, FINANCIAL IMPROPRIETIES AT PRESTIGIOUS UNIVERSITIES; HIGH-TECH ECONOMY EBBS—MANUFACTURING JOBS LOST, BALANCE OF TRADE IN HIGH-TECH GOODS TURNS NEGATIVE. Unlike other episodes in the 1980s that have important and specific historical precedents (e.g., conflicts over the commercialization of academic research), the scandals and the economic problems do not. In their novelty, these issues dashed expectations about the scientific community: Science is the pursuit of Truth. Basic research leads to technological innovation.

Of course, such issues are more subtle, less epigrammatic. But in the context of a flagging national economy, a growing distrust of governing institutions, and a relatively stringent fiscal environment for federal spending on domestic programs, the very salience of these issues eroded their nuance. Even if many details escaped observation, or were conspicuously or negligently ignored by self-serving participants, a distinct core of trouble remained. The federal patrons of research were confused. They appreciated the sound bite simplicity – and scientists encouraged them in their appreciation – that science is the pursuit of Truth and that academic research leads to technological innovation. It was as if, convinced for decades that they were steering with Polaris at their back and headed toward a warmer, brighter future, politicians poked their heads out of their cabins and found instead the weather was colder and stormier. They wanted to know if this unpredicted change was a minor aberration that would blow over soon, or whether some major course correction was needed.

This book is an analysis of science policy confronted with these disturbances – "analysis" rather than "history" or "sociology" because my approach is multi-disciplinary. I set a historical context, relating how politicians and scientists behaved when they first encountered the problems in the 1880s and providing some detail of how they attempted to settle them in the immediate postwar period. I delve into sociological detail to describe the performance of new institutions created to help politicians and scientists construct the boundaries and pursue mutual goals between politics and science. I apply a political-economic model of organizations to elaborate my perspective on the durable structure of science policy and propose a mechanism for encouraging stability at the boundary between politics and science. But all the while my goal is to illuminate the process of making science policy and, by casting a new light, help to improve that process.

The durable structure of science policy is grounded in the difficulties the patrons of research and the performers of research have in dealing with one another. The patrons, often ignorant of the content of research, have to make sure they are getting their money's worth on their investment. The performers have to make sure they can demonstrate the sufficiency of their performance to their patrons. I characterize this mutual problem by using principal-agent theory (also known as ideal contracting theory), which examines organizational relations as if different parts of an organization made contracts with one another. In other fields of inquiry, principal-agent theory helps explain why firms are organized the way they are. For example, it explains why some goods and services are provided by outside suppliers but others by vertically integrated departments of the firm; why health insurance companies attempt to exclude from coverage people with preexisting conditions; or why fire insurance companies employ arson investigators. In the case of science policy, it helps explain why members of Congress hold hearings to investigate allegations of research misconduct, or pass laws to allow researchers to profit from the commercialization of their federally funded work.

A primary aim of science policy is to respond to two difficulties created by this situation: one, to assure the integrity of the performance of publicly funded research and two, to assure its productivity. As I will elaborate in the first chapter, both of these ends can be expressed as unavoidable consequences of the delegation of authority from the research patron to the performer. That is, they can be described by principal-agent theory. They are also ends shared by politics and science, in the sense that both are better off if research is conducted with demonstrable integrity and productivity.

I argue that it is how the government accomplishes these two tasks that should define any periodization of science policy, rather than, for example, funding trends or partisan priorities for research.[3] The period prior to World War II largely ignored these difficulties, except on the early and prominent occasion of the Allison Commission of the 1880s when patrons in the federal government recognized their significance for the first time. The postwar period until the 1980s developed an elegant ideology, often called "the social contract for science," that, while not entirely ignoring the problems, submerged them by assuming their automatic solution. In the current period, they have resurfaced and the automaticity of their solution has been forcefully rejected.

These periods are what could be called regimes for science policy. Something like the "republics" of the United States that Lowi delineates in the "end of Liberalism" (1979) and the "end of the Republican Era" (1995) but in a narrower domain, these regimes consist of a complex set of institutions and ideas. The institutions can be organizations of brick and mortar, like the National Institutes of Health (NIH) or the National Science Foundation (NSF). Or they can be less concrete institutions like rules, policies, and procedures, which accompany their daily routines. The ideas are simply what participants and observers think about the nature of the institutions, and the nature of their own roles, and the nature of Science and Government writ large.

I argue that the boundaries of science policy are to be found or, more precisely, to be made in these institutions. Within their walls and under their rules is the sheltered space where the awkward coupling of politics and science occurs. As I will also elaborate in Chapter 1, there are some institutions at this boundary of politics and science that help mediate between the two and bring stability to what otherwise might be intrusion or tumult. These boundary organizations, not contemplated in the functional scheme of Price, mediate between politics and science by engaging in the assurance of mutual goals such as the integrity and productivity of research.

How a science policy regime goes about specifying these assurances and boundaries is unique – different types of accountability required by different times. In the 1880s, Congress created the Allison Commission to sort out that era's form of accountability. The commission debated whether the scientific bureaus of the federal government should be treated differently from the other bureaus, and it concluded the scientific bureaus should be subject to the same type of oversight and control through the appropriations process. The postwar social contract for science, however, was a tacit agreement between government and science that science is a little more special than other domains. It held that scientific integrity and productivity are more or less an automatic function, steered by some invisible hand. Acceptance of this tacit agreement was prescriptive of certain types of institutional relations that attempt to impose a distinct boundary between politics and science. Rejection of the agreement is prescriptive of different institutions. Beginning in the late 1970s, politicians felt that expectations of integrity and productivity were unmet, and they began to question and then reject this tacit agreement. They then created institutions at the boundary of politics and science to mark a new science policy regime.

In this new regime, the tacit agreement about the automatic integrity and productivity of science has evaporated. To put it more starkly, politicians stopped trusting science to have integrity or be productive all by itself. In place of trust is now the need to oversee, to measure, and, in the bureaucratese that so often accompanies the loss of trust, to "incentivize." Getting used to oversight, measurement, and incentives is a difficult task for both politicians and scientists. It requires different institutional forms, different types of information, and different kinds of behaviors. This book is thus not about the politicization of science, broadly speaking. Rather, it is about distinguishing the present system from the past system, based on a specific analytical approach.

The particular question of the integrity of sponsored research in the United States attracted the attention of the research patrons even as far back as the 1880s. The Allison Commission inquired into whether military discipline was necessary to ensure the integrity of data collection and reporting in the Army Signal Service, and whether John Wesley Powell, director of the Geological Survey, maintained appropriate relationships with contractors in universities who analyzed and stored materials collected by government employees. In the postwar period, the integrity of research was not prominent on the formal agenda of science policy, but the meaning of the political accountability of research was an important source of controversy and the important texts of the period show that concern for integrity was not far from the surface.

Indeed, the relative invisibility of the question of integrity from this period for the next several decades is an important fact. Scientific fraud had occasionally aroused professional and even public interest, as the relatively familiar cases of Piltdown man, the midwife toad, the patchwork mouse, and the twin studies conducted by the late Sir Cyril Burt had all done.[4] But a spate of cases in the late 1970s and the early 1980s involving federally funded researchers triggered not just a small publishing industry but congressional investigations as well.[5] At that time, representatives of the research community assured the congressional principals that the delegation of authority inherent in research grants was safe. Philip Handler, then president of the National Academy of Sciences, declared before Congress that the research community handled cases of misconduct "in an effective, democratic and self-correcting mode" (U.S. House 1981: 11). But as Senator Paula Hawkins (R-FL) later admitted, these episodes of misconduct raised in members of Congress "latent suspicions and doubts" (U.S. Senate 1981: 242). In response to these initial inquiries, Congress passed legislation emphasizing the role of research agencies and applicant institutions in investigating and adjudicating cases of research misconduct (Guston 1994b).

Cases of research misconduct continued to mount, however, and a prominent allegation involving a Nobel laureate and a maltreated whistle-blower attracted more hostile congressional inquiries.[6] The apparent shortcomings on the part of universities in investigating and adjudicating cases led Congress to prompt NIH, NSF, and other research agencies to create their own capacities to oversee the universities and investigate and adjudicate allegations of misconduct independently. These new capacities – in NIH, the Office of Research Integrity (formerly the Office of Scientific Integrity), and in NSF, a unit of the Office of Inspector General – perform exactly the kind of monitoring that principal-agent theory would lead one to expect from a patron concerned with the integrity of research. They are also the boundary organizations within which the science policy front is negotiated and eventually stabilized.

The question of what good or value is derived from the federal investment in science has similarly been present in all eras of science policy. In the 1880s, the question concerned the economic value of sponsored research: if it had value, why was it not privately funded? And if it had no economic value, why was it publicly funded? One of the primary enterprises of government science, mapping the still unfamiliar expanse of the country, seemed to have direct commercial implications. It made advocates of limited government and unfettered markets uncomfortable, even as it encouraged the supporters of a more ambitious government role in industrial expansion.

After World War II, flush with the successes of the atomic bomb, radar, and penicillin, advocates of federally sponsored science argued that basic research is a unique source of military, commercial, and medical innovation, and such innovation would flow naturally out of the support of research in universities.[7] But after the late 1970s brought economic malaise, politicians began to focus more on how to increase the economic consequences – the productivity – of federally funded research. Politicians recognized the benefits that might flow from science were not free of cost, as the earlier models assumed (Alic et al. 1992), and President Carter asked Congress for uniform patent rules and the retention of patent ownership by universities and small businesses on government-sponsored inventions in order to facilitate the commercialization of sponsored research.

Most of the consequent changes have restructured incentives for the performers of research. For example, they granted more consistently liberal intellectual property rights over innovations underwritten with federal money, and offered monetary inducements and other incentives for government researchers to engage in technology transfer to industry and cooperative research with private-sector partners in pursuit of science-based commercial innovations. As in the monitoring of scientific integrity, this technology policy legislation plays out the logic of principal-agent theory by attempting to provide incentives to researchers who themselves had been successfully engaging in commercial innovation.[8] It also created organizations in which the boundary between politics and science could be complicated and clarified with every new innovation.

Under the old regime of the social contract for science, the institutional arrangements attempted to enforce a clear separation of politics and science, akin to the functional and analytical demarcation that Price exploited. This separation was rationalized by certain ideas about science developed by sociologists – and accepted by politicians and scientists alike – that science is a distinctive community, like the one characterized by sociologist Robert Merton (1973: Chapter 13) as abiding by norms of communalism, universalism, disinterestedness, and organized skepticism. As science policy scholar Sheila Jasanoff (1987: 196) has written, "Much of the authority of science in the twentieth century rests as well on its success in persuading decision-makers and the public that the Mertonian norms present an accurate picture of the way science 'really works.' " But the new arrangements, rather than attempting to clearly separate politics and science, questioned these ideas of science and brought the two into even more intimate contact. In dealing explicitly with the integrity and productivity of science, the last two decades have reconfigured science policy both practically and ideologically. The state's new role in science policy has become a collaboration with scientists to assure the integrity and productivity of the science it funds. The creation of new institutions to manage integrity and productivity across the boundary of politics and science has made that boundary more flexible, allowing it to be negotiated within and contained by the new boundary organizations.

To render this argument, I reinterpret a good deal of the traditional literature of postwar science policy in the principal-agent context. I also offer two detailed and original case studies, grounded in extensive documentary review and more than three score interviews with political actors, scientists, and the science policy specialists between them. The primary reason for investigating in tandem the integrity and the productivity of science is their connection as two aspects of the difficulty of delegation inherent in science policy. They are related, as Price (1979: 77) explained, to the means and the ends of that delegation: the means of a science free from governmental fetters and the ends of research as a foundation for technological innovation. Thus, the policy changes in the 1980s regarding the integrity and the productivity of science demand scholarly attention, and they reward it by offering a window on the new and more nuanced relation between politics and science that has evolved. Nevertheless, I cover but a small part of the complete dimensions of the integrity and productivity of science, which extend across all federal agencies sponsoring research and many pieces of federal legislation beyond those discussed in this book.

I apply this analysis of the structure and boundaries of science policy to case studies about the assurance of the integrity and productivity of biomedical research, specifically activities of the National Institutes of Health. NIH warrants this scrutiny not because of any failures on its part, although some of the most spectacular issues in scientific integrity and the commercialization of federally sponsored research have involved NIH and provide rich material for study. Rather, I focus on NIH for a suite of more positive reasons. First, as I describe in later chapters, NIH is characterized well historically and politically, and its position regarding the issues of integrity and productivity has been one of entrepreneurial leadership. Second, the scale of its enterprise is enormous and represents a considerable share of all research activity. Its proposed research budget in fiscal year (FY) 2000 of more than $15 billion includes $9.3 billion to universities and colleges, or 60% of federal support to academic institutions and one third of all research support to academic institutions, as well as more than half of all federal civilian research characterized as "basic" (AAAS 1999: 97).[9] Third, the research performed by both its grantees, as well as by its employees in its own intramural laboratories, seeks fundamental knowledge in the pursuit of NIH's public health mission. Characterized as "use-inspired basic research," this orientation has helped NIH mitigate radical changes in the political environment that threatened federal research and can serve as a model for NSF and other research sponsors (Stokes 1997). Not only do these characteristics of leadership and the scale and character of research make NIH interesting to study in its own right, but they help make arguments derived from its study more generalizable because of its actual and potential influence over the research enterprise derived from them.

I present this argument according to the following plan. Chapter 1, as I have alluded, provides background in principal-agent theory and boundary work necessary to sustain the later discussion. The chapter describes how the difficulty of delegation, formalized by principal-agent theory, is the primary problem of science policy and how it can thus structure a great deal of science policy analysis. It also points to a potential shortcoming in principal-agent theory when applied to science policy, which it suggests can be remedied by adding a more detailed sociological approach to the somewhat stylized political-economic core. This approach, a constructivist one to the sociology of science that emphasizes the observation of how actors attempt to demarcate science from nonscience, allows me to propose the idea of a boundary organization at the frontier between politics and science. I conclude the chapter with a historical prelude of sorts. A short account of the Allison Commission of the late nineteenth century presages aspects of my argument.

Chapter 2 attempts to fathom the "social contract for science," a term for the old regime of science policy and its major effort to solve problems of integrity and productivity. First, I demonstrate the plausibility of even discussing a social contract with respect to science and then elaborate the connotations of its terminology as used by scholars and policy makers. Next I delve into history, searching beneath the conflict between Vannevar Bush's *Science: The Endless Frontier* and its political opponents – to which scholars usually attend – and seeking the perspectives about science and governance they held in common. I argue that the social contract for science was the agreement in the immediate postwar era about the terms of the new relationship between science and government: the scientific community can best manage the integrity and productivity of its enterprise by allowing automatic or self-regulatory mechanisms to engage these challenges. I install this agreement as the baseline, to use as a measure for changes in the relationship between politics and science.

In Chapter 3, I hold the variety of potential challenges to its authority during the postwar era up to the baseline. To judge them, I developed criteria focused on the distinction between blunt and refined manipulation of science by political patrons as suggested by principal-agent theory. The challenges began almost immediately with inquiries into the loyalty of federally sponsored researchers. They also included questions about how agencies such as NIH disbursed their escalating appropriations, attempts by Congress to provide programmatic direction to research agencies in exchange for still more funds, and the potential hazards posed by new lines of research, for example, recombinant DNA, on society. Yet for all the political strife these challenges caused, I argue that they did not compromise the social contract for science because they failed to alter the basic structures of how the sponsors of research deal with questions of the integrity and productivity of science. The challenges all focused on clumsy attempts to manipulate the inputs to science, rather than more refined attempts to intervene in interactions among scientists.

Throughout this period, Congress struggled to acquire more information about the burgeoning research enterprise. In response to its own role in growing science, as well as to keep pace with growth in the executive branch, Congress began to institutionalize an ability to oversee and manage science and technology on its own. New committees and congressional agencies helped Congress reduce the information gap between it and the research agencies, a gap that had made it much more difficult to oversee and manage their activities. Although these new congressional institutions in themselves did not cause the changes I describe in subsequent chapters, they assisted Congress in overcoming the lack of information that plagued its delegatory relationship with science. Ultimately, they helped in overhauling the social contract for science by providing a greater capacity for the more information-intensive policies of monitoring and incentives implemented in the 1980s.

Chapter 4 analyzes this overhaul with respect to the integrity of science. Subsequent to its first inquiries about integrity, Congress provided legislative guidance to the scientific community about how it was expected to deal with problems of scientific integrity. But as cases of alleged misconduct continued to mount, Congress pressed for bolder solutions, and NIH responded by creating the Office of Scientific Integrity, later reorganized as the Office of Research Integrity (ORI). The chapter relates how Congress discredited the attempts of the scientific community to regulate its own integrity, and how the creation of ORI served as the focal point for boundary conflicts over the procedures used to investigate allegations of misconduct. Responsible both to political principals in Congress and in the scientific community, ORI is an example of what I call a boundary organization. Its existence is evidence that the scheme for the automatic management of scientific integrity under the social contract for science has been overthrown and replaced by a more formal system of incentives and monitoring, as the principal-agent framework would suggest. ORI represents a new space for science policy by being a formal mechanism for the management of scientific integrity, and by internalizing the boundary between science and politics over the issue of adjudicating research misconduct.

Chapter 5 analyzes the overhaul of the social contract for science with respect to the productivity of science. Congress discredited the old model of directing the productivity of science from the distance of appropriations – applied from the time of the Allison Commission to the time of the War on Cancer but with mixed success – and applied principal-agent reasoning to create specific incentives within the traditional reward system of science to encourage productivity as Congress defined it. This chapter relates the story of a new policy toward technology transfer consistently pursued since 1980. Through the example of the boundary organization of the Office of Technology Transfer (OTT) at NIH, I show how a more collaborative relationship over boundary work between scientists and nonscientists can produce a more stable relationship between the two. OTT represents a new space for science policy by formally managing the productivity of research and by internalizing the boundary between politics and science over the creation of economic value and its indicators.

In Chapter 6, I extend some of the major themes of this book. To complete the argument about the social contract for science, I review a number of previously elaborated schemes for the periodization of science policy, arguing that the claim presented in this book surpasses the others in the clarity and appropriateness of its criteria of change and its breadth of coverage. I go into further detail about the nature of boundary organizations, comparing the experiences of ORI and OTT at the frontier of politics and science. I also explore the limits of the new system of monitoring and creating incentives and the additional elements of policies for integrity and productivity beyond the boundary organizations. I conclude by speculating that the more formal system, built on cornerstones of an eroded trust, could be the foundation for a renewed trust between politics and science.

1

Science Policy: Structure and Boundaries

Our survival depends on our ability to judge things by their results and our ability to establish relations of confidence and responsibility so that we can take advantage of what other people know. We could not live in modern society if we did not place confidence daily in a thousand ways in pharmacists, surgeons, pilots, bank clerks, engineers, plumbers, technicians, lawyers, civil servants, accountants, courts, telephone operators, craftsmen and a host of others. . . . Democracy is like nearly everything else we do; it is a form of collaboration of ignorant people and experts.

– E. E. Schattschneider, *The Semi-Sovereign People* (1960: 137).

Introduction

To E. E. Schattschneider's characterization of democracy as a form of collaboration among the ignorant and the expert we might add, so too is science policy. The nature of science policy as a delegation of authority from patron to performer has befuddled both from the very beginning. Ignorant patrons worry about getting their money's worth for their delegation of funds and authority to the researchers. Expert researchers face the similarly unenviable task of performing for patrons who might not appreciate it.

Another way of inquiring about the centrality of delegation in science policy is by asking how nonscientists get scientists to do what we, as citizens, have decided. By focusing on the "how?" of science policy rather than the "how much?" of research funding, this line of inquiry appears to step away from the traditional center of conflict in science policy. It is true of course that budgets are the epicenter of political debate about research and the sites where analysts have found expression of differing political priorities (e.g., Barfield 1982). But science policy analysis often has been too involved in the question of "how much?" to the neglect of the question of "how?" The question of "how?" must be asked and answered for any answer to "how much?". Moreover, in the developing "steady state" of research funding, "how much?" is a question settled by increments at the margin of an overall budget and "how?" becomes ever more important (Cozzens, Healey, Rip, and Ziman 1990). My account of science policy is concerned with the structure of science policy – with its relatively durable processes and institutions – rather than with its budgets, which may be alternatively incremental or irrelevantly volatile.

The first section of this chapter describes an analytical framework for examining problems of delegation known as principal-agent theory, which has become an important analytic tool for casting the relationship between politics and science.[1] Roughly put, principal-agent theory as applied to science policy means the government is the principal who requests the agent – science – to perform certain tasks because the principal is not capable of performing them directly. The agent performs the delegated task, out of self-interest, but with some of the consequential benefits accruing to the principal as well. Because of the implicit exchange in this delegation, principal-agent theory is also known as ideal contracting theory. The centrality of the research contract or grant, provided by a public institution to a private institution or individual performing scientific research, is prima facie evidence that principal-agent theory should be an important analytical method for science policy. The contracting aspect also hints at some ways of managing the problems of mutuality and of stability across the boundary between politics and science.

An account of science policy must be informed by an account of policy making in general. The institutions of governance were not created to govern science alone. The apparatus of science policy has historically been largely the apparatus of economic policy, health policy, security policy, and so forth.[2] We need some understanding of the broader structure of policy making in order to understand the specific structure of science policy making. Fortunately, principal-agent theory provides such a broader structure because, as discussed below, the problems of delegation are not limited to scientific agents, although they may be exacerbated by them.

An account of science policy must also be informed by an account of science in general. The idea of science as an objective enterprise populated by an apolitical elite informed the first generation of science policy studies.[3] Political scientist Harvey Sapolsky (1975: 79) argued that "advocacy" in this literature "often substituted for analysis," and it consequently failed to produce useful policy instruments or to generate much cumulative scholarship. The contrary idea of science as a political enterprise populated by an interested elite followed, promoted by journalistic accounts of the scientific establishment.[4] But this idea overplayed the difference between the ostensibly political behavior of scientists and our expectations of an apolitical science. The role of this literature was its repositioning of science as an interest, but its value was mostly shock value. Its message still appealed to the earlier model: if only scientists would be less venal and live up to their creed, then science policy would be better made.

The second section of the chapter appeals to a better account of science, called constructivism. Derived from techniques in anthropology and sociology and from newer answers to old problems in the history and philosophy of science, constructivism takes an empirical and skeptical – indeed, a scientific – view of science.[5] The constructivist approach casts science as a social activity much like any other occupation or profession, and it provides social explanations for why this particular profession manages to produce knowledge that is reliable. Constructivism is valuable for science policy because, contrary to claims by those who have examined only its margins, constructivist studies of science provide the close, empirical, reasoned, and unvarnished account of scientific work that is necessary for informed policy making.

Additionally, the constructivist perspective on science leads to a helpful perspective on the problem of boundaries between politics and science. For as clearly as principals and agents seem to map on to politicians and scientists, respectively, the principal-agent approach does not exhaustively or exclusively demarcate the conceptual territory they inhabit into politics and science. Constructivism provides a more nuanced approach to the boundary between politics and science straddled by science policy. Indeed, if science were as entirely objective and politics as entirely venal as the early model suggested, then science policy would be impossibly reduced to the simple appropriation of funds and the mindless following of advice. Pragmatism demands the ability to account for institutions of science policy such as those discussed in this book, and constructivism fits this bill. These institutions are the boundary organizations I introduce in later chapters, and they satisfy the need for nuance in science policy by satisfying principals on both sides of the boundary.

Structure: the Problem of Science Policy

In 1884, the eminent geologist, ethnologist, and explorer Major John Wesley Powell appeared before a special commission of Congress investigating the organization of government science. Powell testified to the Allison Commission that because institutions conducting scientific research required constant modifications by those conducting the research, "[i]t will thus be seen that it is impossible to directly restrict or control these operations by law" (quoted in Guston 1994a: 38).

In his testimony, Powell pointed at the primary analytical fact of science policy: scientists know things about the conduct of research that politicians and administrators do not. This fact is too often either used as an apology, as Powell did, for a laissez faire policy for science, or overlooked entirely. The asymmetry of information between those who would conduct research and those who would govern it presents the central problem of science policy. It means the patrons of research have a hard time understanding whether the recipients of their largesse are doing their bidding, and if so, how well. It also means the recipients have a hard time providing evidence of their integrity and their productivity to their patrons.

The asymmetry of information between performers and patrons is not unique to science policy. Rather, it is characteristic of all delegatory relationships. For the purposes of this book, it matters little whether the study of science policy is conceived as merely a subset of the study of delegation, or whether science policy is in some way unique. Any singularity of science policy is likely derived from the position of science in the nexus of claims about a unique epistemological status, the unpredictability of advance, the difficulties in discerning productive consequences, and the delivery of products through such intermediaries as educated students or an external market rather than directly to the principals. Any of these claims, if true, would serve simply to increase the asymmetry of information. Thus, the problem of delegation may loom even larger for the principal of research.

Other scholars have recognized the centrality of the problem of delegation in science policy. In discussing "forms of patronage," theorist Stephen Turner (1990a) has suggested that politicians looking to fund science suffer from a mismatch in the distribution of knowledge and discretionary power. To substitute for the elements of science they cannot grasp, these politicians focus on trust, public attestations, personal relations, and metonyms of overall performance such as financial accountability. Patrons trust researchers based upon their personal relations or their ability to demonstrate adherence to their public statements or standardized rules of accountability. This trust substitutes for the ability of patrons to understand the substance of research and to trace its impact. In a more literary vocabulary, Turner, like Powell, describes the logical outlines of the principal-agent view of science policy.

The advantage of principal-agent theory over Turner's formulation is its facility in formalizing and generalizing discussions of delegation. Borrowing from transaction-cost economics, principal-agent theory takes a contractual approach toward explaining organizations and hierarchies.[6] That is, the relationship between institutions, or among individuals within an institution, can be described as if those parties had entered into a contract specifying the rights and obligations of each party. Such a contractual perspective has metaphoric significance in science policy. Analysts and policy makers often speak of a "social contract for science" as the promise of science "to deliver goods to society in return for its patronage with no strings attached" (Rip 1990: 399). The contractual perspective also has a great deal of procedural significance for science policy because of the centrality of contracts and grants in the actual relationships between sponsors (principals) and performers (agents).

As in more formal models, in principal-agent theory it is important to specify what parts of the model correspond to which parts of the real world. The principal is an actor who requires a task to be performed but lacks the ability to perform it directly. The agent is an actor to whom the principal delegates the performance of the task, or with whom the principal engages in a contract for its performance. In commercial application, clients or consumers of goods and services are the principals, and professionals and other producers are the agents. I cannot grow vegetables, so I delegate the task of providing them to my greengrocer and sign a contract for the delivery of fruits and vegetables. I cannot practice medicine, so I delegate to my physician the task of healing me when I am ill, and we agree to the provision of diagnostic and prescription services. Politicians cannot perform research, so they delegate to scientists the task of investigating the natural world and contract for the performance of inquiries, analyses, innovations, etc. Table 1 provides a summary of such principal-agent relationships.

Anywhere there is a delegatory, contractual, or representative relationship, there is potential to apply the principal-agent perspective. Think of Dashiell Hammett's *The Maltese Falcon*, a story in which the problems of agency plague the characters. Casper Gutman, also known as "The Fat Man" and played by Sydney Greenstreet in John Huston's familiar movie version, is a very rich man who has spent seventeen years pursuing the valuable statuette. He has been betrayed by agents acting on his behalf, including the sultry blonde of many names who tries to seduce the twitchy private detective Sam Spade (played, of course, by Humphrey Bogart). Gutman suspects that Spade can help him retrieve the falcon, but he wonders if Spade is the right agent. Gutman tests Spade by offering him alcohol. Spade passes the test by accepting a full glass from Gutman, who mutters, "I distrust a man that says when. If he's got to be careful not to drink too much, it's because he's not to be trusted

Table 1 *Typical Principal-Agent Relationships*

Principal	Agent
Patron	Performer
Customer	Greengrocer
Patient	Physician
"The Fat Man"	Sam Spade
Voters	Politicians
Politicians	Researchers
Congress	NIH
Congress	Researchers

when he does" (Hammett [1929] 1972: 94). After deciding Spade is the right agent, Gutman must still assure himself that, after he provides Spade with information about the falcon, Spade will not double-cross him and use the information to take the falcon for himself. So Gutman offers Spade a smaller amount of money down, and a share of the profit from the eventual sale of the statuette, the burden of which Gutman will bear.

"The public is like a very rich man," Schattschneider (1960: 139) mused, "who is unable to supervise closely all of his enterprise. His problem is to learn how to compel his agents to define his options." Gutman's problem with Spade is like the public's problem in representative government. Table 2 illustrates how this problem of agency is iterated throughout representative government, as the public chooses representatives, who create executive agencies and delegate authorities to them as the next agent. Executive agencies perform some of the requirements of the delegated authority directly, and they let grants and contracts to other performers, who in turn are their agents.

The delegation from the government to the scientific community is the most abstract principal-agent perspective in science policy. Although at this level there is no single principal or agent, we can still discuss the systems for expressing goals for the relationship and assuring they are being pursued. At finer levels of resolution, we can view particular institutions within those systems: legislative bodies, executive agencies, and other public and private research performers such as universities, firms, and hospitals. The legislative bodies are usually specified as the principals for executive agencies, as well for all of their subsequent agents.

Table 2 *Iterated Principal-Agent Structure of Representative Government*

Principal	Agent
Electorate	Representatives
Representatives	Executive Agencies
Executive Agencies	Grantees/Contractors

That is, the agencies are themselves principals in providing grants and contracts to the performers, but since the funding agencies are agents of the legislature, the performers are also agents of the legislature.[7] At the finest level of resolution, individual principals and agents become visible: the chairpersons of legislative committees, the administrators and professionals in the executive agencies, and the individual researchers. This level of analysis is important for two reasons. First, organizations are not unitary actors, and the activities of principals can provide resources to particular agents within an organization who are more likely to share their perspective. Second, because analysts can sharpen the resolution of the principal-agent perspective to individual relationships as embodied in actual grants, contracts, legislation, policy statements, and other less tangible social relations, the application of principal-agent theory bears little risk of reifying the institutions it examines.[8]

Where the principal is governmental, it usually needs its agents to produce things that the market does not produce in an optimal quantity, for example, the public good of scientific knowledge upon which technological innovation is supposed to be predicated. Without the ability to refer to market prices for the delegated chore, the principal is assumed to be relatively ignorant of the manner and cost of production (Tullock 1966, Niskanen 1971, Turner 1990a). But even where there might be a market, for example, in vegetables, the asymmetry of information between the agent who supplies my vegetables and myself is apt to be large. Keeping track of the growing season, knowing how to identify produce of the finest quality, and other tacit knowledge of greengrocery is difficult for me to learn. Given the challenge of providing technical information and analysis to legislators who usually have a generalist's background, the assumption of an asymmetry of information about research between principals and agents is not hard to justify.[9]

Further, the agent may not share the goals espoused by the principal, but might prefer to conduct research on anything intellectually interesting or personally lucrative, regardless of its technological potential. The traditional research practice of "bootstrapping," reserving funds intended for one project for use in another, usually a more exploratory project, is an example. Or the agent – because of the principal's ignorance and the agent's desire for reward – may in fact be the wrong agent to accomplish the goal. My ignorance of medicine may lead me to choose a physician who provides me with an intoxicating but otherwise ineffective elixir over one who offers a debilitating but eventually effective treatment.

The potential conflict of goals and the asymmetry of information create two regular problems of delegation known, through terms derived from their original use in insurance theory, as "adverse selection" and "moral hazard."[10] In the adverse selection problem, the principal has difficulty selecting the appropriate agent because of an original lack of expertise or information. It is difficult and costly for the principal to discover which potential agent most completely shares the principal's goals. The classic example is when persons most likely to apply for health insurance are those most likely to require it, thus costing the insurer money. Or the least expensive vegetables may be of the poorest quality or grown with the greatest amount of pesticides. Or a mercenary detective like Sam Spade may not be trusted with a priceless bauble.

In the moral hazard problem, the delegation by the principal provides not only an incentive to perform the required task, but also an incentive to cheat, shirk, or otherwise act unacceptably. It is difficult and costly for the principal to know whether the agent will continue to pursue the principal's goals after the principal has made the delegation of authority. The classic example is the incentive to commit arson that fire insurance perversely provides. Or physicians may perform medically unnecessary procedures, for which they are remunerated, only to make it appear as though they are thorough diagnosticians. Or the Fat Man, in hiring Spade to recover the Maltese Falcon, may have given Spade the opportunity to abscond with the bird.

There are a variety of ways of solving these problems. Indeed, I maintain that how the relationship between government and science is structured to solve these problems is the most important way to measure change in science policy, and Chapter 6 offers a new periodization of science policy based on such a change. Historically, principals began by simply grappling with these problems and educing, as Turner describes, attestations and other signifiers of integrity and productivity. After World War II, both patrons and performers tacitly agreed that integrity and productivity were automatic products of an autonomous scientific community. But if this agreement breaks down, as it did from the late

1970s, the patron has other options, such as requiring a degree of monitoring and reporting by the performer. For example, providers of fire insurance employ investigators to discover the causes of fires on insured property and thus deter arson. Providers of health insurance employ physicians to examine applicants and attempt to enforce restrictions against preexisting conditions to prevent coverage of persons likely to be ill. None of the characters leaves Spade's residence, so that each may monitor the others while the falcon is delivered to them. My task here is to explore the steps the public patron of research has taken to assure the integrity and productivity of the scientific agent.

A set of related questions about who should conduct publicly funded research exemplifies adverse selection in science policy. In the United States, these questions were already contentious by the 1880s, as politicians and scientists argued over the character and conduct of research in civilian agencies such as the Coast and Geodetic Survey versus military agencies such as the Hydrographic Office of the U.S. Navy, or the Geological Survey's practice of contracting out the analysis of collected material to university scientists rather than government employees (Manning 1988; Guston 1994a). In the immediate postwar period, the questions were primarily over whether government agencies or universities would conduct the bulk of federally funded research continuing from the War.

Examples of decisions about the choice of agents include, among others, choices between: military versus civilian research; intramural versus extramural research; mission or programmatic research versus disciplinary research; large firms versus small firms; and peer-reviewed versus earmarked (or pork barrel) research. In practice, such decisions are rarely unidimensional; that is, decisions about military versus civilian research, for example, often contain elements of the choice between peer-reviewed versus earmarked research as well.

Although these choices are important ones in science policy, this book will not dwell on them because they are derivative of the questions of integrity and productivity, properly conceived. Questions of the integrity and productivity of science must be asked and answered across each of the dimensions of choice listed. Patrons must be able to assess the integrity of research, regardless of its location intramurally or extramurally. They must be able to perceive the productivity of research, whether it is conducted by military or civilian agencies.

Furthermore, the choice of agents is a problem that can extend far outside the domain of science policy, because a great deal of even basic research is conducted in pursuit of missions and is therefore competitive not with other research projects but with other projects in pursuit of that particular mission.[11] That is, there is a step prior to the selection of a research agent that involves selecting a method for achieving a mission, be it research, procurement, a service program, or some other expenditure. This step, taken in public health policy, security policy, energy policy, and elsewhere, needs to be informed by an understanding of the integrity and productivity of research. In this sense, science policy as understood here must inform policy decisions in these other substantive fields.

Regardless of the agent selected, problems of the conduct of research by that agent still remain. Even agents who espouse the goals of the principal, and who are provided with incentives to keep them aligned with that goal, might conduct their research sloppily or fraudulently or might pursue other goals and interests that divert them from the contractual ones. The two primary concerns of the patrons of research about this moral hazard are: 1) how the patron can tell that the research will be conducted with integrity; and 2) how the patron can tell that the research will be conducted with productivity.

The governmental principal's concern with productivity is evident. Research must at least push back the frontiers of knowledge and often must also contribute to higher education, military security, public health, economic advantage, or other missions. The government would not want to squander public monies by funding the meanderings of researchers. As Price (1979: 80) wrote about the authority delegated to researchers, "it depended on the continued confidence among elected politicians in the assumption on which the tacit bargain was founded – that basic research would lead automatically to fruitful developments."

But what of the patron's concern with the integrity of research? It has two elements. First, the principal is concerned to the extent that it affects the productivity goal. Research is the basis for myriad applications ranging from regulations to new drugs to military hardware. Fraudulent research can compromise the integrity of these applications and threaten the policy goals to which they contribute.[12] Moreover, fraudulent research may simply waste the time of other researchers.[13] Second, the principal has a symbolic or ideological concern for the integrity of science. Since the twin birth of liberal democratic thought and modern science in the English Enlightenment, science has been held as something of an exemplary community of freedom and cooperation in the pursuit of a common goal. As a result, it has served as a model of integrity for the larger society and of the efficacy of instrumental action and values, upon which representative government relies (Ezrahi 1980; 1990). If the public cannot trust science to have integrity, what can it trust?

The concepts of integrity and productivity, however, are not fixed, but they will vary over time and circumstance, as will what is taken as evidence of integrity and productivity. Yet it will remain in the durable interests of the principal to be concerned about the integrity and productivity of sponsored research, regardless of the fact that the specific questions and answers relevant to those concerns will be flexible and even contested. Similarly, it will remain in the durable interests of the agents to be able to demonstrate integrity and productivity.

In scholarship about politics and public policy, principal-agent theory is usually applied to the relationship between a congressional committee and a particular executive agency under its jurisdiction. An important starting point is economist William Niskanen's *Bureaucracy and Representative Government* (1971), which stands as a neoclassical translation of the Weberian warning against the "overtowering" expert bureaucracy (Weber 1946: 232).[14] Niskanen adopts the standard assumption of political-economic analysis – that individuals act to maximize their utility – to model the relationship between a legislative committee and an executive agency. In this "bilateral monopoly," a single bureau promises a set of expected outputs in exchange for a budget granted by a single patron committee. The asymmetry of information is the crucial characteristic of Niskanen's bilateral monopoly. The bureaucrat needs little information, most of which can be garnered from the preferences legislators reveal in campaigns, proposed legislation, floor debates, and other public pronouncements. The patron, however, needs information to set a budget, and yet has little access to such information because there is no market price to use as a reference for bureaucratic services. Bureaus therefore command budgets larger than those that, had legislators possessed complete information, would provide the greatest net benefit. In such situations, Niskanen reasons, bureaus consume too much of their patrons' resources, and they produce too much as well.

Legislative principals can manipulate institutions and incentives to align the bureaucratic agent's goals with their own. For example, structural changes can increase competition among bureaucracies that produce similar outputs. Multiple bureaucracies fracture the bilateral monopoly on one side, making information about the costs of production more available and putting budgets at risk if one bureau lags in comparison to others. Although Niskanen argues that such competition does not directly reduce bureaucratic overconsumption, it does increase the chance that one bureaucracy will "end run" around the committee principal to other committees or the legislature at large, thus also breaking the bilateral monopoly at the legislative end.[15]

Changes in incentives can encourage bureaucrats "to maximize, not the total budget, but the *difference* between the obtainable budget and the minimum total costs of the service" (Niskanen 1971: 201; emphasis in the original). Niskanen therefore recommends incentives to encourage agents to cut costs while maintaining output, such as rewarding thrifty bureaucrats with a portion of the budgetary cuts, or residuals, they make. Such bureaucrats would hunt for waste, fraud, and abuse, and they would share in any amount of money they saved their principal. This scenario of sharing residuals with cooperative bureaucrats is the logic behind Gutman's offer to Spade of a percentage of the sale of the bird. It is the logic behind the institution of Inspectors General in all the cabinet departments and many of the independent agencies, as well as the offices created to investigate scientific misconduct.[16] It is also the logic behind sharing royalties from licenses with the federally funded inventor to help assure scientific productivity.[17]

The Two-way Street

In the principal-agent literature on the relationship between Congress and the bureaucracy, Niskanen represents what is generally known as the "bureaucratic dominance" school of thought, which emphasizes the asymmetry of information and the consequent and costly autonomy of the bureaucracy. There is also a school of thought favoring "congressional dominance," which argues that Congress possesses sufficient tools – budgets, new authorizing legislation, confirmations, and oversight – for liberating information and otherwise bending the bureaucracy to its political will. A detailed examination of the debate between the two schools is not in order here, especially since the concept of schools on this issue simplifies both the empirical work and the principal-agent framework behind it too greatly.[18] But the debate is symptomatic of a broader pathology, albeit a curable one, of the principal-agent framework. As Morris Ogul and Bert Rockman (1990: 21), two long-time observers of the struggle between Congress and the bureaucracy, conclude, "The logic of the principal-agent relationship . . . is its great advantage; its stylization of facts is its vulnerability."

Terry Moe, an important clarifier of the application of the principal-agent framework for the study of political institutions, provides a helpful metaphor to elaborate a more subtle use of it. He describes principal-agent relations as "a two-way street" and argues that each of the schools has elaborated only one direction.[19] If Moe's sense of principal-agent theory as a two-way street means reciprocal causation or mutual influence, as for example Dodd and Schott (1986) portray it, an additional perspective more sensitive to the ebb and flow between principal and agent is called for. After all, we are interested in the relationship between politics and science, and no relationship monopole exists. At the very least, the inquiry must consider the reciprocal hazards of the agent-principal framework, if you will: How does the agent demonstrate that the research is conducted with integrity? And how does the agent demonstrate that the research is conducted with productivity? These questions are part of the problem of mutuality between politics and science that Price overlooked.

In my analysis of science policy, I attempt to address the problem of mutuality. But I also go further to combine the political-economic approach of principals and agents with more sociological insight.[20] This insight is derived from the constructivist approach to the study of science. Constructivism, or social constructivism, maintains that science is not the simple result of an immediate and objective understanding of the natural world. Rather, science has an invariably social component, which makes it subject to a wide array of influences, from the theory-laden aspect of observations, to the demographic characteristics of the scientific community, to the interpersonal, organizational, and technological processes through which knowledge is certified.

Sheila Jasanoff (1992) describes a small set of central tenets of the constructivist view of science that are important to understand about science as it impinges on policy arenas. First, constructivism holds that scientific claims are contingent upon certain local or background conditions of production. It is difficult – some would say impossible – to separate what is contingent about science from what is not. Second, constructivism holds that the process of inscription, by which scientists represent reality through a series of highly mediated interactions with machines, is problematic. Nature does not speak directly to scientists, but scientists use machines to write down what they manage to wring out of experiments. Third, constructivism holds that, because there are contingent components and practices embedded in scientific claims, these claims may be deconstructed by revealing these contingencies. Scientists involved in controversies, adversaries engaged in legal or policy proceedings, and scholars applying constructivist methods use similar techniques of deconstruction.[21] Fourth, constructivism holds that one particularly common manner of deconstruction (related to inscription) is "experimenters' regress," in which critics reveal the contingencies of experiments such that no experiment could actually stand up to scrutiny. Thus, the certainty of the critical processes of replication and falsification is illusory because no pair of experiments could be truly identical. Finally, in large part as a consequence of these other tenets, constructivism holds that what counts and what does not count as science does not correspond to any essential endowment of necessary and transcendent characteristics. Rather, constructivism encourages analysts to observe how participants themselves attempt to demarcate science from nonscience.

Although all of these tenets of constructivism are relevant to my analysis, and the third one is particularly important to understanding the role of Congress in my case studies, the final tenet is crucial for my overall approach. As sociologist Thomas F. Gieryn (1995: 393–94; emphasis in the original) writes, "the boundaries of science are drawn and defended in natural settings often distant from laboratories and professional journals – a process known as 'boundary-work.' Essentialists *do* boundary-work; constructivists *watch* it get done." A good deal of the empirical work upon which my analysis is based has involved watching, in various ways, how the participants involved in science policy tasks related to the integrity and productivity of science go about their work.

Boundary Work and the Problem of Stability[22]

Whether by Popper's falsification, Merton's norms, or Kuhn's paradigmatic consensus, claims for the demarcation of science from nonscience help construct and preserve the cognitive authority of science (Gieryn 1995).[23] Thus, the constructivist argument that boundaries between science and non-science are not essential, but instead provisional and ambiguous, has important consequences. One is the fear that constructivism erodes the cognitive authority of science. Some believe the tenets and methods of constructivism admit or legitimize a dangerous relativism. If constructivists manage to convince people that science is not a rational, objective, truthseeking and, indeed, truthfinding enterprise, then science will have lost its role as ultimate arbiter of Nature and its competitive position against religion, politics, and other traditionalist enterprises for providing a world view.

On a less prosaic but more immediate level, a feared consequence of constructivism is that it opens the tent of policy to the nose of the camel of irrationality. This fear is a variant of Yaron Ezrahi's more robust (but less apprehensive) argument about the decay of the productive relationship between science and liberal democracy in the Anglo-American tradition.[24] It is also at the root of policy-relevant discussions by a number of antagonists in the recent, so-called science wars.[25] For example, the editors of *The Flight from Science and Reason* argue, "The health of liberal democracy depends on the general use of reason. Reason must not be the cognitive tool of the few: if the integrity of science and reason are undermined among the majority, then democracy itself is in peril" (Gross, Levitt, and Lewis 1996: 491).

Central to these fears is the threat of instability – that the objective role of science is necessary to prevent human activities from undermining the rational foundations of society and freeing them to slip down into some abyss of unreason. This threat is akin to political scientist Langdon Winner's (1977) concept of "apraxia" – the danger of large-scale technological failure should certain conditions for the management of technology, such as technocratic forms of governance, not be fulfilled. It holds that if science gives an inch to the dark forces of irrationality, there is no remaining fallback, no next position of compromise or stability. Philosopher Mario Bunge (1996: 110) argues, "Spare the rod and spoil the charlatan. Spoil the charlatan and put modern culture at risk. Jeopardize modern culture and undermine modern civilization. Debilitate modern civilization and prepare for a new Dark Age."[26]

The appropriate response to the charge that constructivism paves the road to the abyss should be a careful cartography of the admittedly unfamiliar territory that lies beyond our often scientistic and exclusionary liberalism, but does not descend so fearsomely. Indeed, a second possible consequence is that constructivist studies of science can improve the position of science in society, for the ultimate benefit of society and perhaps of science as well. By clearly portraying science as it is practiced, constructivism can recover the human face beneath science's rationalist mask. And even if the creature revealed is a little disfigured, greater familiarity with this phantom will bring sympathy rather than contempt. This hope grounds the work of a number of scholars who argue that constructivist approaches can actually aid the rationalists' perennial goal of scientific literacy and the public understanding of science.[27] It also grounds constructivist perspectives on questions usually addressed by more traditional approaches to science policy. For example, Jasanoff's (1990) study of science advisory committees to U.S. regulatory agencies finds, in situations where scientists and policy makers insisted on the realist's clean demarcation between the science and the policy components of their task, policy making became more difficult. When those boundaries were intentially blurred, policy making was easier.[28]

Such cartographies of constructivism in the policy arena are critical for providing an alternative to realist accounts and fears. It is thus imperative for constructivism, both intellectually and politically, to map the toeholds, ledges, plateaus, or even the vast plains that are accommodatingly stable and level. They may overlook the abyss, but they are not slippery slopes into it.

Scholars drawing on the concept of boundary work have seemingly intuited this problem and concretized aspects of it, finding toeholds without reifying the boundary. The primary example is the identification by Star and Griesemer (1989: 393) of "boundary objects" that are "both plastic enough to adapt to local needs and constraints of the several parties employing them, yet robust enough to maintain a common identity across sites." These boundary objects allow members of different communities to work together around them, and yet maintain their disparate identities. Boundary objects can be such things as tomatoes, which are familiar to both me and my greengrocer, but which convey different specific meanings to the horticulturalist selling them and to the shopper looking to make a marinara sauce. Or they can be things like the Maltese falcon, which represents wealth and prestige of legendary proportions to the Fat Man, but to Sam Spade is a way of paying the bills and saving his own skin. Or they can be things like an article in a research journal, in which unsubstantiated claims may represent research fraud to a congressional investigator, but merely unwarranted speculation to a research colleague.

The use of boundary objects, however, is almost infinitely flexible. Sociologist Joan Fujimura therefore expands them into "standardized packages," which are more adept than boundary objects at stabilizing facts. A standardized package "is used by researchers to define a conceptual and technical work space which is less abstract, less ill-structured, less ambiguous and less amorphous" (Fujimura 1992: 169). The standardized package combines boundary objects with common methods in more restrictive but not entirely definitive ways. Unlike boundary objects, standardized packages are robust enough to change local practices. But as "interfaces" among a set of actors from diverse social worlds, standardized packages emphasize the collaboration of those actors to "get work done" and simultaneously to maintain their integrity in their respective social worlds. Although Fujimura's focus remains on the use of standardized packages among scientists, the diverse social worlds that mutually partake in them can easily be populated by policy makers as well. Under such circumstances, examples of standardized packages might include a patent for a recombinant bacterium, which a researcher pursues because it represents priority in discovery after long years of research. But the same patent also represents to a policy maker the prospect of a commercial pharmaceutical, and the policy maker treats this kind of research more generously as it produces more patents.

In the next incremental step, sociologist Kelly Moore (1996: 1598) broadens the scope of analysis from objects and their aggregates to organizations, likening the latter to the former in their ability to "provide both an object of social action and stable but flexible sets of rules for how to go about engaging with that object." In Moore's historical account of public interest organizations such as the Scientists' Institute for Public Information, the relationship between politics and science is the crucial site of boundary work. These organizations allowed scientists to present themselves both as members of a knowledge community and as advocates, bridging the boundary between politics and science while allowing both enterprises to continue operating without substantial change.[29] The organization became the boundary object.

Each of these elaborations contributes to a discussion of stability, but none provides a compelling general hypothesis of how the objects, packages, or institutions stabilize the potential chaos of the politics/science boundary.[30] As Gieryn (1995) points out, the extent and productiveness of boundary work in Jasanoff's account varies among cases. In such a collection – one example of boundary work is too much, one too little, and one just right – there are no instructions to follow in reproducing the right measure. For Star and Griesemer, as long as there is some local agreement over these boundary objects, the boundary may be relatively stable around them. But this stability is based entirely on consent, and there is a large and unexplained gap between the fully consensual boundary object and the other means of satisfying conflicting social worlds, including "imperialist impositions of representations, coercion, silencing and fragmentation" (Star and Griesemer, 1989: 413).[31] And Moore's (1996: 1621) conclusion that "the boundaries between science and politics were redrawn [by the public interest organizations] to suggest that the content of science was untainted by subjectivity but that scientists had a moral obligation to serve the public good" still does not allow her to explain why some of the organizations she studied succeeded and others collapsed. It remains an open question how the politics/science boundary becomes, or can become, stabilized.

In this book, I introduce the concept of a boundary organization as one route to stabilization. Boundary organizations are institutions that straddle the apparent politics/science boundary and, in doing so, internalize the provisional and ambiguous character of that boundary. Negotiating these elusive qualities becomes the daily work of the boundary organization, which in fact involves the use of boundary objects and standardized packages as a collaboration between the interests of the principal and those of the agent. The success of the boundary organization is judged by principals on either side of the boundary, both of whom rely on the boundary organization to provide them with necessary resources. A successful boundary organization will thus succeed in pleasing two sets of principals and remain stable to external forces astride the internal instability at the boundary. The success of the organization in performing these tasks can then be taken as the stability of the boundary, while in practice the boundary continues to be negotiated at the lowest level and the greatest nuance within the confines of the boundary organization.

My concept of the boundary organization differs in subtle but important ways from German political scientist Dietmar Braun's (1993) description of intermediary agencies. In his comparative study of mission agencies that sponsor research in the United States, Great Britain, France, and Germany, Braun appropriately critiques the dyadic structure of principal-agent theory and situates the mission agencies as intermediaries between a political system and a scientific system. He concludes that this three-part or triadic structure improves the communications between politics and science, but continues to concede significant power to science over the choice of research. Rip (1994) has a similar vision of the dual nature of research councils between the scientific community and the government, embodying values from both sides. Moreover, Rip (1994: 12–13) generalizes from this observation, arguing that "because they have two patrons, the state and the scientific community, the research councils are relatively independent with respect to either of them."

The analyses by Braun and Rip, however, are more apt for the European agencies studied than they are for the United States (where Braun studies NIH and Rip generalizes about NIH and NSF). The European agencies or research councils are semipublic, whereas NIH is a fully public, governmental institution. The available resources for all three parties in the triad are therefore somewhat different, and the extent of "capture" (Rip 1994: 8) of the councils by the scientific community varies greatly among nations. Moreover, these authors attribute to the research councils narrower functions – apart from funding research. Braun introduces the triadic structure merely to account for complexity, and the need of his intermediary agency for the scientific system is limited to the latter's providing reputational assistance to the former. In the case of the boundary organization, however, the professionals in the agency and the scientists on the outside collaborate to produce mutually instrumental boundary objects and standardized packages. To the extent that Rip focuses on the consequences of the dual nature of the research councils, he argues that it permits them an independence they can exploit in an entrepreneurial way. Although the boundary organization may behave entrepreneurially, its key characteristic is the stability it induces in the science/politics boundary by successfully internalizing the boundary negotations.[32]

This boundary organization also differs from the boundary-spanning organization previously defined in the sociology of organizations (Aldrich 1979; Bozeman 1987). The concept of the boundary-spanning activities helps explain how organizations insulate themselves from external political authority. Organizations engage in such activities to exploit opportunities or respond to threats from their environment. The boundary organization I elaborate draws its stability not from isolating itself from external political authority, but precisely by making itself accountable and responsive to opposing, external authorities. The boundaries most important to the sociologist Aldrich, for example, are those of the organization itself, which determine its membership. The most important boundaries here are the ones between science and politics that the organization internalizes in order to be flexibly undifferentiable from either politics or science.

Historical Prelude: the Allison Commission

To explore the plausibility of my approach, which emphasizes the problems of agency between politics and science, I provide a brief historical probe of the Allison Commission of the 1880s. Although the cast of characters in this episode is radically different than today's – small-government Democrats, free-spending Republicans, and well-traveled, interdisciplinary geologists – their concerns and the interplay of their institutional interests will be remarkably familiar. That, of course, is the point. This century-old struggle reveals that the asymmetry of information and the concern for the integrity and the productivity of science are durable elements of the structure of science policy.

The Allison Commission was an ad hoc, joint committee of Congress established in July 1884 to examine the organization of the federal research effort.[33] The Allison Commission, eponymous for its chairman Senator William Boyd Allison (R-IA), was formally known as the Joint Commission to Consider the Present Organizations of the Signal Service, Geological Survey, Coast and Geodetic Survey and the Hydrographic Office of the Navy Department. The Signal Service of the Army Department included the Weather Bureau and maintained a school of meteorological training at Fort Myer, Virginia. The Geological Survey of the Department of the Interior mapped public lands and conducted research in geology, ethnology, archaeology, and paleontology under the direction of Major John Wesley Powell. The Coast and Geodetic Survey, created in 1807 and thus one of the oldest federal bureaus, charted coastal waters and lands and conducted a transcontinental triangulation. The Hydrographic Office also conducted coastal mapping, but its domain was restricted to foreign coasts. Together, these four agencies accounted for the vast majority of the federal government's very modest budget for research, spending about $3 million in annual appropriations in the years before the billion dollar budget.

The ostensible reason for Congress's study of these agencies was their apparent overlap in jurisdiction. Conflict roiled between the Hydrographic Office and the Coast Survey, spurred by the Secretary of the Navy, who believed everything on the water belonged to the Department of the Navy, and reasoned the Coast Survey should not perform coastal mapping but be restricted to geodesy – the science of measuring the size and shape of the earth. The Coast Survey's geodetic work, however, conceivably overlapped with the finer resolution mapping performed by the Geological Survey. Meanwhile, the bureaucratic location of the Signal Service was under dispute. Many members of Congress felt it did not belong under military supervision in the War Department, but should instead be a civilian agency because its purposes were no longer military. Supporters of the status quo argued that making scientific observations in remote places, on a regular schedule, and with the required precision necessitated military discipline – a problem of delegation unto itself. Given the uncomfortable jurisdictional problems and the scientific character of each of the disputed agencies, prominent voices from the scientific community called for at least the consolidation of the surveys or even for the creation of a new Department of Science.

To answer these and other questions, the six members of the Allison Commission delved into the minutiae of bureaucratic detail, from the rate of subsistence payment to employees of the Coast Survey to the quality of the coffee at Fort Myer.[34] But they also heard testimony from the scientists and bureaucrats about the nature of research and its quality as conducted by their agencies. Major Powell, for example, lectured the Commission on the two classes of scientific work conducted by the government: the "constructive work" of "applied science," performed, for example, by the Army Corps of Engineers (which was not under scrutiny); and the "original investigation" that "purely scientific institutions" such as the Geological Survey, the Coast Survey, and the Signal Service were "designed for." Because such scientific institutions required constant modification as dictated by scientific inquiry, Powell argued, "[i]t will thus be seen that it is impossible to directly restrict or control these scientific operations by law." Powell was not alone in this opinion, but at least he was far more subtle than other scientists who supported the bureaus. In a mode still common today, these scientists personalized the asymmetry of information, accusing members of Congress of ignorance and antiscientific attitudes. "It is a shame," one scientist wrote, "that a Congressman whose brain is not more than two kitten power can kick [the Coast Survey] around like a foot ball [sic]" (quoted in Guston 1994a: 30). Powell and his supporters reasoned that because scientists had a monopoly on the information needed to direct their inquiries – and perhaps even on brain power itself – Congress as the principal would have to trust the details to the agents. Congress could provide only the most general of guidance.

For Powell, however, it was not merely that the character of science exceeded legislative grasp, but the character of scientists themselves made extending that grasp unnecessary. "[S]cientific men are, as a class, the most radical democrats in society," he argued, and they become "restive and rebellious when their judgments are coerced by superior authority." As "radical democrats," scientists could be trusted to act with the same values and goals as their patrons. Powell therefore concluded, "Bureaus engaged in research should be left free to prosecute such research in all its details without dictation from superior authority" (quoted in Guston 1994a: 38). By alleging the unique character of science, its organization and composition, Powell advanced what historian George H. Daniels (1967) called "the pure-science ideal" as a rationale for a laissez faire science policy.

The Allison Commission nevertheless pressed its investigation, inquiring into the integrity with which the bureaus were implementing their delegated authority. Using the few avenues of entry open to them, the commissioners questioned whether reimbursements for the out-of-pocket expenses of Coast Survey employees were too high, and why particular numbers of Signal Service officers had been promoted. They also questioned Powell's technique of contracting out work to scientists such as O. C. Marsh at Yale University, who had been accused of using materials collected with government support for private museum collections, and of double-dipping by receiving salaries from both Powell and the university. Whereas the former charge may have had some merit, Marsh was not guilty of drawing two salaries.

Just as the Allison Commission began to touch on these questions of integrity inherent in the delegatory nature of science policy, it likewise began to touch on questions of productivity. In a minor example, the Allison Commission examined the nature and number of the publications of the Geological Survey and wondered whether it was necessary for the government to fund this kind of output. At a grander level, the Commission wondered what the relationship among science, government, and the economy should be. Whereas Powell staked his claim to the "pure-science ideal," J. E. Hilgard, the director of the Coast Survey, took a different tack. Hilgard stressed the Coast Survey's work "is economic, of practical value . . . for practical purposes, though some science comes of it" (U.S. Senate [1886] 1980: 54). Neither Powell's position nor Hilgard's route was clearly successful to some members of Congress who saw government science as caught on the horns of a dilemma: If science is of practical value, then why must it be publicly rather than privately funded? And if science is purely scientific, then why must it be publicly funded at all?

As a result of its inquiry, the Allison Commission introduced several reports and bills in the House and Senate. Although the bills themselves were never debated on the floor of either chamber, many of the provisions eventually found their way into appropriations bills and then into law, limiting the printing performed by the bureaus, restricting the number of promotions in the Signal Service and eliminating funding for its school at Fort Myer, and requiring greater itemization of the appropriation for the Geological Survey. Although Major Powell was superficially correct that members of Congress did not have the detailed knowledge necessary to govern the day-to-day operations of science, the Allison Commission nevertheless identified certain mechanisms – namely, the joint committee itself – and certain metonyms (a la Turner) – namely, the appropriations process and financial integrity – that endure through the history of congressional science policy. The Allison Commission established that a science policy of laissez faire did not mean *laissez bon temp roulette*.

Conclusion

As the episode of the Allison Commission indicates, principal-agent theory provides a durable framework with which to structure science policy analysis. The critical elements of this framework are: 1) an asymmetry of information, which creates the need for a contract or delegation from a principal to an agent; 2) the problem of moral hazard, translated in science policy as problems of the integrity and productivity of research, faced by the principal; 3) the reciprocal problems of demonstrating integrity and productivity faced by the agent; and 4) a variety of mutual strategies to solve these problems, including attestations and metonyms, trust, and monitoring and incentives.

In many applications, however, principal-agent theory tends to stylize the relationships it attempts to explain, and the sociological nuance of boundary work is a critical admixture to temper this tendency. The crucial aspects of boundary work are: 1) the contingent, rather than necessary, character of the demarcation of science from nonscience, especially including politics; 2) the methodological proscription for constructivists to refrain from doing the boundary work that demarcates science and politics, but rather to engage in observing it; 3) the ability of boundary objects and standardized packages to unite actors on both sides of that boundary and thus begin to solve the problem of the stability of the boundary; and 4) the possibility of boundary organizations to further stabilize the boundary by internalizing the boundary work performed by participants and by being an agent, monitored and given appropriate incentives, by principals on both sides.

These aspects of principal-agent theory and boundary work do not exhaust the potential contributions of each approach. Indeed, they may do little more than provide a useful and theoretically compelling set of organizing principles for the analysis of science policy. In the historical prelude of the Allison Commission, they did at least that. They reveal the historic concern of Congress for the integrity and the productivity of the science it funds and the reciprocal frustration of the scientists, who did not quite understand why members of Congress substituted financial and moral integrity for scientific integrity and who clashed with each other on how to explain the productivity of their work. With respect to the detail of boundary work, the Allison Commission obliged Powell to some extent, as it affected only the bureaucratic conditions under which scientific work was done, without intruding into the scientific work itself (Guston 1994a: 48). In the 1880s, there was no boundary organization, no fuzzy office between politics and science responsive to both. When there was a question or a difficulty, members of Congress sat at the dais and the scientists – the same ones who collected specimens and charted territory – sat across from them and gave testimony.

This confrontational arrangement would be repeated a century later when members of Congress would investigate allegations of misconduct in science. In the late nineteenth century, Congress did its best to exert just a minimal amount of influence over the bureaus. In the late twentieth century, Congress possessed a greater wealth of experience in and depth of institutional resources for dealing with science, and it instigated a defensive scientific community into creating a new boundary organization, in an attempt to secure a stable boundary. Between these two examples, however, lies a time period in which, more than any other, Powell's apologies for the independence of science and scientists took hold as policy. The social contract for science institutionalized trust in the previously articulated attestations, as well as in the demonstrated material successes, of science. The next chapter explores the creation of this relationship between politics and science.

2

Understanding the Social Contract for Science

> The problem then is to visualize and create linkages between the search for scientific truth, and the desire to achieve justice in our society. . . . [To do this] the scientific community must seek to establish a new contract with policy makers, based not on demands for autonomy and ever-increasing budgets, but on the implementation of an explicit research agenda rooted in [social] goals. . . . [S]cientists and policy makers must work together to make certain that research programs stay focused on policy goals . . . [and] that success of research is measured by progress toward a better quality of life for humankind, rather than by number of publications or citations or research grants.
>
> – Representative George E. Brown, Jr. (1992: 780–81).

Introduction

Economist Kenneth Arrow (1991: 48) makes clear in an overview of principal-agent theory that the costs of overcoming the asymmetry of information between the ignorant principal and the expert agent can be very high. Moreover, even if such costs could be overcome, the opportunity for principals to use specific monetary incentives is very limited (Braun 1993). These difficulties create pressure for simple contracts that do not necessarily incorporate monitoring, incentives, or other features required for an efficiently structured relationship. This chapter is about the simple contractual solution to the problem of delegation in science policy, from its institutionalization just after World War II to its termination in the 1980s.

This simple contractual solution can also be considered an ideology, in either the economic sense of ideology as a substitute for the gathering of costly information (Downs 1957), or in the anthropological sense of ideology as a map to guide actors through a complex social reality (Geertz 1973). Although all such maps are to some degree ideological, they are of crucially different complexity. As principals uncover more information about the performance of a simple contract, they can negotiate new, more complex contracts and restructure the conditions of their delegated authority to assure the agents perform as instructed.

Like paper maps of geographic territory, maps of social reality portray different phenomena – routes, activities, locations – as extant or absent, possible or impossible, known or incognito. And as with such maps, they also portray boundaries between separate domains or jurisdictions. But whereas a current map of the United States would show the Mason-Dixon line clearly between a red-hued state of Pennsylvania and a blue Maryland, a mid-eighteenth-century map might have shown no clear boundary between the claims of the respective Protestant and Catholic colonies. There might instead have been a dotted line, a cross-hatching, or perhaps even a purple boundary area. Changes in maps reflect changes in social reality.

This chapter describes the charting of the social reality of science policy in an ideology known as "the social contract for science." This map portrays the domains of politics and science as neatly cleaved, like Pennsylvania and Maryland after the survey by Mason and Dixon, or like a hearing room between members of Congress on the dais and scientists across at the witness table. The problems of the integrity and productivity of research appear on this map, but they do not loom very large and they are easily avoided by relying on particular conceptions of science and the scientific community.

The first part of this chapter elaborates the social contract for science, beginning with a bit of social contract theory and continuing on to describe how scholars and policy makers deploy it to shape the debate over science policy. I want to scrutinize its usage, origins, and implications closely because language can be used for either simple or strategic purposes (Habermas 1979), and because the language used by policy participants often plays a significant role in how policy problems are framed, argued, and resolved (Edelman 1977).

The second part of the chapter delves into historical detail about confronting the problem of delegation in the immediate postwar period and the construction of the social contract for science. The story of the creation of the federal research enterprise is often told, but I focus on the elements the designers of the postwar system shared, rather than those about which they disagreed. These shared elements involved solutions to the problems of integrity and productivity in science, which then became part of the ideology embedded in the map.

Among my hopes for studying the social contract for science in this way is to establish it as a baseline from which to measure change, and to hold its annunciators to some kind of accountability. If the social contract for science has any meaning, it denotes a map of institutional arrangements and their intellectual underpinnings that dominated science policy from the end of World War II until roughly 1980. These institutions and their rationales did not attempt to overcome the costs of asymmetric information or apply specific monetary inducements. If the social contract for science has this meaning, then science policy makers must confront the changes that overturned it in the 1980s and move on, both rhetorically and practically.

Constructing the Social Contract for Science

Any amount of reading in the science policy literature or traveling in the science policy circles of Washington, DC reveals the ubiquity of the social contract for science. The epigraph by Representative George Brown (D-CA), the long-time member of the House Science Committee, is just one example from one politician. Scientists use it as well. For example, the zoologist Jane Lubchenco (1998: 491), in her inaugural address as president of the American Association for the Advancement of Science, called for a "new social contract for science" that would commit "all scientists to devote their energies and talents to the most pressing problems of the day, in proportion to their importance, in exchange for public funding." Some even attach a specific provenance to it, as physicist and former president of the University of Michigan James Duderstadt (1996) defined "the remarkable social contract . . . laid down in Vannevar Bush's report, *Science: The Endless Frontier*."

Researchers have actual contracts with the sponsors of their research. But these sponsors are not policy makers per se, but rather the operating arms of federal research and development (R&D) agencies, private foundations, and, increasingly, private firms. Furthermore, these actual contracts are usually made between the sponsor and the scientist's institution and not with the individual scientist or with some broader community. So what are we to make of references to a social contract between the scientific community and policy makers?

I will first describe the general aspects of contractarian thought that are important for understanding any social contract for science. Given this description, I will ask whether a particular social contract for science is plausible. I will then attempt to plumb the meaning of the social contract for science by examining what policy makers think of the concept and by searching for additional clues to its meaning in the history of the postwar establishment of science.

Plausibility of the Social Contract for Science

A social contract is a theoretical device used to explore principles of political and civil relations. In some circumstances, as with the familiar social contracts of the liberal theorists Locke, Rousseau, and Rawls, these principles concern rights, justice, or other constitutive aspects of society. At other times, these principles concern duties and obligations at a lower level of organization, for example, within voluntary associations. In either case, as Rawls (1971: 16) writes, "a contract view holds that certain principles *would be* accepted in a well-defined initial situation." I emphasize "would be" because as a theoretical device the social contract is merely a hypothetical agreement. That is, arguments from a social contract hold its principles are valid not because actual people actually agreed to them, but because people, had they the opportunity to agree to them, would have. Only in the United States do we have the parchment illusion that our Constitution is a real social contract.

A social contract needs just a few basic elements to begin to take polemical force. As Rawls alludes, the first need is a "well-defined initial situation." Although the situation itself is hypothetical, the realism of its parameters has positive bearing on the force of argument. That real people could imagine themselves in this situation can only encourage their receptivity to the argument.[1] The second element is a rationale for the acceptance of the proffered principles, usually in the form of an appeal to the reasonable interests of the contracting parties. A third element, which strengthens the applicability of a social contract but which may not be necessary to explicating it, is an opportunity for occasional renewal by the people subject to the principles it rationalizes.

Locke ([1689] 1963), for example, defined the initial situation as a state of nature with certain characteristics, and he appealed to natural law and the ability of reason to interpret it as the rationale for accepting the principles he articulated. Locke also offered the opportunity for renewal by tacit agreement, for example, by partaking of the material benefits of the state constituted by the social contract, as well as the opportunity to dissolve the social contract by throwing off the yoke of government.

With this understanding, it seems clear that a social contract for science is plausible. We could imagine, for example, representatives of the government and of the scientific community coming together, in an initial condition characterized by mutual disengagement but newly threatened by Fascism, and agreeing the government would employ scientists to produce knowledge and instruments of war in order to secure the future of the free society that exists to their mutual benefit. It is to the benefit of the state because it aids its continued existence, and it is in the interests of the scientists, who believe they flourish as scientists and human beings under such a regime and not under Fascism. This social contract for science would be renewed every time a scientist accepted a wartime contract from the government. Similarly, we could imagine, after the war, the same groups coming together and agreeing to change the terms of association given the changed conditions – producing a greater variety of knowledge and instruments for a greater variety of social goals including public health, economic growth, and social change in addition to national security. This social contract for science would be renewed every time a scientist accepted a grant from the government to support research.

This brief probe suggests that speaking of a social contract for science is a plausible way to explore the relations of government and science. It is not exact enough about the initial position or the interests of either side to detail the exchange of obligations and authorities. But it would also be plausible to say, in each case, the government would clearly offer a reasonable if not generous amount of funding, and the scientific community would offer to be subject to a greater amount of control in the first social contract – given the greater risk – than in the second contract. But in both cases, the scientific community would reciprocate by offering to contribute to the requested products.

One particularity about this social contract for science as presented is that, unlike those of Locke, Rousseau, or Rawls, it is not an agreement among persons for each of them to incur obligations and be subject to a new authority in order to each receive benefits. Such a social contract is what sociologist James Coleman (1990: 328) calls a "conjoint constitution" because the beneficiaries are the same persons as those subjected to the authority of the agreement. A social contract for scientists, a tacit agreement to abide by norms of knowledge production discussed below, is a conjoint constitution. But Coleman also describes a "disjoint constitution," in which the beneficiaries establish the scope of the obligations and authority, which apply to other persons.[2] The social contract of Hobbes, made between a sovereign and hopeful subjects, is a disjoint constitution, compared to the social contract of Locke to establish an "umpire" to enforce rules among persons.

But just how disjoint is the social contract for science? Is it the case that science, in agreeing to accept government funding, has agreed to accept the absolute authority of some Leviathan? Or is there a greater degree of mutuality to the social contract for science, in which the government has delegated authority to the scientific community to produce goods crucial to national goals, without which the government would fail in its obligation to its principals, the citizens? Such a delegation could exist, akin to that described by political scientist Charles Lindblom (1977: 170–89), that leads to the production of crucial economic goods by the market and the subsequent "privileged position of business." It could also lead to a situation in which the scientific community's privilege is competitive with the government's power of the purse. For not only does the government rely on the scientific community to contribute substantially to economic well-being and the production of other valuable goods; it also relies on the scientific community to contribute to the ideological well-being of liberal democracy. Science provides a working example of the nonviolent and progressive formation of consensus, and it clarifies the nature of cause and effect relationships, both of which are necessary for legitimating representative government (Ezrahi 1990).

The social contract for science might thus be called a "mutually disjoint constitution." Over time, the parties to it are engaged in a mutual struggle to stretch its bounds or further articulate its terms in ways supportive of their own interests – engaged, in the words of Don Price (1979: 96), in "mutual recrimination beween the worlds of politics and of science." Because the social contract is an implicit constitution, there are no terms etched in stone to which the parties to this struggle can appeal. It is therefore likely that any description of the social contract for science itself – including mine – will be used strategically in some sense. Politicians might use the social contract for science to attempt to bind scientists to their idea of accountability. Scientists might use it to attempt to bind politicians to their idea of privilege. I use it to offer a new scheme for the periodization of science policy, one related to the central fact of delegation and the insights of principal-agent theory and boundary work and, in some respect, to umpire in an admittedly self-appointed way in the "mutual recrimination" between the politicians and the scientists.

Origins of the Social Contract for Science

Two Hypotheses. If the mutually disjoint social contract for science is the object of continual struggles over meaning and influence, a closer examination of its derivation, usage, and connotations is warranted. I do not propose, as Merton (1965) did with Isaac Newton's "on the shoulders of giants" aphorism, a romp through centuries of literature and art in search of the definitive genealogy of the phrase. But there are two plausible hypotheses about its origins, neither of which may be correct, but both of which are enlightening.

I look again to Don Price to derive the first hypothesis. In *Government and Science* (1954), Price analyzed the "dynamic relation" between political institutions and scientific ones. He described his support of the government's active, postwar role in science in counterpoise to two extremes:

> The lawyers and accountants and reformers who fear the predatory private interests argue that private institutions must not be allowed to profiteer on government grants. Suspicious capitalists and scientists who are jealous of their academic freedom say that he who pays the piper calls the tune – that the government, whenever it puts funds into research, is bound to destroy the liberty and initiative of those who receive the money.
>
> These two points of view, while superficially at opposite poles, are fundamentally in agreement. They both hold that the public interest is necessarily opposed to private interests, and that government cannot ever provide funds without destroying the independence of the institutions that receive them. But this is only another version of the idea that power is indivisible – the old idea that . . . is the basis of the organization of unitary states (Price 1954: 65).

Instead of revolving around a central and unitary sovereign, the American system developed a layered form of sovereignty called federalism, in which a federal government shared political power with its constituent states. By inventing a grant and contract system that "gives support to scientific institutions that yet retain their basic independence," Price (1954: 67–68) argued, "the United States has improvised a new kind of federalism for the conduct of research." This relationship resembles the mutually disjoint constitution discussed previously.

At the heart of this new system were the grants awared by the Public Health Service (PHS) and the National Science Foundation (NSF) to universities and other research laboratories to perform science "for its own sake," and contracts from such military agencies as the Office of Naval Research (ONR) that amounted to the same thing.[3] Military contracts might not even be awared for each project; rather, one master contract would be negotiated with each institution. "The 'master contract' is the basic charter of the new federal relationship" (Price 1954: 70). Contemporary analysts, for example the sociologist Edward Hackett (1990: 275), apply this perspective to federal funding of academic research, focusing on "resource relations and the quest for legitimation" as the basis of "the 'contract' between the university and its patrons." Price's focus on the mechanism of the contract as a charter and on the freedom retained by institutions despite the contract system is a plausible kernel to the more expansive social contract for science.

In the second hypothesis, the idea of a social contract for scientists is the kernel for a social contract for science. Mentioned above, this idea concerning a conjoint constitution among scientists – offered by the seventeenth-century English historian Thomas Sprat to describe the Royal Society as "a union of eyes" – is roughly the same vintage as the political social contract (Ezrahi 1980). The English chemist and philosopher Michael Polanyi ([1946] 1964) adopted and expanded it, as did American sociologist Harriet Zuckerman (1977; 1984). Polanyi, for example, describes the scientific community as an agreement among scientists on which the freedom and ultimate success of science hinge. Like citizens in Rousseau's social contract, scientists are equal partners in, but submit to, a General Will represented by scientific opinion. "This absolute submission leaves each free," but all are obliged and devoted to the "ideals of scientific work" (Polanyi [1946] 1964: 64). The message about scientific integrity in this formulation is implicit but powerful.

The social contract for scientists might be the germ of the social contract for science because the former may provide a rationale for the latter. The constitution of a group as a profession, like medicine, law, the clergy, or science, under a social contract among its members is a strong argument that such a group should have a privileged relationship with the state as well. For scientists, the debate over the safety and desirability of recombinant DNA experiments might have been "the starting point for a new social contract both within the professions and in its external relations" (Goodfield 1977: 209). But whereas other professions have formal links to external accountability, "an external accountability is missing from the social contract between the scientific profession and society" (Goodfield 1977: 79). That lack was central to the recombinant DNA controversy.

The essays collected by the American Academy of Arts and Sciences in *Limits of Scientific Inquiry* (Holton and Morison 1979) addressed these emerging difficulties with genetic research and the relationship between society and science. In the letter sent to solicit participation in the original American Academy Advisory Group, the organizers quoted the words of physicist Walter Rosenblith that "scientists and scholars have long had a bargain with society by which they have produced ideas and devices with few constraints, but that now this bargain is in danger of breaking down or in need of revision" (quoted by Graham 1979: 1). Contributors to the *Limits* volume variously referred to this relationship as: "an implicit bargain" or a "tacit bargain" (Price 1979: 25, 79–80); an "implicit contract" (Culliton 1979: 152); "this postwar contract"

(Nelkin 1979: 193);[4] an "old bargain between science and society" (Holton 1979: 236); and, quoting Price (1961), a "concordat" (several authors). These descriptions invariably referred to the postwar relationship and many, as James Duderstadt did, invoked the government report that helped encourage and structure it, *Science: The Endless Frontier*.

At about the same time, Harriet Zuckerman's work on questions of norms and deviance in science further explored the notion of a community of scientists contractually bound to one another. Zuckerman (1977: 113) asserted that the "institution of science involves an implicit social contract between [sic] scientists so that each can depend upon the trustworthiness of the rest." In a retort, philosopher Warren Schmaus (1983: 15) pushed the argument one step toward a social contract for science: if "the norms of science [are to be considered] as contractual obligations . . . [and] are to be considered special moral rules, . . . it is helpful to think of scientists as participants in a larger social contract among all members of society." But Schmaus (1983: 16) did not complete the transformation of the social contract for scientists into a "larger social contract" because he thought the potential contractors "would immediately confront two [intractable] problems: (1) defining precisely the role of the scientist, and (2) agreeing upon the importance for society of carrying out the functions attached to that role, whatever they may be." In other words, transforming the social contract for scientists into a social contract for science would mean confronting the difficult relations between politics and science.

Refining the Vocabulary. Harvey Brooks (1990b: 12) polished the definition of the social contract for science:

> Science was to be supported largely through grants and contracts to private institutions, leaving "internal control of policy, personnel, and the method and scope of research largely to the institutions themselves" [citation omitted]. Overall, this suggested a kind of social contract between the scientific community and the American people as represented by the federal government (including the Congress). The social contract promised widely diffused benefits to society and the economy in return for according an unusual degree of intellectual autonomy and internal self-governance to the recipients of federal support.

In this description of the transaction, the elements of the integrity of science (with respect to the guarantee of autonomy and self-governance) and the productivity of science (with respect to the social and economic benefits) are central, just as they are in the more formal description of the transaction within the principal-agent framework.

To ask policy makers about the social contract for science is to elicit a remarkably similar perspective.[5] According to a professional staff member with a subcommittee of the House Science Committee, "The deal was, after the War, 'we [the government] will give you [the scientists] money and leave it in your capable hands to get the most amount of progress.' " A former official of the National Institutes of Health (NIH) described the social contract for science, "in its crudest terms, the government will give scientists money to do what they want to do; in return, scientists will try to work on things that are going to be good for . . . the people whose money they're spending. It is a contract which is relatively new [and] certainly did not exist before the Second World War." And a former House Science staffer defined the terms of the contract pithily as "science gets the pleasure of serving society by doing what it wants with other people's money."

James Wyngaarden, who directed NIH through much of the 1980s – the turbulent times covered later in the book – explained his view in more detail:

> I think it runs something like this: that there are many views as to why the government supports science. I . . . would like to think that [the government supports] science for science's sake, and that they're doing the Lord's work, and that it's of such great interest to society that society should give them the money and move them along, and never tell them what to do. On the other hand, in Washington, it's clear that with some exceptions, that the government – Congress [and the] White House – looks upon the support of scientists [and believes] that science gets done for [its] utility. Now they all have to recognize that you have to give fundamental scientists a lot of freedom because there's a long time-frame with what they do. Nevertheless, it's supported with the firm belief that it will be useful to society in time.[6]

Descriptive Power and Analytic Shortcomings

As the brief discussion of its possible evolution and usage may suggest, the terminology of the social contract for science displays some of the descriptively important themes in the relationship between the federal government and scientific community in the United States. But each of these themes is also analytically incomplete. Below, I elaborate on four of the most important themes, each recurring like an *obbligato* in general discussions of science policy. Users of the rhetoric of the social contract for science appeal to these themes, intentionally or not.

The Social Contract for Scientists. Zuckerman's (1977: 113) view of "an implicit social contract [among] scientists" reflects a strain of thought in the sociology of professions that generalizes a "tacit social contract among professionals" to justify norms of professional conduct. Kuhn, for example, envisions that the maturity of a research field depends upon a social contract among practitioners that certain fundamental questions are off-limits (Funtowicz and Ravitz 1992: 266). In this sense, the social contract for science is not a unique phenomenon; as Coleman (1990) suggests, there could be social contracts between society and any professional specialty that could demonstrate a social contract among its members.

But the relationship between society and other professional groups is at once more and less formal than society's relationship with scientists. For example, physicians are licensed, attorneys examined, and accountants certified by government boards in cooperation with professional advisors. No similar public authentication of scientists occurs. Yet some scientists are chosen by their peers, who are themselves selected by the government and in concert with professional advisors, to be supported by the state in their professional activities.[7] The claim by scientists for a social contract with the polity seems made in a more absolute way. Whereas other professional groups can be self-regulating through an internal social contract, the scientific community, as Polanyi intimated, must be in order to satisfy the rigorous production of truth.

Critics (e.g., Bayles 1983 and Schmaus 1983) argue that the social contract model cannot sustain professional norms for two reasons. First, they claim that the model presupposes the norm that contracts should be adhered to. Supporters respond that pragmatism or self-interest facilitates adherence to the contract among professionals.[8] But this response begs the question of whether pragmatism or self-interest is sufficient justification for identifying norms. Indeed, this critique is part of sociologist Michael Mulkay's (1975: 653–54) attack on the norms of science as an ideology or "vocabulary of justification" for essentially self-interested behavior.

Second, critics point out that a social contract among professionals could not justify norms of conduct toward persons outside the profession, for example, clients. Supporters suggest that the profession of science, unlike medicine, law, or accounting, lacks specific clients and is therefore relieved of the standard professional obligation to specify conduct toward them (Zuckerman 1984). It may, however, be the case that the polity is in fact the client for science. In the United States, it is not only the case that the government funds the greatest share of basic research and subsidizes basic research in other sectors of society through tax credits and nonprofit status. But again, as political scientist Yaron Ezrahi (1990) argues convincingly, a liberal democracy gets a good deal on this investment on ideological as well as instrumental grounds. Use of the social contract for science connotes a possible social contract for scientists that presupposes a particular and perhaps problematic relationship among scientists.

Science as a Public Good. A basic aspect of the contractarian view of the government-science relationship involves the provision of a public good, research, by the scientific community. Versions of the public good argument – that the private sector will not invest in research at an optimal level because it is difficult for private sponsors of research to appropriate the return on their investment – have been used in science policy in the United States from the beginning of the Republic.[9]

Yet designating something a public good is the commencement rather than the completion of public policy. Analysts (e.g., Rottenberg 1968) distinguish between public productive goods, which are investments for future payoffs, and public consumption goods, which are investments for culture like museums, fountains, and parks. But does the potential of science as a productive public good justify investment in rocket science rather than cities? Is the scale of the public investment in science as a consumptive activity appropriate compared to other public investments?

With the growing investment by government in science – especially during a time through the 1980s and 1990s when Keynesianism fell into disrepute and the funding of public consumption goods that it inspired collapsed – arguments justifying or supporting the continued expansion have tended to rely on findings that science as a productive investment is uniquely profitable (Lederman 1991; Mansfield 1991; Narin, Hamilton, and Olivestro 1997).[10] Current arguments for an expanded federal role in the creation and dissemination of new technologies motivate the public good argument as well (Branscomb and Keller 1998).

Public goods like science, however, are not necessarily free goods (e.g., Alic et al. 1992; Callon 1994). Taking advantage of their public quality usually requires resources – like education, scientific sophistication, or a technological capacity – that are themselves difficult or expensive to come by. The investment in science as a public good therefore has important distributionary consequences. How available is this capacity to take advantage of publicly sponsored research? To whom does the benefit of the public investment in research accrue? Are the social consequences of new knowledge – both the costs and benefits – appropriately distributed throughout society?[11] The rhetoric of the social contract for science evokes only the superficial description of research as a public good and elides these more subtle details.

Generational Equity. The distributional questions also have generational overtones that resonate with more traditional perspectives on social contracts. For example, in Rawls' (1971) work, individuals who are party to the social contract deliberate behind "the veil of ignorance," unaware of a number of particular interests that could bias their thinking. Among the facts they are ignorant of is their location in time. If only to ensure their own well-being regardless of when in the historical trajectory of a society they live, these individuals must consider questions of generational equity. That is, they must plan for a well-ordered society over the long term, understanding that decisions about the allocation of resources affect the quality of life of descendants as well as contemporaries.

Similarly, a social contract for science commits money, highly trained individuals, and sophisticated equipment in the expectation of a return on the investment for a future generation.[12] As in the public good discussion, this investment in progress is often connoted by the social contract for science rhetoric. The vague promise of fundamental research suggests a long time horizon for a return on the investment, but it also threatens the loss of other investments or current consumption because of the uncertainty inherent in any individual project. Future generations who may reap the benefits from current investments in research will also bear any social, environmental, and other costs of such research applications as genetic engineering or nuclear power as well. Therefore, these questions of generational justice are embedded within the decisions to fund scientific research in particular ways. This relationship among science, technology, and progress motivates the critique by former congressional aide Daniel Sarewitz (1996) of myths of contemporary science policy in the United States, many of which he traces to Vannevar Bush and *Science: The Endless Frontier*. Especially in an era of severe budgetary constraint and sensitivity to both the positive and negative sequelae of technological change, generational equity in the funding of scientific and technological progress is a vital question that the social contract for science could frame better.

Consensus and Change. Finally, the social contract for science can express an original consensus against which change can be measured and evaluated. If anything approaching a social contract for science can be identified, delineated, or rationalized, then the premises on which it rests can serve as a theoretically rich base from which to measure change over time. But because no one has yet focused on explicating the social contract for science in order to develop criteria against which to measure change, no consensus has been possible.

Brooks (1990a: 33), for example, believes that:

> Many times in the last forty-five years commentators have predicted the imminent dissolution of the "social contract" between the scientific community and the polity which was so cogently formulated in the Bush report. The year 1971 was a particularly acute time of "doom and gloom" in this respect, and yet the relation has not deteriorated to the extent anticipated. Today many of the same negative signals that existed in 1971 are again evident. Will science recover to experience a new era of prosperity as it did beginning in the late seventies, or has the day of reckoning that so many predicted finally arrived? Only time will tell.

Political scientist Richard Barke (1990: 1), however, maintains that "allegations of reneging on the 'compact' between science, technology, and government often are based on rather selective interpretations of Bush's message . . . ; yet some fundamental changes do appear to be emerging in the relationship between the scientific enterprise and its public patron." In times of trouble, spokespersons for the scientific community such as Frank Press (1988: 2), then the president of the National Academy of Sciences, assert that "[s]cience has been faithful to that compact – that the American people for their support of science could in time expect a better life and a stronger nation. And we continue to honor that compact."

There have been some more formal attempts to argue for a periodization of science policy based on the idea of a social contract. Science policy scholar Bruce L. R. Smith (1994) has argued that the postwar social contract for science actually met its end in the late 1960s, only to be resuscitated in the early 1980s. The late political scientist Donald E. Stokes (1997: 91) alleged that "the postwar compact [between science and society] has crumbled only in the 1990s."

Those who augur changes in the social contract for science do so with apprehension for the continued success of the old system. Those who trumpet its durability do so with the apprehension of future challenges. The remainder of this chapter seeks to engage this apprehension by articulating appropriate criteria to measure change. Subsequent chapters will examine potential challenges to the social contract for science against these criteria, and I will return to assess the claims by Smith and Stokes in Chapter 6.

A History of the Social Contract for Science

The beginning of this chapter demonstrated three things: it is plausible to speak, in a theoretical sense, of a social contract for science, but the terms of that contract are subject to ongoing dispute; some shared understanding of the meaning of such a contract exists among policy makers and scholars, but over the issues of change this consensus breaks down; and the social contract for science connotes important but incomplete themes in science policy, as we should expect from an ideology or a map stripped of its complexity.

Since I intend the social contract for science to serve as a historical baseline against which to measure changes in the relationship between science and society over time, I must remedy this situation. But it is not the case that I must show that a social contract for science existed in any real sense. It would then be a contract or constitution, and one could refer more concretely to its terms in debate – not that the terms of a written constitution are fully determined either. Rather, after meeting the plausibility test as it did above, the social contract for science need be precise enough only to educe criteria of evaluation from it. To draw these criteria out, one could extend the plausibility probe into a full-fledged philosophical treatise, clarifying the initial position and the interests of the parties to such a refined extent that one could specify the obligations and authorities in detail. But the abstract derivation of such obligations is a daunting challenge after Locke and company, and even their analyses remain debatable.

An alternative, however, exists: to return to the historical setting metaphorically represented by the social contract for science and examine the rhetoric of actual people and the actual decisions and agreements they made. If the hypothesized actions of hypothetical individuals can provide normative guidance for real people, then the actual conduct of real people can provide analytical guidance for theory.[13] This method searches for convergence among a number of different lines of argument: the theory of delegation, the device of the social contract for science, and the rhetoric of analysts and scholars, which have already been discussed; and the history of change in science policy, from the end of World War II when the current enterprise was conceived, to the 1980s when the enterprise changed in a critical way. I take such convergence as strong evidence for the validity of the approach.

Contract and Founding Myth

The social compact of Thomas Hobbes promised to relieve humanity of the war of all against all by creating a commonwealth that would foster commerce, leisure, and science. The Federal Constitution defended by Publius promised to counteract the impending chaos by implementing a new science of politics and a new "constitutional technology" (Wolin 1989: 100) to promote tranquility and the general welfare. Vannevar Bush's report, written toward the end of World War II and implemented during the Cold War, promised military superiority and domestic prosperity through science-based technology. The original position for the social contract for science was a dangerous and threatening place, but beyond the chaos lay a secure, enterprising, and prosperous order.

If there is yet little consensus about the terms or duration of a social contract for science, there is remarkable agreement that Vannevar Bush's *Science: The Endless Frontier* codifies it. This conclusion is illusory, as a social contract cannot be codified, at least not without becoming a real contract. But Bush's report does loom large in the mythos of American science policy.[14] In this mythos, if the most revered positions in the pantheon of science are reserved for laureate scientists, then Vannevar Bush is like Hephaestus, an artificer who provided the more powerful Olympians with the chariots, thunderbolts, and other tools of their trades. Bush invented the institutional machinery of the golden age of American science and was, according to his biographer G. Pascal Zachary (1997), the "engineer of the American Century."

The history, of course, is not as clear as the myth. But it is hard to say that the polemical force of myth ever suffers for its lack of historicity. Nevertheless, a brief recounting will help delineate the approach Bush and his colleagues took to facing the problems of science policy. The issues over which Bush and his opponents disagreed are quite familiar. Those issues about which they agreed are less so. But it is in their agreement, and thus not in Bush's hand exclusively, that the social contract for science is written.

The uncertain domestic political context must be included to understand the creation of the contract and its fulfillment. The central conflict was a struggle between liberal reformers who wanted to organize science for the purposes of the state, and conservative scientific and business interests who wanted to curtail the public domain and keep science private and free.[15] During World War II, Bush directed the Office of Scientific Research and Development (OSRD), which managed the federal sponsorship of science and technology for the war effort through its several committees. Popular for its successes but criticized for neglecting the ideas of independent inventors and small colleges and universities, as well as for allowing its contract recipients to retain patent rights from war research, OSRD fell squarely within the academic-industry-military alliance that opposed the liberal reformers.[16]

Leading the liberal reformers in Congress was Senator Harley M. Kilgore (D-WV). Dissatisfied with war mobilization policies, Kilgore proposed an Office of Technological Mobilization in 1942. The next year he expanded his vision to include science and postwar considerations. His Science Mobilization Act would have established an Office of

Scientific and Technological Mobilization to finance education and research and to compel the disclosure and dissemination of technical information from the recipients of federal research assistance. Assistant Attorney General Thurmon Arnold heralded Kilgore's bill as "the magna carta of science."

The bill was greeted less enthusiastically by the scientific leadership who, in an unsubtle sense of the coming principal-agent relationship, were "unalterably opposed 'to being made the intellectual slaves of the State' " (Kevles 1977: 10–11). Bush was ambivalent about the bill: he found some aspects of the peacetime provisions to his liking; but as director of OSRD he could not abide by its wartime provisions. Bush also thought that Kilgore underestimated the threat that political control posed for science. Kilgore's activity prodded his opponents into action and, in November 1944, after a flurry of drafting by OSRD and White House staff, President Franklin D. Roosevelt sent a letter to Bush requesting a report on the organization of postwar science.[17] Bush established committees to correspond to each point of the four-point letter. The reports of these committees, prefaced by Bush's magisterial synthesis, constituted the June 1945 response to President Harry Truman in *Science: The Endless Frontier.*

Although Bush had originally planned to involve Kilgore in legislation to implement his report's recommendation of a National Research Foundation, he instead arranged for Wilbur D. Mills (D-AK) to introduce a bill in the House (Zachary 1997). Warren G. Magnuson (D-WA) introduced the Senate companion (S. 1285). Feeling abandoned by Bush, Kilgore introduced his own bill (S. 1297) a few days later. The two Senators, initially at loggerheads over the issue of presidential control over the proposed foundation, compromised and Kilgore introduced a new bill (S. 1850) in February 1946. The compromise passed the Senate, but it died in the House largely because Mills introduced a new bill akin to Bush's original proposal. Bush felt no regrets and looked forward to the 1946 elections in which Republican prospects were high (Kevles 1977: 24–25).

In the fall of 1946, Truman tried to regain the momentum for the reformers by appointing his own Scientific Research Board, with presidential aide and economist John R. Steelman as the chairman. Steelman reported in August 1947 in five volumes of *Science and Public Policy*, surpassing Bush's report in scope, detail, and even in optimism about the possible influence of scientific research on economic and social progress.[18] Bush, who had been invited to participate in Steelman's deliberations, was hostile to the project, and the report had less legislative impact than its patron and its author might have hoped (Blandpied

1998). The 80th Congress, the first Republican Congress since before the Depression, delivered a new Bush bill by the summer of 1947. But Truman, on the advice of Bureau of the Budget director James E. Webb and based on a memo by Don Price, pocket-vetoed the bill because it failed to provide for Presidential direction.[19]

In addition to the conflict over the governance of the new foundation, the issues that kept the debate alive included the question of geographic distribution of research funds, the role of the social sciences, and the status of patents in federally funded research. The most important of the three for the purposes here is the status of patent rights.[20] Magnuson's bill had left patent policy to be decided by the foundation's governing board which, under his plan for an independent board, would most likely have resulted in contractors' and grantees' being able to claim title. Kilgore's bill had provided government ownership and nonexclusive licenses.[21] The compromise bill kept patents public under normal conditions, but the administrator of the foundation could vest rights in the contractor or grantee under certain circumstances. There was general support in the scientific community for the compromise bill, but Mills' maneuver in the House, for which Bush bore some responsibility, killed it and delayed the establishment of the foundation (England 1982: 58–59). This delay had ominous consequences.

The Democrats regained control of both chambers in the 81st Congress of 1949–50, but conservative Democrats maintained a working majority with the Republicans, especially as anti-communist fervor flared. The patent issue receded, however, because legislators realized its reduced stakes as it became clearer the foundation would support only basic research, which they perceived as being of less immediate commercial potential. Loyalty also overran other issues. The Senate passed its bill easily. The House bill had to be forced out of the Rules Committee, only to be amended to include an affidavit of loyalty and a Federal Bureau of Investigation (FBI) check on potential grantees. The conference committee deleted the FBI check but retained the affidavit. In his signing message in 1950, Truman (1965: 338) cited *Science: The Endless Frontier* and, despite disputes over governance and patents, the broad consensus "concerning the objectives to be sought."

The Plural System

While Bush, Magnuson, Steelman, Kilgore, and Truman were taking two steps forward and one step back, the bureaucrats were not merely wallflowers at this dance of legislation. The two most important research agencies of the immediate postwar period began as bureaucratic, rather than legislative, initiatives, and they were well-established by the time of NSF's long-awaited birth.

As early as 1943, the Navy troubleshooters known as the Bird Dogs began to plan for a research office after the war. Although this planning in itself led to naught, Truman signed legislation creating the Office of Naval Research (ONR) in August 1946. ONR was intended to be an organizational base from which Vice Admiral Howard G. Bowen could build a nuclear Navy. But Bowen lost jurisdiction over the nuclear propulsion program, and he took terminal leave shortly after ONR was created. Lacking its intended mission, ONR turned to funding a wide array of research because of "nothing more than a bureaucratic accident" (Sapolsky 1990: 118). ONR's approach exceeded even the flexibility developed by OSRD for letting contracts to universities, to the point where "the formal distinction between contracts and grants [was] inconsequential." From its establishment in 1946 until NSF's creation, ONR served more as the "Office of National Research" (Sapolsky 1990: 43, 35).

Similarly, the Public Health Service (PHS) scrambled to protect its stake in the postwar research system. PHS had established an enviable wartime record with its role in the development of penicillin, gamma globulin, adrenal steroids, cortisone, and blood plasma. Planning began in August 1944, shortly after the passage of the Public Health Service Act, which gave PHS "broader authority for investigations of all types in the 'causes, diagnosis, treatment, control, and prevention of physical and mental diseases and impairments of man' " (Steelman 1947d: 17–18). Although Bush had established a Committee on Medical Research, the committee failed to consult PHS in its deliberations and recommended a separate institution to fund medical research – distinct from both the proposed NSF and the extant PHS. Bush, however, opposed the idea. PHS lept into the breach much as ONR had done. When OSRD was terminated on January 1, 1946, PHS received jurisdiction over many of its outstanding contracts in medical research.

Within months, NIH established its Office of Research Grants. With funds remaining from its penicillin contracts because the price of the drug had fallen under mass production, PHS advised medical school deans of the availability of money for grants. Newly decommissioned physicians and scientists overwhelmed the two professional grant officers with more than one thousand proposals in the first year (Strickland 1989). By October 1946 the NIH grants program had authorized 264 projects for $3.9 million (Steelman 1947c: 190–91). Shortly after Truman signed the NSF legislation, including a division of biological and medical science, NIH received essentially unlimited authority to expand in the Omnibus Medical Research Act (Strickland 1989). By then, NIH had established a track record of providing flexible grants for basic research. NSF came in a poor second for the chance to fund medical research on a large scale.

The few years between the end of the war and the creation of NSF also saw the passage of the Atomic Energy Act, which created the Atomic Energy Commission. These agencies, "firmly entrenched" by 1950, assured the nation's support of basic research would occur in a pluralistic manner (U.S. House 1986b: 35).

Framing the Social Contract for Science

If postwar legislation for the federal sponsorship of research was a "magna carta" or social contract for science, Vannevar Bush and the others competed to be its framer. There was a consensus that laissez faire for science would end: the only scientist who testified in opposition to the federal role was Frank Jewett, president of the National Academy of Sciences and of Bell Laboratories. In this sense, the competitors were on the same side.[22]

Bush and Kilgore both wrote forceful, hopeful rhetoric about the promise of science-based technology. Bush, a founder of Raytheon Company, had a Hamiltonian vision of the vitality of small manufactures. Yet Kilgore, untrained in science and a practicing populist, was not merely an advocate of the yeoman farmer. He instead did yeoman's duty drafting and compromising and redrafting legislation for seven years before his efforts helped lead to the federal role in basic research.

What yoked Bush and Kilgore together was their opportunity, at the end of what historian Thomas P. Hughes (1989) calls "a century of invention and technological enthusiasm," to create another special American century based on the continuing promise of science-based technology. Bush wanted the new order to look more like the old Republican order of the 1920s (Reingold 1991: Chapter 13). Kilgore wanted a national research foundation with the new view of the nation introduced by the New Deal – a state whose idea of general welfare was not limited to bettering business. But they both wanted to harness their concept of the new order to the morally and instrumentally powerful shoulders of science.[23]

Is it reasonable, then, to say that Bush wrote the social contract for science, as many people seem to think?

Historian Nathan Reingold (1991: 321) writes that "*Science: The Endless Frontier* was more honored than literally heeded." Reingold is indeed correct that on many important points Bush was forced to yield, by legislative necessity or by political circumstance. NSF did not adopt OSRD's patent policy. The plurality of funding agencies created a plurality of patent policies, ranging from the military agencies following liberal wartime policies to NIH and AEC, which did not generally allow recipients of funds to patent research products for the quite different reasons of propriety and security, respectively.

Reingold (1991: 304–05) argues that "[w]hat Bush did not propose (nor countenance afterward) was what Don K. Price later dubbed 'government by contract.' Those arrangements could and did violate Bush's sense of the proper, differing roles of industry, government, the universities, and the like." But here Reingold confuses what was intended and what resulted. Bush and OSRD invented the full cost contract without advertising and implemented a liberal patent policy. Bush wanted to continue these relationships after the war. Price praised the system Bush and OSRD invented because it granted the fullest measure of independence possible to the funded institutions thrown into a relationship that was novel for both partners. Bush was in this sense less a "creative anachronism" (Reingold 1991: 321) than a reasonable incrementalist who only over the long run may have lost to the tyranny of little decisions.[24]

The irony is that just when scholars and policy makers have been disputing whether or not Bush's social contract for science was coming to an end[25] – mourning its passing or questioning how it should be renegotiated – Bush's ideas had only recently come to their most complete fulfillment. The Patent and Trademark Amendment Act of 1980 unified patent policy across the pluralistic research system and allowed contract and grant recipients to more easily obtain title to the fruits of sponsored research. Bush had sought just this policy. The Federal Technology Transfer Act, authorizing the cooperative research and development agreements between federally employed scientists in government laboratories and researchers in private firms, might have been too much for Bush during peacetime, although this relationship is not so different from the wartime relationships that Bush himself had fostered among industry, universities, and government. But neither is it much more than an incremental step beyond the Patent and Trademark Amendments.[26]

The irony can be accounted for by realizing what I have argued: the patent provisions were not part of the social contract for science because Bush lost this part of the conceptual and legislative battle. The social contract for science was constituted by the noncontroversial views about science that he shared with Steelman, Kilgore, and the others. If the social contract for science had been Bush's alone, then the patent policy for all agencies would have been like that at OSRD and there would have been no need for the changes in the 1980s. Bush was not the framer of the social contract for science; nor was *Science: The Endless Frontier* its complete or sole articulation. Bush was one of several apostles of science, along with Steelman and Kilgore, and his report was but one part of the good news of the federal role in science funding.

A Reciprocal Boundary

Looking back through the lens of history and seeing such a fractured reality, does it make sense to draw a sharp line differentiating the present from the past? After all, " 'Vannevar Bush and John Steelman and Senator Kilgore didn't sit down in a room over at the Capitol to negotiate this contract. In fact if that's what happened, then it really isn't a social contract' " (Hamlett 1990: 31).[27] But one can articulate a clearer sense of the mutual obligation of the parties to even the tacit agreement. Although all the parties (but Jewett) agreed to extend elements of the wartime relationship, there was little agreement on the outlines of the intervention.[28] But with the end of both the negative prewar commandment of laissez faire and the wartime supremacy of the military imperative, some new boundary was needed. The idea was to make the new relationship merely one of financial support, to construct a boundary between politics and science through which only money could pass in one direction and science-based technology in the other. What transpired on the science side of this boundary was quite immaterial to the politics side of the boundary. When and precisely what technologies would pass were unspecified, but it was an article of faith that they would in fact pass. Figure 1 provides a schematic of this semipermeable boundary.

In designing and erecting this boundary, Bush and Steelman were in substantial agreement, and this agreement prevailed. With respect to the overall structure, they agreed the relationship between the federal government and basic research would be exclusive, providing the "bilateral monopoly" that Niskanen (1971) emphasizes is crucial for the asymmetry of information in principal-agent theory. Basic research was a unique source of innovation. Bush argued that "new products and processes are not born full-grown. They are founded on new principles and new conceptions which in turn result from basic scientific research. Basic scientific research is scientific capital" (Bush [1945] 1980: 6). Private firms would not create enough of this capital because they could not channel its flow once they had created it; private investment in research was not easily appropriable. Similarly, Steelman (1947a: 3–4) wrote that "[o]nly through research and more research can we provide the basis for an expanding economy, and continued high levels of employment." Be-

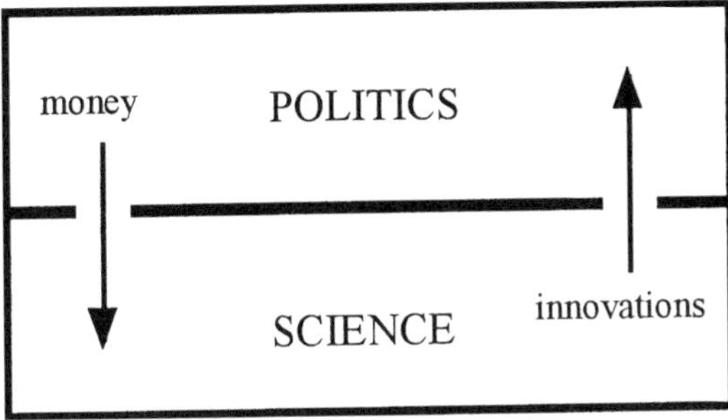

Figure 1 The Boundary Between Politics and Science

cause belief and circumstance proscribed other federal activity in stimulating industrial productivity, basic research monopolized government attention to innovation.

Furthermore, the federal government was the only appropriate patron because "in order to be fruitful, scientific research must be free – free from the influence of pressure groups, free from the necessity of producing immediate practical results, free from dictation by any central board" (Bush [1945] 1960: 79). The federal government was the only patron thought capable of promising this kind of freedom.[29] Industry would misdirect basic research because "there is a perverse law governing research: Under pressure for immediate results, and unless deliberate policies are set up to guard against this, *applied research invariably drives out pure*. The moral is clear: It is pure research which deserves and requires special protection and specially assured support" (Bush [1945] 1960: 83; emphasis in the original).[30] For Steelman (1947a: 26), the unique government role was based on the provision of public goods by science: "It is difficult to think of any other national activity which more directly benefits all the people or which makes a larger contribution to the national welfare and security" than research. The federal government was the only entity with the foresight and the ability to provide special protection and assurance for basic research and its provision of public goods. With the support of basic research constructed in this way, researchers had no obvious alternative principal, and the federal government had no obvious alternative agent, thus fixing the status of the bilateral monopoly.

With respect to the concern of the government about what transpired on the science side of the boundary, Steelman (1947a: 50), referring to both NIH and ONR, wrote that "grants – a gift made to individuals or institutions whose competence has been demonstrated for the purpose of an investigation whose outcome cannot be known precisely in advance" are the appropriate mechanism for the support of basic research. Some administration of science is necessary. But with a perception worthy of Niskanen, Schattschneider, or Powell, Steelman wrote that administrators suffer from two common maladies when confronted by science: awe and ignorance. Neither have positive administrative results and therefore "[t]he inevitable conclusion is that a great reliance must be placed upon the intelligence, initiative, and integrity of the scientific worker; and that he must, by the nature of things, be much less subject to the usual controls and regulations imposed in governmental administration than most other government employees" (Steelman 1947b: 129). Similarly, for Bush ([1945] 1960: 9), the new foundation "should recognize that freedom of inquiry must be preserved and should leave internal control of policy, personnel, and the method and scope of research to the institutions in which it is carried on." Steelman recognized the principal-agent dynamic, if only out of pragmatism. Bush recognized it, if only out of distrust of politics.

Steelman and Bush were equally enthusiastic about the productivity of basic research in the creation of new technologies. Steelman (1947a: 48–49) fit the federal support of science into a constitutional frame, viewing research as "necessary to the effective performance" of defense, standards, and commerce, not to mention the "sweeping general welfare clause." He found it "difficult to think of any other national activity which more directly benefits all the people or which makes a larger contribution to the national welfare and security" (Steelman 1947a: 26). Not only did science serve this broad national purpose, but it "is equally the basis for our progress against poverty and disease" and "the basis for an expanding economy, and continued high levels of employment" (Steelman 1947a: 3–4). But the government could expect these results only if it recognized that applying pressure to achieve them is counterproductive. Upon this recognition "rests the wise decision to maintain a relatively high degree of segregation organizationally for basic research" (Steelman 1947c: 99).

Such results were serendipitous, and important implications could come from even unlikely sources. Steelman (1947b: 3–4) provided an example of "biological experimentation to develop a fungus-resistant tomato [that] led to the discovery of 'tomatin' which was analyzed and found to contain the same ingredient as substances used to counteract ringworm, *immediately resulting* in the development of an impregnating agent in military boots and footwear" (emphasis added). In his extended discussions of administration for science, Steelman (1947c: 12) acknowledged the need for a "liaison between operating units . . . for interchange of ideas and experience between both the scientific and administrative personnel." Such liaisons were particularly important among scientific fields and for project initiation within a particular field. Steelman did not identify, however, the need for liaison work in disseminating scientific work, in linking the different sectors in which research is performed, or in linking the different types of research, for example, in linking plant biologists in government laboratories who discover tomatin with industrial chemists who fumigate army boots.

Bush's attitude was similar. "Basic research is performed without the thought of practical ends," and "is necessarily speculative" (Bush [1945] 1960: 18; 32). Science must be, to use Steelman's word, "segregated" or as Bush wrote ([1945] 1960: 79) "free from the influence of pressure groups, free from the necessity of producing immediate practical results." Nevertheless, despite its detachment from practical ends and its inherently speculative and therefore vulnerable character, basic research creates "the stream of new scientific knowledge to turn wheels of private and public enterprise" (Bush [1945] 1980: 18). Therefore, "[t]he simplest and most effective way in which the Government can strengthen industrial research is to support basic research and to develop scientific talent" (Bush [1945] 1960: 21). Without basic scientific research supplied by the government, industrial development would "stagnate" (Bush [1945] 1960: 18).

Furthermore, both Bush and Steelman understood an interrelation between the privileged position of science and the productivity of science. For Bush ([1945] 1960: 12), "[a]s long as . . . scientists are free to pursue the truth wherever it may lead, there will be a flow of new scientific knowledge to those who can apply it to practical problems in Government, in industry, or elsewhere." But even the "free play of free intellects" "must be responsible to the President and Congress [because o]nly through such responsibility can we maintain the proper relationship between science and other aspects of a democratic system" (Bush [1945] 1960: 12; 33). Steelman (1947c: 27) is even more explicit about a privileged yet responsible science:

> However, in organizing scientific effort, the administrator must recognize the special characteristics of research and development work and the special qualities of the scientific mind. Otherwise, he cannot function effectively. For their part, scientists must accept the organization which is essential to all large scale operations, and – in the Federal Government – the necessity for rules and regulations which accompany public operations of great scope.

> Neither public administration nor modern science can exist or function in a vacuum.
>
> After conceding the special status and vital role of the scientists in our society, it is important to note also that society and its organization are important to the scientist. Science is a functional part of the framework of the community. Scientists are members of society living within limits set by social responsibility, economic reality, and democratic government. The democratic ideals of our society have fostered science and helped to give it its present place in the world at large. It is the obligation of scientists, in turn, to give willing aid to the tasks involved in making our system work well.

Both Bush and Steelman shared ideas about a reciprocal relationship between science and politics: one that involved the "free play" of scientists in an environment "segregated" from political and market pressure; and also one that, if given this freedom, would be productive for the political community because its investment in science would provide welfare and security.

Conclusion

The relationship that both Bush and Steelman conceived, the social contract for science, can therefore be described as follows: the political community agrees to provide resources to the scientific community and to allow the scientific community to retain its decision-making mechanisms and in return expects forthcoming but unspecified technological benefits. Both Bush and Steelman plotted their campaigns for the federal role in science on this map, and others have used it since, implicitly or explicitly, to legitimate this role. While not an actual agreement, this social contract for science represents a plausible agreement and summarizes a dominant ideology of the postwar era. As the words of the science policy makers and analysts earlier in Chapter 2 attest, these very ideas continue to have currency.

But did the social contract for science continue to endure as policy, rather than as rhetoric? I argue that it did, despite its being faced with its first of several challenges even as it was being framed. These challenges, which I elaborate in Chapter 3, changed some ways in which science was done in the United States. But they did not alter the underlying mechanisms for treating the problems of the integrity and the productivity of science. Crises over loyalty, appropriations, programmatic research, and the safety of genetic research, as Chapter 3 shows, provided the opportunity for a great deal of political activity and soul-searching, but they did not amend or redraft the social contract for science. They did not alter the position of science policy between politics and science.

3

Challenges to the Social Contract for Science

> Despite much debate, and much apprehension and cries of alarm from the scientific community, it appears to me that the basis [sic] outlines of the 'social contract' between science and government proposed in Bush's famous report to President Roosevelt, *Science the Endless Frontier*, have remained more or less intact, and are still broadly accepted by public and politicians. Reality has changed much less than rhetoric. True, there has been some intrusion of government into the management of the extramural scientific enterprise, but after many threatening draft regulations and bursts of threatening rhetoric in the Congress, the end result has not been much real change, certainly not as great as the alarmists feared.
>
> – Harvey Brooks (in Brooks and Schmitt 1985: 17)

Introduction

In Chapter 2, I located the social contract for science in the broad consensus among Vannevar Bush, his political allies, and his political opponents that although funding science was a public responsibility, maintaining the integrity and the productivity of the enterprise was to be left to the scientists alone. Contrary to the epigraph from physicist and science policy scholar Harvey Brooks, the outline of the social contract for science was not limited to Bush's report. Neither were all the major tenets of *Science: The Endless Frontier* part of that outline. But the social contract for science can serve, as Brooks suggests, as the basis for assessing change in the relationship between the political and scientific communities over time.

Having established that baseline, in this chapter I assess a number of challenges to it in the postwar era, for the broad agreement on the automatic solution to the problems of the integrity and productivity of research did not preclude serious conflicts that challenged the ideology of the social contract for science. With McCarthyism, as the history of the NSF legislation makes clear, the challenge of the loyalty of scientists began even before the ink on the social contract for science was dry. A second challenge occurred within a decade: as NIH funding doubled and redoubled, Congress began to investigate grant-giving practices and financial accountability at NIH. A third challenge arose as federal funding for R&D crested through 1967. Congress, better equipped institutionally to deal with science, scrutinized the productivity of this investment and attempted to push more practically oriented research through the Mansfield Amendment and programs like Research Applied to National Needs and the War on Cancer. Finally, in the 1970s, just as the language of the social contract for science was fully developing, scholars were questioning its durability under the challenge of risky DNA research and the "limits of scientific inquiry."

Although these cases show the social contract for science has been embattled since its origin, they also demonstrate its continued durability until the late 1970s. Furthermore, they demonstrate the variety of tactics employed by Congress to control and direct scientific research within its framework. In a science policy regime emphasizing the separateness of politics and science, attempts to manipulate appropriations for science and threats and bluster were among the few avenues of influence open to politicians. The "alarmists," as Brooks called them, cited a contract with the implication that changes in science and government threatened the agreement – whatever it was. Brooks more clearly defined a social contract for science that he saw as broader, more robust, and more durable. Yet Brooks refined this optimistic rhetoric just at the period when, as I argue in subsequent chapters, politicians were altering the set of arrangements and ideas that constituted the social contract for science. In the 1980s, Congress reached beyond these blunt tactics in favor of a more refined strategy that altered the relationship between politics and science, using explicit monitoring and incentives to assure the integrity and productivity of research.

This chapter performs two primary roles in the argument of the book. First, it derives and articulates criteria for evaluating change in the social contract for science, focusing on a distinction between the blunt attempts by the political principal to exert influence, which I will call macroeconomic controls, and the more refined or microeconomic attempts characteristic of the new regime. Second, it surveys a set of issues posing possible challenges to the social contract for science, including loyalty, NIH funding, programmatic research, and genetic research. These challenges remained at the macroeconomic level, failing to institutionalize any more refined monitoring and incentives prescribed by principal-agent theory, and therefore the social contract for science remained intact until at least the late 1970s.

Premises and Criteria

The social contract for science delineated in Chapter 2 has at least two implicit premises. One is that the scientific community is actually capable of being allowed to retain its decision-making mechanisms. That is, the social contract for science is premised in part on its being what is often referred to as an autonomous or self-regulating scientific community (I prefer the latter term because I view autonomy as a concept more aptly associated with individuals than with communities). The second premise is that under this arrangement, the scientific community can produce the technological and other benefits expected by the political community. These two premises are the basis of the social contract for science.[1] When the political community begins to tamper with them, or when the scientific community evidently fails to live up to them, the social contract for science erodes.

Is there a coherent conception of science underlying these premises, in addition to the rhetoric of Bush and Steelman? There are attempts to justify the premise of self-regulation with the social contract for scientists, discussed above. Michael Polanyi offers another variety of this defense in his duly famous essay, "The republic of science" (1962), which provides a political economic model of the scientific community. Polanyi (1962: 54–56) argues that the "free cooperation of independent scientists" is, like an economic market, a "special case of coordination by mutual adjustment." The rules of Polanyi's republic of science keep order, as in a market, despite competing interests. Polanyi's model specifies a science that corrects its mistakes and regulates the conduct of its members, recalling Bush's "free play of free intellects." As the workings of the market are separated from political interference, so are the workings of science.

Admitting a close relationship to and influence from Polanyi's work, economist Gordon Tullock articulates a more specific economic vision of the social organization of the scientific community. Like Polanyi, Tullock (1966: 11) supposes the interrelation of scientists is based on "voluntary, and almost unconscious, co-operation," and therefore it is familiar terrain for economists because the lack of planning or hierarchy in science, as in a free economy, does not mean a lack of social organization. Among the concerns Tullock evinces are the two central concerns here: the integrity and productivity of science. With respect to integrity, Tullock holds the marketlike organization of science responsible for the ability of society to "depend upon scientists not only to refrain from faking research results, but [also] to exercise the most extreme precautions to insure accuracy." It is therefore "quite safe to leave [scientists] free of other supervision," with the exception of the same auditing functions that Bush and Steelman admitted (Tullock 1966: 6; 7). With respect to productivity, Tullock expounds on the ability of patents and other monetary arrangements to "induce" curiosity among researchers who otherwise would confine themselves to pure research rather than applied, or to the narrow bounds of their own curiosity rather than more socially linked curiosity.

Tullock's work enjoyed very little follow-up. Much of the scholarly domain regarding the social organization of science, as Tullock noticed even as he was publishing, was inhabited by sociologists, and only recently have economists returned to it.[2] But some of these sociologists admit the power of the economic metaphor for the organization of science – even if their constructivism leads them in different directions than Tullock's or Polanyi's positivism.

Sociologists Bruno Latour and Steve Woolgar, for example, extend the economic perspective of Polanyi and Tullock by providing a more complete account of transactions among scientists within the pseudo-marketplace of science. Latour and Woolgar (1979: 204) "had the distinct impression that the constant investment and transformation of credibility taking place in the laboratory mirrored economic operations typical of modern capitalism." They describe a credibility cycle, which traces the flow of scientific "capital" through a heterogeneous circuit of domains: recognition, grants, money, equipment, data, arguments, articles (which are also products), and recognition.[3] Within the scientific community, the free flow of such capital is permitted and encouraged, and successful scientists efficiently convert their capital into products such as scientific papers which, if credible, are demanded by other scientists. A market is thus created, with a supply of and demand for credible information.[4] Furthermore, an important implication of such a market is that any policy regime that interfered with the microeconomic transactions would, from the perspective of the scientific community, threaten the economic structure of science by intruding upon the exercise of scientific judgment that converts one form of capital into products and other forms of capital.[5]

The role of the government in this market is limited to the provision of money for grants – a monetarist macroeconomic policy if you will. Thus there is no strict laissez faire, as Bush and Steelman agreed. But the microeconomic aspects exclude government action because they require the exercise of a sort of scientific judgment that Major Powell, Bush, and Steelman all thought was beyond the ken of administration. For example, the conversion of recognition into grants, and articles into recognition, requires the judgment of peer review. Similarly, the conversion of money into equipment involves the judgment of choosing experimental problems. As the application of judgment by scientists is said to moderate economic exchange and transformation, and as credibility is cyclical, the system could be said to be self-regulating.[6]

But the claim to self-regulation is meant to be even more powerful than this economic analogy. It is meant to regulate the integrity of the conduct of research. Recognition does not evolve into grants without a peer-reviewed proposal. Data do not evolve into a paper without a peer-reviewed journal. Papers do not evolve into recognition without successful replication or extension. At any point, the mechanisms of review and experimental checking are supposed to flush out shoddy or fraudulent work, which is then not rewarded or, worse, is punished, and the unfit or miscreant scientist falls by the wayside – unable to convert a soiled reputation into other forms of scientific capital.

In Polanyi's republic of science, the premise of self-regulation is inextricably bound to the premise of productivity. Polanyi argues that only by allowing science this free association can the rest of society expect the benefits that science can provide. First, relying on the "invisible hand" metaphor, Polanyi (1962: 56) claims that this organization of science is "the most efficient possible." This organization also drives the "maximum advancement of science," just as the Smithian market produces the maximum satisfaction possible. Second, "that research would no longer be conducted for itself as an end in itself" but would instead be guided "into socially beneficent channels" is an "impossible and nonsensical" aim (Polanyi 1962: 62). One could not guide, direct, or plan science because one cannot predict the uses to which scientific discovery might be put.

Third, because of this unpredictability, Polanyi (1962: 62–63) concludes:

> Any attempt at guiding scientific research towards a purpose other than its own is an attempt to deflect it from the advancement of science. . . . You can kill or mutilate the advance of science, you cannot shape it. For it can advance only by essentially unpredictable steps, pursuing problems of its own, and the practical benefits of these advances will be incidental and hence doubly unpredictable.
>
> . . . . In describing here the autonomous growth of science, I have taken the relation of science and technology fully into account.[7]

The "relation of science and technology" is summarized by Polanyi here as "incidental."[8] But the technological product is directly derived from the advancement of science, and one cannot, according to Polanyi, increase the former by attempting to manipulate the latter. In this view, the only possible way to increase the technological yield from research is to conduct more research, which is another way of stating what is known as the "linear" or "pipeline" model described in detail in Chapter 5. Bush's model was this sort, in which the government would "put money into pure science at the front end of the process. In due time, innovation will come out of the other end" (Wise 1986: 229). As Chapter 5 will show, belief in the linear model meant that policy makers paid little attention to innovation.

In this political-economic model, both the maintenance of the integrity of science and the contribution of scientific advance to technological innovation are unproblematic. They are managed by the normal, automatic functions of science – the self-regulating system with respect to integrity and the linear model with respect to productivity. Figure 2 alters the earlier figure to emphasize these aspects. The point here is not whether Polanyi was right or wrong in his conception of free science as regulating integrity and being productive. Rather, Polanyi provides an intellectually coherent vision of science of this kind, akin to the vision manifest in the social contract for science, and elaborated in the same metaphor by analysts as distant from Polanyi in time and outlook as Latour and Woolgar.

With the political economic metaphor, one can sketch a map such as Figure 2 that helps articulate the criteria for measuring change. The criteria are the following: First, a challenge to the social contract for science must involve one of the premises of integrity or productivity. This criterion is justified by the centrality of integrity and productivity to the structure of principals and agents – a structure the basic element of which is widely shared across time and perspective. It is also justified by the common and related treatment of integrity and productivity by contributors to the intellectual force behind the social contract for science, including Bush, Steelman, Polanyi, and Tullock. Second, a challenge must be effectively directed at the microeconomic activity of research – the activities in the bottom half of Figure 2 – and more specifically at the automaticity of integrity and productivity. This criterion is justified by the dual claim implicit in the social contract for science that a macroeconomic policy for science is necessary and that a microeconomic policy is not merely unnecessary, but destructive.

In the challenges to the social contract for science described in this chapter, the politicians or principals who want something more or different from the scientific agents will only deal with the input to the credibility cycle and not cross that semipermeable boundary. They will

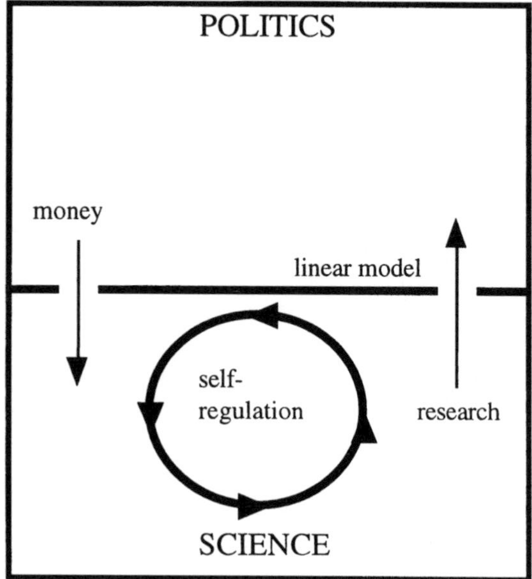

Figure 2 The Automatic Functions in the Social Contract for Science: Self-regulation for Integrity and the Linear Model for Productivity

attempt to influence the goings on beyond the boundary by manipulating the amount of money available for certain delegations of authority. And in these efforts, they will only be marginally successful at best.

Loyalty

Beginning in June 1952, about two years after Truman signed the National Science Foundation Act that included an affidavit of loyalty for grant applicants, the Department of Health, Education, and Welfare (DHEW) inaugurated a policy to deny or suspend grants "where it is established to the satisfaction of this Department that the individual has engaged or is engaging in subversive activities or that there is serious question of his loyalty to the United States" (quoted in Edsall 1988: 24). DHEW backed this policy well into the Cold War attack on the loyalty of scientists. The House Un-American Activities Committee (HUAC) had begun its campaign against Communism in 1947. But although the prominent cases of scientists pursued by HUAC – including J. Robert Oppenheimer (Stern 1969; Smith and Weiner 1980) and Edward U.

Condon (Wang 1992) – generally involved security clearances for classified research, DHEW's action did not. And unlike NSF's affidavit, DHEW gave no forewarning to its action. It could deny or suspend a grant without the applicant or grantee knowing the cause.

DHEW's policy did not surface publicly until the spring of 1954, when it was rumored at the annual meeting of the National Academy of Sciences (NAS) that several scientists had lost or been denied grants from NIH because of loyalty questions (Wilson 1983). After press coverage of the NAS meeting and an official NAS request for information, Secretary of Health Oveta Culp Hobby issued a statement describing the policy and reporting that "fewer than 30 persons have been denied support" among the 14,000 persons supported on more than 2000 PHS grants (quoted in Edsall 1988: 24). Members of the scientific community, most prominently John Edsall of Harvard University, attacked the action because "grants for open, unclassified research were being revoked or denied, on grounds apparently political and unconnected with the competence or integrity of the investigators involved" (Edsall 1988: 24). Indeed, Edsall (1988: 25) argued that the "action taken against [these scientists] has often involved the breaking of a moral agreement, if not a legal contract, by the supporting agency."

Edsall acknowledged, however, that security checks seemed reasonable for classified research, and that technically the grants were discretionary actions by the Secretary. Furthermore, the approach he took in his rhetoric against DHEW's action was oriented more toward the maltreatment of scientists as citizens of a democratic polity than the maltreatment of scientists involved in a special relationship with the federal government: "The policies attacked here violate a long tradition – a tradition deeply rooted in English and American law" (Edsall 1988: 26). So Edsall invoked a three-tiered rhetoric about the question of loyalty: he accepted the demands of classified research; he pointed out the scientific community has mechanisms to determine if "a man is trusted and respected by his colleagues and neighbors" (Edsall 1988: 26); but he contextualized both the security demand and the internal governance aspect of the social contract for science within a broader idea of the responsibility of a democratic government to its citizens. Although the action by DHEW may have been in violation of a social contract for science, it was abhorrent not necessarily because it crossed the boundaries specified by the contract, but rather because it crossed the boundaries specified by Anglo-American legal traditions and liberal government in general.

In effect, Edsall and DHEW were fighting over what constituted scientific integrity. Was it something that referred only to the conduct of scientists in the laboratory, and thus the scientific community has the mechanisms to determine "if a man is trusted?" Or is it something broader, where scientists who do not take part in a common societal morality are suspect in their science as well? If Major Powell could argue for exemption from scrutiny based on his claim that scientists are "the most radical democrats in society," where does that leave scientists who are not democrats?

The revelation of DHEW's policy prodded NSF into action because, although NSF had implemented the loyalty oath, it remained possible that scientists whom DHEW found unacceptable could have obtained NSF funding, which would have put NSF in an awkward position. NSF reconsidered security checks but decided not to implement them for two reasons: its sponsored research was unclassified; and institutions and not individuals were the legal grantees, so the institutions (and not NSF) were responsible for the conduct of their faculty and staff (Wilson 1983).[9] The American Association for the Advancement of Science endorsed NSF's policy, as did NAS in a 1956 report requested by the White House (Cochrane 1978). The Eisenhower administration opted to implement the Academy's recommendation across the federal agencies, resolving the issue.

Measuring this case against the two criteria, the issue of loyalty is about competing ways to construct integrity, and therefore it is worth considering. But did it involve macroeconomic or microeconomic issues? Edsall equivocates, although he shades on the side of the macroeconomic level by recognizing the discretionary nature of grants and the importance of Anglo-American legal tradition. But even if the loyalty issue constituted an intrusion into the microeconomic workings of science, its resolution was quick and occurred through action by the scientific community. Indeed, the conclusion, that the mechanisms of science are more relevant to the construction and identification of integrity than are the categories of politics, sided with scientists.

NIH Accountability

Questions about NIH grant practices and financial accountability became a source of conflict between Congress and the burgeoning agency during the 1960s. NIH's budget doubled three times from 1951 to 1960, through the combined efforts of the "disease lobby," headed by Mary Lasker, and the chairmen of the health appropriations subcommittees, Representative John Fogarty (D-RI) and Senator Lister Hill (D-AL).[10] Representative Lawrence H. Fountain (D-NC), chairman of the Intergovernmental Affairs Subcommittee of the House Government Operations

Committee, suspected that these rapid increases were not being put to good use.[11] Fountain conducted several inquiries in a partially successful attempt to demonstrate that NIH financial management was too loose.[12]

The initial inquiry began in 1959, and in April 1961 the Fountain Committee recommended thirteen actions to NIH for tightening its financial management. The next year, Fountain held hearings to determine what NIH director James A. Shannon had done to respond to the recommendations; the answer he received was that NIH had not done much (Greenberg 1967; Henderson 1970; Strickland 1972). Fountain issued a second report in June 1962 that took Shannon to task for his position that financial oversight was a concern secondary to choosing the right researchers (Strickland 1972) – in other words, that solving the problem of adverse selection solved the problem of moral hazard.

The impact of Fountain's inquiry was seemingly twofold. First, NIH tightened up its information requirements on its grants. It required the itemization of equipment expenditures and the specification of travel budgets, mandated that salaries paid by grants reflect only time spent on research and not be higher than the grantee's university pay rate, and required prior approval for grantees to change research plans. "By non-scientific standards, none of these requirements was onerous," but the biomedical community complained loudly nevertheless (Greenberg 1967: 277). Second, Greenberg attributes the relatively weak increase in NIH funding, from $930 million in FY 1963 to $974 million in FY 1964 to the scrutiny brought by Fountain. Thus, according to Greenberg (1967: 271–72), the Fountain Committee was a significant part of the change from the "old politics of science," which was "predicated on government and scientific sovereignty," to the "new politics of science," which was "characterized by the diminution of the *de facto* sovereignty that pure science had nurtured though the postwar period." But the social contract for science is not involved with sovereignty so loosely defined.

Strickland (1972: 173) disagrees, suggesting that Fountain's inquiry "was not a lethal blow to the Cause [of independent biomedical research], by any means, but for a time it was staggering." This interpretation is more sound, particularly when it comes to evaluating the impact of Fountain's inquiries on the social contract for science, which neither specifies levels of funding nor frees scientists from the obligations of good financial practice. Both Steelman and Bush recognized in their reports that some administrative practices might need to be tailored to accommodate scientific practice, but neither suggested that scientists should be free from financial accountability. Nothing in the new paperwork requirements crossed the exercise of scientific judgment that Powell and the others found essential to protect. They did, however, allow

Turner's (1990a) financial metonym to take on a more precise form. Loose administration, as practiced by NIH, was at odds with the social contract for science, not Fountain's inquiries.

Fountain, however, stirred up hope as well as trouble for the biomedical research community. In the summer of 1963, President Kennedy charged Dr. Dean E. Wooldridge to investigate the quality of research at NIH, in what may have been a direct response to Fountain's inquiries (Strickland 1972). The Wooldridge Committee saw as the cardinal points the examination of "[a]dministrative relations between NIH and recipient or contractee institutions" and "[a]dministrative procedures used to disperse [sic] and control NIH funds" (Wooldridge 1965: xv). Given the question of the quality of financial controls at NIH, the word "disperse," from the Latin, "to scatter" – presumably for the word "disburse" – from the Latin for "out of the bag," is a malapropism that seems unfortunately telling about the attitude of biomedical researchers toward federal largesse.

After meeting with more than 600 scientists funded by NIH and 150 administrators, the Wooldridge Committee concluded "that the activities of the National Institutes of Health are essentially sound and that its budget of approximately one billion dollars a year is, on the whole, being spent wisely and well in the public interest" (Wooldridge 1965: 1). The report found that "[d]espite the tenfold increase in NIH support of research during the last eight years, there is no evidence of over-all degradation in quality of the work supported. On the contrary, there is good evidence that the average quality is steadily improving" (Wooldridge 1965: 3).[13] It also assured that "NIH funds and equipment allocated to a project are ordinarily well related to the task to be accomplished, and the funds are expended with care and probity by the investigator" (Wooldridge 1965: 4).

Two years after Wooldridge vindicated NIH, Fountain commenced a new investigation, questioning both financial management and the quality of some grants. Fountain's October 1967 report charged NIH with "weak central management," geographically elitist funding, "inept handling" of indirect cost reimbursement, and a general "laxity" in administration. He also attacked the quality of scientists and research projects, saying NIH spent too much money on too many projects.[14] Fountain concluded that Congress was still appropriating too much for NIH.

Despite Fountain's harsh conclusions, Congress took relatively gentle action, especially given the larger context of a "crisis" in government-science relations spurred by conflicts over military R&D and the increasingly apparent guns-and-butter problem wrought by deepening involvement in Vietnam. Furthermore, appropriations subcommittee chairman

John Fogarty had passed away in 1967, depriving NIH of its man in the House. In the appropriations battle for FY 1969, President Johnson and the Bureau of the Budget cut less from the NIH request than in previous years. The House trimmed Johnson's request by $40 million, but Lister Hill, still active in the Senate, replaced the $40 million and added $10 million more. The final appropriation fell between the Senate and House figures, a $20 million cut (Strickland 1972: 222). Some of this cut, however, was undoubtedly attributable to the $8 billion budget cut required by Congress in exchange for Johnson's Vietnam War tax increase, rather than to Fountain's attacks. Indeed, health research showed the smallest downward increment among the three largest government R&D programs in FY 1969: defense R&D fell 3.2% in current dollars; space R&D fell 10%; and health R&D fell only 2.9% (NSB 1973).[15]

Strickland declares 1968 the "end of an era." Fogarty was a year gone, and Fountain was seemingly having an impact on the budget. Senator Hill decided not to seek reelection after 45 years in Congress. NIH director Shannon would retire with the change in administrations. Strickland's assessment is more apt than Greenberg's, although given the budgetary context and other R&D spending, he overestimates the impact of a $20 million cut from a wartime budget. The era Strickland sees ending was the pre-Watergate Congress, dominated by appropriations and committee barons. This era would pass completely with the election of the Watergate class of 1974. Yet even with the demographic changes in Congress, and the structural ones to follow, NIH funding would recover and continue to grow, if only in small real terms, through most of the 1970s. As Figure 3 shows, however, NIH would have a budgetary renaissance in the 1980s. It would continue to lead most other R&D accounts, even as R&D spending outperformed the remainder of domestic spending in the more stringent 1990s.

The turnabouts, from Fountain to Wooldridge to Fountain to later renewal, suggest the technique used by Greenberg and Strickland of assessing the overall relationship between Congress and NIH, or for that matter between Congress and science more broadly, by measuring appropriations is not precise enough. Even though the appropriations process instutionalizes a great deal of oversight, and indeed is often the site of scientists offering those public attestations so important to Turner, the size of the delegation is no good guarantee of its performance with integrity. Spending is a blunt instrument for Congress to achieve qualitative control because it is so dependent upon other factors and because it can be so easily manipulated by other contemporary and future actors. For Fountain, however, there was no legislative action that could be taken against NIH from the Government Operations Committee other

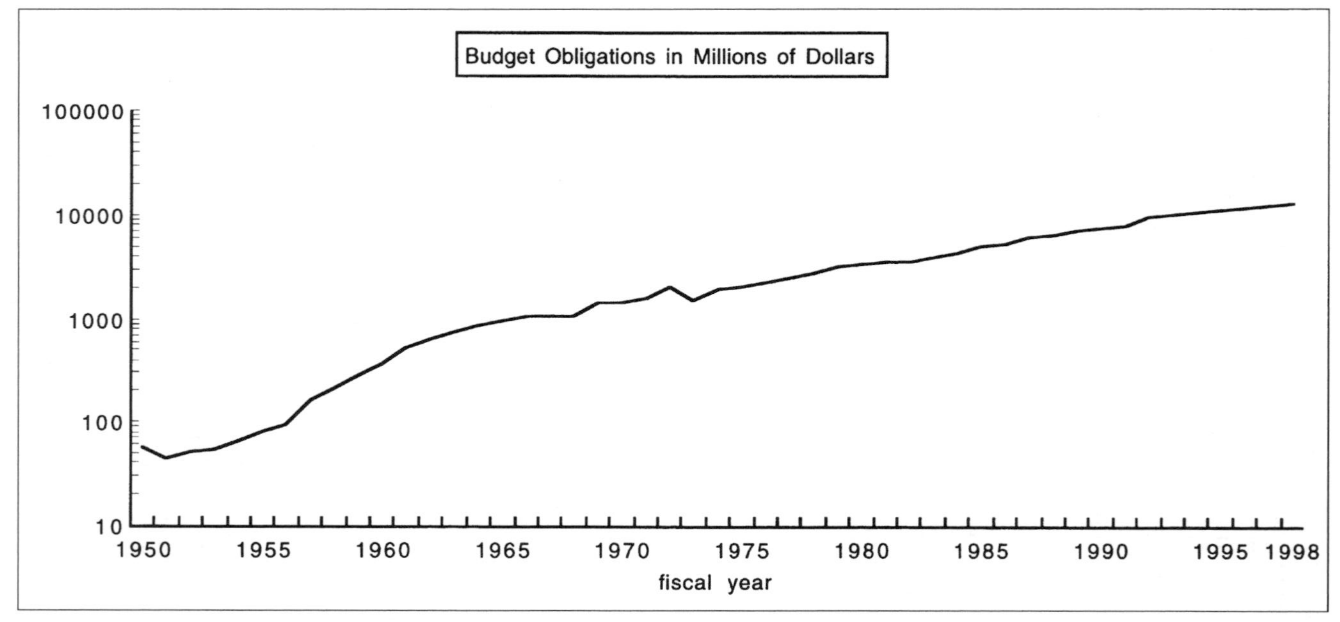

Figure 3 Growth in NIH Budget, 1950–1998

than stirring up trouble and hoping for a budgetary impact (Henderson 1970).

The challenges to NIH accountability in the 1960s did not implicate the social contract for science properly understood because they involved merely the size of the financial delegation and the means to account for it. The only members of Congress who might have wanted to institute a more controlled relationship lacked the institutional means to do so. Fountain's attention perhaps encouraged NIH to rise to the expectations of financial integrity of any agency. But without the ability to intervene in any more permanent way than by spooking the House into making incremental cuts, which were compromised by the Senate, during times that were tough anyway, Fountain did not institutionalize any damage to the social contract for science.

Congressional Organization and Scrutiny

The mid- to late-1960s, however, did witness some changes in the relationship between science and government most broadly conceived. The Kennedy and the Johnson administrations often embodied a heady instrumentalism in their programs and approaches. Broad-based cultural critiques, some trenchant and some trivial, tempered the technological enthusiasm in American culture that had driven Bush and Steelman.[16] But focusing on the cultural trends misses the activity at the organizational and programmatic level, as members of Congress tried both to reassert their policy prerogatives in areas of science policy that were increasingly falling under executive sway, and to rein in and redirect an expanding scientific bureaucracy.

In September 1963, to "strengthen their body's role in formulating scientific research and development policy" (U.S. House 1986b: 48), members of the House of Representatives created a Select Committee on Government Research. Carl Y. Elliott (D-AL) led the effort and became its chairman. The Select Committee held a number of hearings and published ten reports during the 88th Congress.[17] Disbanded after the moderate Elliott suffered defeat in his 1964 primary, it left but a modest jurisdictional impression. It had recommended Congress establish a Joint Committee on Research Policy as a counterweight to executive expertise in the Office of Science and Technology (OST) and the rest of the President's science advisory apparatus.[18] The thought of such centralization aroused the territorial instincts of the authorizing committees responsible for the fragments of the plural system of science policy. The House Science and Astronautics Committee had established a new Subcommittee on Science, Research, and Development in response to the plans for the Select Committee, and the House Armed Services Committee also created its own science subcommittee (U.S. House 1980f; 1986b).[19] In parallel to the new committee structures and at the urging of the new science subcommittee, the Legislative Research Service created its Science Policy Research Division in 1964 (U.S. House 1980f). But the joint committee never materialized.

The Subcommittee on Science, Research, and Development, headed by Emilio Daddario (D-CT), became active in a number of reviews and innovations in science policy. Most prominent were several reports requested by Daddario of the National Academy of Science's Committee on Science and Public Policy (COSPUP), which began to address in a more contemplative manner the issues of science and government.[20] In 1968, Daddario also worked with Senator Edward Kennedy (D-MA) to revise NSF's charter. The revision led to increased efforts in the social sciences and in applied research (U.S. House 1980f; Wilson 1983) as well as to an annual reauthorization cycle at NSF (Smith 1990).

It was not only Congress that was trying to come to terms with the federal role in science organizationally and informationally. The agencies supporting research, in particular the Department of Defense (DOD) and NSF, began to examine the connection between the support of basic research and technological products. DOD instituted Project Hindsight, which attempted to discover the character of the innovative events that had led to current critical weapons systems.[21] Hindsight concluded that only nine percent of the 700 events identified could be classified as scientific rather than technological, and that only two events in total could be classified as basic research. These conclusions engendered a great deal of controversy both over the methodology of the study, the twenty-year time horizon of which was deemed too limited to uncover the real contribution of basic research, and over its findings, which seemed contrary to the technological premise of the social contract for science, in other words, the linear model. Moreover, the findings were punctuated by the notorious Mansfield Amendment to the 1970 military authorization bill, forbidding the use of military funds to support research unless it has "a direct or apparent relationship to a specific military function or operation" (quoted in U.S. House 1986b: 62).[22] The amendment was a successful coalition of the ends, uniting the liberal Mike Mansfield (D-MT), who was trying to reduce military-university tensions, with conservatives who were skeptical of the military impact of basic research in any event. But the coalition fractured, and Congress watered the amendment down in the next year's authorization.[23]

NSF also engaged in a retrospective of the relationship between science and technology, entitled *Technology in Retrospect and Critical Events in Science*, or TRACES.[24] Its conclusion was more "supportive of the assembly-line view" of the role of basic research that had been articulated by Bush (Wise 1986: 233). But NSF also suffered a short-term programmatic change in the wake of congressional change and the scrutiny of TRACES. Following the charter newly amended by the Daddario Subcommittee to include applied research, NSF began a program called Interdisciplinary Research on Problems Relevant to Our Society (IRPOS), which was expanded and reestablished in 1971 as Research Applied to National Needs (RANN). Funds under RANN constituted 8.6% of NSF money in 1972 and rose to 13% in 1974; their share then fell to 10% in 1976 (Smith and Karlesky 1977: 34) and in 1978 the program was discontinued (U.S. House 1986b: 68). Although the academic research community was initially uncomfortable with RANN as an applied research program, it gradually became accustomed to both the new money involved and the fact it was distributed in much the same way as other NSF money.[25]

NIH also received programmatic impetus toward supporting more applied work, following an attempt to increase information about scientific productivity for policy analysis. In 1970 Congress amended the Public Health Service Act to set aside up to one percent of the funds to a program authorized under the act for program evaluation. NIH has since maintained several computerized databases to assist in such evaluation (OTA 1986). Although not causally related to the move toward evaluation, NIH was also moved toward more socially relevant work with the advent of the Nixon administration's War on Cancer. The Johnson administration had tried to reorient NIH in a more applied direction (Lambright 1985), but the Nixon administration succeeded by allying with congressional liberals like Senator Kennedy and with the disease lobby in mobilizing the biomedical resources at NIH for a crusade against cancer (Rettig 1977). Like RANN, the War on Cancer consisted of a large amount of money for an applied goal and was initially opposed by the relevant scientific community. A tougher case than the Fountain inquiry because it involved actual appropriations rather than simply the bluster of a congressional overseer, the War on Cancer nevertheless demonstrates the continuing currency of the social contract for science. Although the funding mechanisms favored contracts over grants and clinical research over basic research, this shift was only in emphasis and not a rejection of grants or basic research as such.[26] As with RANN, the community initially protested, but scientists took the money and performed the research – thus tacitly accepting the continuation of the social contract – and then came to accept the program as it grew familiar.[27]

Hindsight, TRACES, and program evaluation at NIH were symptomatic of a discomfort – general in society and specific in Congress – about the automaticity of the technological premise of the social contract for science. In an effort to ease the symptoms, Congress made some programmatic changes that emphasized mission-oriented and socially relevant research. My claim is not that the programmatic changes were directly and causally related, and in fact they were probably dependent on both the larger cultural context and the organizational changes in Congress. Rather, my claim is simply that new ideas and new tools were being tried. The tactics used were different from the attacks by Fountain. Instead of simply targeting the size of the research budget, the Mansfield Amendment, RANN, and the War on Cancer tried to direct scientists to produce relevant research. By changing the conditions on the input flowing from the political community, Congress hoped to influence the outputs from the scientific community.

This attempt to program research still abides by the same logical structure of delegation and thus the same problems of moral hazard and adverse selection, even if the expected output of the contract is marginally better defined. It demonstrates the principal's struggling to write a more specific agreement for delegation, something that principal-agent theory recognizes as problematic. The output is, however, not assured, and the same money is spent regardless of whether IRPOS or RANN or the War on Cancer has actually achieved the programmatic goal. Like a novice at computer programming, Congress did not know machine code and thus had little concern for what went on inside the black box of science. Indeed, that scientists seemingly took the money and ran with their own research agendas suggests the moral hazard and adverse selection problems were as robust as ever. Even the establishment of a new research agency or, in the case of NIH, an institute dedicated to the study of a particular disease – however politically motivated that might be – still faces the problems of integrity and productivity of the delegation of authority.

Furthermore, these mechanisms left the internal reward system of the scientific community intact. They were still in the realm of the macroeconomic management of science. But they did presage the more complete set of instructions and incentives provided by the technology policy of the 1980s. These changes were temporary – very temporary in the case of the Mansfield Amendment. The scientific community eventually took to both RANN and the War on Cancer. These changes did show, however, how the new organization of Congress could respond to the challenges of governing scientific programs in more direct ways. They also showed science itself was subject to study and attempts could be made to scrutinize the technological promise of the social contract for science. But they did not constitute a break in the social contract for science.

Research Risks and the Limits of Scientific Inquiry

The concern over research risks, particularly those from new recombinant DNA techniques, presented another challenge to the social contract for science in the 1970s. This concern was expressed in a set of essays published by the American Academy of Arts and Sciences in 1978 and later as a separate volume, *Limits of Scientific Inquiry* (Holton and Morison 1979).[28] Titled in counterpoint to *Science: The Endless Frontier*, the *Limits* volume may have done as much to disseminate the language of the social contract for science as it did to describe its possible renegotiation. Likewise, June Goodfield's (1977) *Playing God* framed the issue of identifying the risks of recombinant DNA and beginning to regulate them in terms of a social contract between society and science.

The primary concern of the two books is the nature of risks from research and the reciprocal impact understanding these risks has on science and on society. It was not new in the 1970s, having begun as early as World War II for physicists in the dual concerns for atomic weapons and secrecy, and for life scientists and physicians with concerns over the conduct of Nazi doctors.[29] The most contentious of these concerns, however, erupted over new techniques in molecular biology pioneered in the early 1970s that led to the ability to recombine genetic material from different organisms in one organism. These recombinant DNA techniques, or genetic engineering, offered prospects of the control of disease at the molecular level, the mass production of pharmaceuticals through biological means, and the specific control of heredity. Along with such possible boons, some recognized, came the specter of accidental epidemics, novel workplace hazards, and a new eugenics.[30] Biologists began to talk, as the atomic physicists had, of knowing sin.

Although in retrospect their actions often appear as an effort to circle the wagons, to their credit, some prominent scientists were instrumental in forcing both their colleagues and the public to recognize the dangers as well as the promise of the new techniques.[31] Scientists first raised questions about hazardous experiments in private as early as 1971, and at a small meeting at the Asilomar Conference Center in California in early 1973. At the Gordon Conference later that year, researcher Herbert Boyer first described the techniques he and Stanley Cohen had been developing – the process that would in 1980 be acknowledged in the Cohen-Boyer patents that sparked the new biotechnology industry. But they could hardly contain the social implications of such research at the meeting. The attendees at the conference agreed to write a letter describing the techniques and their concerns about them to NAS and the Institute of Medicine (IOM), and they also agreed to "go public" by sending the letter to the journal *Science*. Responding to the Gordon Conference letter, NAS decided to establish a study panel and invited Paul Berg, a Stanford researcher intimately involved in developing recombinant techniques and a principal in the 1973 Asilomar meeting, to lead it. Berg gathered a group of scientists, many of whom had track records in issues of social concern, and the group met at MIT in the spring of 1974. The panel published a set of recommendations (the Berg letter), including a moratorium on the riskiest techniques and the establishment by NIH of an advisory committee to perform oversight, procedural, and regulatory tasks.

Following the Berg letter, NAS charged a second meeting to be convened at the Asilomar Conference Center. The meeting, in February 1975, is known generically as "Asilomar" and although its interpretation is contested, it stands as something like a benchmark of scientific responsibility. What is agreed upon is, as Krimsky (1982: 99) writes, "No single event has had more impact on the public-policy outcome of rDNA research than this four-day conference. It was a key point in the transition . . . from informal scientific to formal governmental channels." The details of Asilomar are far too numerous to relate here, but it is clear from Krimsky's (1982: 99) account that scientists at Asilomar engaged in consequential boundary work: "The objective was not necessarily to close off debate and discussion on other aspects of the research – the social, ethical, and political considerations, for example – but only to separate those issues from the task of establishing the conditions under which the research would be conducted." But in the recommendations that the conferees agreed upon:

> the organizers of Asilomar had accomplished two objectives: (1) they defined the issues in such a way that the expertise remained the monopoly of those who gain the most from the technique, and (2) they chose to place authority for regulating the use of the technique in the agency that is the major supporter of biomedical research in the United States (Krimsky 1982: 153).[32]

In October 1974, a few months after the Berg letter and still several months before Asilomar, DHEW Secretary Caspar Weinberger implemented the scientists' recommendations and created the Recombinant DNA Molecule Program Advisory Committee (later the Recombinant DNA Advisory Committee or RAC) in NIH. The first meeting of the RAC was held on the tail of Asilomar in February 1975.

Congress did not become involved in recombinant DNA issues until Senator Kennedy, chairman of the Health Subcommittee of the Committee on Labor and Public Welfare, held hearings late in April 1975. RAC meetings continued through 1975, and in July 1976 DHEW published the Guidelines for Recombinant DNA Research in the *Federal Register*. City council hearings in Cambridge, Massachusetts in the summer of 1976 vented the issues of the containment of hazardous experiments and the role of public participation in decisions about siting hazardous research.[33] In September 1976, Kennedy held additional hearings jointly with the Judiciary Committee. President Gerald Ford also established a Federal Interagency Committee on Recombinant DNA Research that met for the first time that autumn.

Scientific and congressional activity accelerated through 1977 as NIH revised its guidelines and an environmental impact statement it had published on their impact. But counter to expectations, and although some dozen bills were introduced, there was no legislation to regulate this new research activity.[34] Lack of support from both the outgoing Ford administration and the incoming Carter administration complicated congressional efforts, and the breadth of the issue, involving not just health jurisdictions but also environment, judiciary, and science in general, caused damaging congressional fragmentation. But the primary reason seems to be that, as illustrated by the great deal of scientific activity prior to the initiation of congressional involvement, the opponents of legislation were better organized and better mobilized than the supporters of legislation. Despite initial expectations, Congress passed no legislation to regulate scientific activities on recombinant DNA because, whether accurate or not, the biomedical community made the case that it could regulate itself.[35]

Conclusion

In the midst of the changes of the 1980s – changes I will argue finally altered the social contract for science – the House Science and Technology Committee, under the chairmanship of Don Fuqua (D-FL), organized a Task Force on Science Policy. Fuqua himself directed the task force, which drew its membership from a large subset of the full committee. Over the course of the 99th Congress, the task force produced twenty-four volumes of hearings and twelve background reports in an attempt to generate a comprehensive view of the research enterprise and help the Committee participate in setting national goals in science policy.

According to a group of political scientists and science policy makers who gathered in 1988 to discuss it, the task force was a congressional activity involved in the renegotiation of the social contract for science, primarily because it examined scientific programs across the research establishment with an eye for their results (Hamlett 1990). Another factor identified by this group, and also briefly engaged by the task force, was the question of scientific integrity.[36] Questioning NIH director James Wyngaarden in writing after the hearings, the task force asked to what extent the social contract applied to biomedical science. Although his response focused on the productivity of research and did not refer to scientific integrity, Wyngaarden averred that "[t]he reciprocal obligations between biomedical scientists and the society that provides their support can indeed be viewed as a social contract" (U.S. House 1985a: 92).

The discussion group did not come to any definitive conclusions about the social contract for science, and it was largely ineffectual in establishing a research agenda around the idea.[37] Nevertheless, the group and the task force further clarified what the other episodes of challenges to the social contract for science demonstrate, that there is a relationship between congressional organization, its ability to gather information and oversee the scientific enterprise, and the bond of the social contract for science. Just as Coleman (1990: 351) notes, a change in organizational capacity within a partner to a disjoint constitution can lead to the renegotiation of the contract. At various times, Congress has attempted to improve its access to and control over the scientific community by making changes in the structure of committees or subcommittees, either permanently or ad hoc. Congress has also experimented with various kinds of oversight and control mechanisms, exemplified by the gadfly technique of the Fountain Committee and the programmatic direction of the War on Cancer. Although these episodes verged on the issues of scientific integrity and productivity that are so crucial for the social contract for science, they brought neither a recognition of the politics internal to the workings of science nor a mechanism for monitoring or inducing appropriate behavior among researchers. That is, even if the interests of the congressional committees and the scientific community appeared to be diverging at times from the postwar consensus, straining the relationship, the committees had not yet invoked the refined mechanisms of control described by principal-agent theory.

Without the invocation of these mechanisms, the social contract for science articulated by Bush and Steelman – the trust in and reliance on the integrity and productivity of science – remained unaltered. The consensus they described was rooted in the self-regulating republic of science whose ultimate provision of technological benefits was predicated on segregation from political and commercial pressure, and was immediate from the production of good science. The social contract for science, together with its premises of self-regulation and unproblematic technology transfer, endured from its postwar articulation to be included in the vocabularies of science policy analysts and science policy makers, as well as to be enabled in the institutional relations between Congress and the scientific bureaucracies such as NIH.

The boundaries established by the social contract for science, necessarily established in the absence of true laissez faire, have been recurrently pushed and tested. Sometimes these episodes took on crisis proportions, like the Fountain Committee whose reputation for causing problems still remains part of the collective memory at NIH. These crises recur because the boundaries of the social contract for science are somewhat plastic and because the old politics of science turns into the new politics of science. Politics and science are similarly expanding and interpenetrating enterprises. Tocqueville ([1848] 1969) described the march of democratic equality through the ages and into the American polity. As Bush and Steelman after him, he prescribed insulating basic research lest it be overcome by a leveling democratic culture. One step in this march is the pursuit by elected representatives in Congress of their goals and their creation of both an expansive set of executive agencies to increase the instrumental success of government, as well as an expansive set of internal and marginal institutions to control them. Latour (1988) described the expanding laboratory of French biologist Louis Pasteur. Pasteur in effect expanded the boundary of his laboratory in an increasing set of contexts to enroll allies in his scientific enterprise.

Each expanding enterprise inevitably encroaches on the other. But the meetings need not be cataclysmic, as both are expansive precisely because they are mutually dependent on instrumental and ideological resources from the other. Some democratic politics will infiltrate into science, and some science will creep into politics. Some scientists will be hired or coopted by politicians, some politicians will be enrolled by scientists. During the course of this reciprocal process, as I will describe in the next two chapters, members of Congress questioned the premise of self-regulation and instigated the creation of formal mechanisms to manage the integrity of science. They questioned the premise of immediate technology transfer and mandated formal incentives to encourage it. These cases will demonstrate that the simple social contract for science has been elaborated to include microeconomic interventions by the political principals into science, and that the boundary between politics and science is even more plastic than before.

4

Assuring the Integrity of Research

> [A]t some point a misconduct in science case came to my attention, and I said, 'How did we handle these kind of cases?' And I am told that if the Director of NIH at the time or back in history felt that someone had really engaged in it, that he made a phone call or two, and that person disappeared from the map of science. I don't know whether it actually happened or who he called and what the process was, and clearly that was not, even if it was true, it was not an acceptable way to proceed.
>
> – Richard Riseberg, Chief Counsel, Public Health Service (PHS 1991: 84).

Introduction

Under the social contract for science, the management of scientific integrity was highly informal and contained entirely within the scientific community, as Richard Riseberg avers. The period "back in history" to which he refers is the time when James Shannon was still director of the National Institutes of Health (NIH), a golden age of the funding increases that Representative Fountain vigorously questioned but never really staunched. Scientists recall it rosily, for it lacked the intrusiveness of the rules and regulations, assurances, and certifications now familiar in every academic and government laboratory.

Yet it is also clear this informality was not an appropriate modus operandi. There was no notice of what constituted misconduct, no procedures for how misconduct was to be determined if charged, and no code of how it was to be punished if determined. Such action was seemingly as secret and precipitous as that protested by John Edsall during the anti-Communist hysteria. A great gulf appears between Riseberg's statement and the 1981 testimony of Philip Handler, then president of the National Academy of Sciences (NAS), before the House Science and Technology Committee that the research community handled misconduct "in an effective, democratic and self-correcting mode" (U.S. House 1981: 11). And there is still more distance between either account and the current situation, in which government employees at NIH's Office of Research Integrity (ORI) and in Offices of Inspectors General investigate allegations of misconduct against federally funded researchers.

These three representations take different perspectives on the boundary between politics and science. Actually, Riseberg and Handler share perspectives, but they interpose different value filters. Both describe a science independent of normative guidance from politics. For Riseberg, science does not take the political idea of due process into account but instead operates in an unspoken and invisible way. For Handler, however, the invisibility indicates deft, Smithian (or Bushian) self-regulation, by which scientific authorities quickly exile "from the map of science" those not worthy of membership. ORI, however, has struggled for years now to define what guidance the determination of scientific misconduct needs to borrow from politics and what from science.

This struggle is important in at least three dimensions. First, it is important in the framework I have introduced because assuring integrity is a crucial transaction between politics and science. In order to understand the role of the state in sponsoring research, we need to understand how this function is performed. Second, it is important because a number of commentators have defined the attention to scientific integrity as anti-scientific and thus part of a "flight from science and reason" that, they claim, increasingly characterizes contemporary culture.[1] In order to understand the politics of science policy, we need to understand the politics of scientific integrity.

But a third important dimension is the lives and work of federally funded researchers and the people who rely on this research. As Vannevar Bush and John Steelman agreed, researchers take on certain obligations when they accept federal funding. But do they relieve themselves of the protections of due process? Can they continue in their careers if they raise questions about integrity? How do the protections required by the producers of research compare to the protections required by the consumers of research – when those consumers may be researchers seeking to replicate or extend work, risk assessors seeking to apply the newest findings to the scientific evaluation of health and environmental hazards, or patients awaiting the results of the latest clinical trials of drugs that may relieve them of a dread disease?

Chapter 4 examines the development of policy regarding the integrity of scientific research in two areas: the origins and immediate impact of congressional investigations and oversight of scientific integrity, and the evolution of policies and procedures for adjudicating accusations of research misconduct. I focus on policy at the Public Health Service

(PHS), part of the Department of Health and Human Services (HHS) that houses the major research agencies of NIH, the Centers for Disease Control and Prevention, and the Food and Drug Administration (FDA).[2] As I will do with the productivity of science, I reveal how Congress drew the conclusion the integrity of science is not an automatic function. That is, Congress realized the social contract for science could no longer be sustained.

Congressional attention instigated the creation of an Office of Scientific Integrity (OSI), which in the course of its brief existence attempted through its policies and procedures to maintain the separation between politics and science that characterized the social contract for science. For reasons to be discussed, however, the separation was untenable, and HHS reorganized OSI into ORI and implemented a more subtle vision of the boundary. As a boundary organization, ORI abides by the characteristics described in Chapter 1, and in attempting to assure the integrity of science, it provides a context for negotiating the boundary between politics and science.

Congressional Involvement in Scientific Integrity[3]

The beginning of congressional involvement in scientific integrity in 1981 should be seen apiece with increasing congressional oversight of the executive branch.[4] Part of this secular trend, it differed from the previous inquiries into the political loyalty of individual scientists and the fiscal integrity of the scientific agencies, scrutinizing instead the integrity of the performance of research and the mechanisms of alleged self-regulation of misconduct.[5] Congress asked if there were scientists on the federal payroll who were not pursuing truth and, if so, what the agencies were doing about it.

The first hearings on scientific integrity in 1981 focused exclusively on events under the jurisdiction of PHS. Al Gore, then a Representative from Tennessee and the chairman of the Investigations and Oversight Subcommittee of the House Science and Technology Committee, and Orrin Hatch, then the junior Senator from Utah but already chairman of the Senate Labor and Human Resources Committee, first raised the issue. Gore and Hatch questioned the adequacy of the detection and investigation of scientific misconduct with respect to cases involving researchers Marc Straus and John Long, both supported by the National Cancer Institute (NCI). The hearings prompted PHS to make changes to help assure the integrity of the science it funded. Perhaps more importantly, the hearings set expectations about how the scientific community should handle misconduct – expectations Congress would find were not being met.

The Origin of Institutional Assurances

Gore's hearing was the first in a series on ethical issues in biomedical research, including biotechnology, human subjects research, and university-industry relations. Much like Representative Fountain a generation before, Gore felt that in matters of integrity the scientific community should be held to the same kind of standards as other recipients of federal largesse. The hearing elicited testimony from spokespersons from NIH, representatives of the broader scientific community, and independent experts on ethical issues in science. Prominent witnesses played down the threat of scientific misconduct. NAS president Handler called the problem "grossly exaggerated" and expressed complete confidence in the existing "system that operates in an effective, democratic and self-correcting mode." NIH director Donald S. Fredrickson testified misconduct was not and would never be a problem because of scientific self-regulation.

Despite the defensive tone adopted by these leaders of the scientific community, the hearing led to identifiable results, if extended in their implementation. It helped subordinates at NIH convince their superiors to take the issue more seriously, and the Institutional Liaison Office (ILO) at NIH began to play a larger role in coordinating investigations of alleged misconduct among the various institutes, which handled allegations in an ad hoc manner.[6] It also resulted in legislation. Working with colleague Henry Waxman (D-CA) on the Energy and Commerce Committee, Gore added language pertaining to misconduct to the reauthorization bills for NIH (H.R. 2350) and the Alcohol, Drug Abuse, and Mental Health Administration (ADAMHA). The latter (P.L. 98–24) passed quickly, but President Ronald Reagan vetoed the NIH bill twice for unrelated reasons, and it did not become law until Congress passed it a third time in 1985 (P.L. 99–158). Both laws underscored the responsibility of universities to manage research misconduct by directing HHS to require all institutions applying for funding to establish misconduct procedures and report investigations of substantial misconduct. Gore's hearing was thus the origin of the institutional assurances, which maintained a significant degree of local control over scientific integrity, under modest federal oversight.[7]

The Origin of the ALERT System

Hatch first became interested in the oversight of scientific work when the Office of Inspector General (OIG) of HHS reported on sloppiness and favoritism in procurement at NCI. Staff investigators, working through regular financial audits conducted by OIG and the General

Accounting Office, discovered that researcher Marc Straus had received a new grant from NCI, despite having been accused of scientific fraud a few years previously. Senator Paula Hawkins (R-FL) ably summed up the committee's perspective: "It is shocking for me to read in the Gore report that falsification involving cancer patient treatment cannot only be ignored, but is, in fact, rewarded. If the relationship between Agency and researcher is so fraternal and cozy that coverups of this magnitude could occur at all, then it is time that the Congress stops winking at wrongdoing" (U.S. Senate 1981: 29).

NCI director Vincent T. DeVita testified that despite Boston University's severance of Straus, the Institute did not conduct an investigation because its former director held that "NCI 'cannot intervene in the internal affairs of institutions' " (U.S. Senate 1981: 55). DeVita's decision not to inform the peer review board considering Straus's application about the case "was based on the fact that the grant was scientifically sound and Dr. Straus was innocent until proven guilty [by NCI]" (U.S. Senate 1981: 36). NCI's conduct reminded Senator Howard Metzenbaum (D-OH) of the "old saying of if you fool me once, you are a fool; if you fool me twice, I am a fool." He told DeVita, "I think you are putting yourself in a position to be fooled twice with $900,000 of the Federal Government's money." Confronted with this logic, DeVita admitted that, if "[I] had to go back and do it again, there is no question that . . . I would have . . . deferred the payment of the grant" (U.S. Senate 1981: 122).

The biomedical community reacted sharply to Hatch's inquiry, in part because of anxiety over what the little-known conservative would do with the new political emphasis on waste, fraud, and abuse in government. Nevertheless, like the Gore hearing, the Hatch hearing strengthened the hand of people at NIH who wanted to address scientific integrity more aggressively. Concretely, the hearing led NIH to create the ALERT system to share information about misconduct cases between grantee institutions and the various national institutes. Institute directors could use the information in the ALERT system on a need to know basis to defer or suspend grants, grant extensions, or renewals for scientists such as Straus whose conduct was gravely suspect.

Reactions to the Hearings

Committee staff were less than satisfied by the reaction to the hearings from the scientific community at large, which they characterized as ranging from denial to hostility. The committees continued to receive reports of misconduct and evidence of the handling of cases by universities that was in distinct contrast with Handler's testimony about effective and democratic self-correction.

But both committees were reasonably satisfied with the response from the agency. PHS began working on a proposed rule for applicant universities to follow when conducting investigations, printing draft guidelines (PHS 1985), and publishing interim guidelines (NIH 1986), ostensibly in response to what had become its obligation under the delayed 1985 law. Congressional staff observed with discontent, however, some backsliding. ILO did not soon receive increased staffing or expertise to handle the increasing number of allegations of misconduct. Nevertheless, the committees took at best minimal steps to continue overseeing the issue for three interrelated reasons: they trusted NIH and the scientific community to act once problems had been pointed out to them; they believed with the implementation of the assurances and the ALERT system, that the self-regulatory nature of science would suffice; and they simply had better things to do than micromanage science. The assurances and the ALERT system were politically instigated ways for the scientific community to formalize its responsibility for self-regulation – to investigate and report episodes of scientific misconduct and to prevent scientists without integrity from benefiting from federal grants.

After these efforts, scientific integrity dropped off the congressional agenda for several years. Even when the House Energy and Commerce Committee investigated alleged fraud involving research relevant to the Clean Air Act standards (U.S. House 1984), it failed to integrate it into the trajectory of the misconduct issue generally. But a May 1986 hearing by the House Task Force on Science Policy became a turning point.[8] This hearing focused on a paper, written by NIH researchers Walter Stewart and Ned Feder, that analyzed the practices of the various coauthors of a scientist who had committed misconduct. The paper (Steward and Feder 1987) claimed to document an extraordinary level of sloppiness and possible misconduct among this constructed sample of collaborators, who had seemingly failed the test of self-regulation by ignoring or overlooking fraudulent data provided by their colleague. It met with vociferous but often uninformed criticism from the scientific community, and its rocky road to publication was obstructed by legal as well as methodological challenges. Members of Congress read this criticism as stonewalling by the scientific community in the face of the empirical scrutiny they saw as necessary to assure the integrity of the public investment in research.

Creating a Boundary Organization[9]

Over the next two years, whatever lid that had been kept on the issue of misconduct blew off. Congress launched new probes, piloted by two of its most aggressive investigators: the late Ted Weiss (D-NY), then chairman of the Intergovernmental Affairs Subcommittee of the House Government Operations Committee, and John Dingell (D-MI), then chairman of the Oversight and Investigations Subcommittee of the House Energy and Commerce Committee.[10]

Weiss served notice of his interest in the fall of 1987 by requesting information about several cases from ILO, particularly those including university-industry relations and conflicts of interest. Dingell's inquiry did not commence until early 1988, when Feder and Stewart informed his staff of allegations of misconduct involving research associated with Nobel laureate David Baltimore at the Massachusetts Institute of Technology. Dingell scrutinized what became known as "the Baltimore case" and the related issue of the protection of whistle-blowers. He chose it from among a number of likely cases largely because Baltimore was "a big fish" to fry. The hearings by Dingell and Weiss accomplished two things of great significance. They publicized a traditionally unseen aspect of science, one involving politics and power in the place of scientific judgment; and by doing so they dashed high congressional expectations in the ability of the scientific community to manage its own affairs. These expectations were perhaps inappropriately high but, in Weiss's words, "the American public depends on science to solve human problems and to help us find ways to make the world a better place. . . . Because we depend on science so much . . . many people expect science to be infallible and scientists incorruptible" (U.S. House 1988a: 1).

Deconstructing Self-regulation[11]

Through the scrutiny it brought to bear in these hearings, Congress "engaged in what might be called the deconstruction of scientific exceptionalism" (Bimber and Guston 1995: 565). That is, members of Congress learned through their own efforts what scholars have found through academic study, that "the science made, the science bought, the science known, bears little resemblance to science in the making, science in the searching, science uncertain and unknown" (Latour 1991: 7).[12] This discovery of the gap between the product of science and its process is particularly disconcerting in light of the principal-agent framework, in which the problem of moral hazard plagues the ability of the sponsor of research to trust the performer.

Specifically, it plagued Dingell's ability to trust scientists to monitor and investigate the integrity of their own:

> In this system, the university gets the first crack at the data or lack thereof, and at the witnesses. . . . In most of the gross and celebrated cases of scientific fraud and misconduct . . . the institutions engaged in what appears to be a cover up effort to protect the institutions and some of their senior scientists. In some cases, the investigations of scientific fraud and misconduct are carried out by the very targets of the investigations, and in other cases, by only the interested parties themselves (U.S. House 1988b: 2–3).

It appeared the mechanisms of self-regulation – to which the social contract for science had delegated responsibility and earlier legislation had reinforced – led not to universalistic decisions based on a skeptical analysis of the empirical evidence, but rather to conspiracies and conflicts of interest. Experience accentuated this perception. Within twenty-four hours after its first hearing, Dingell's subcommittee received more than a dozen calls about new cases of scientific misconduct.

Because of the apparently poor performance of the universities in investigating misconduct allegations, and NIH in overseeing them, Representative Ron Wyden (D-OR) presaged a more active role for the government in monitoring science. He held that the institutional assurances resulting from the Gore hearing did not go "anywhere near far enough" and promised, in the next reauthorization, he would pursue "a new, independent program for quality assurance in research" (U.S. House 1988b: 4). Commented one staffer about Wyden's reaction, "Congress does not take kindly to an abuse of delegated authority."

Dingell also attacked the idea of self-regulation through the experiences of whistle-blower Margot O'Toole. O'Toole had brought to light problems in the paper published by Thereza Imanishi-Kari, David Baltimore, and others. O'Toole testified about her surprise, confusion, and dismay over Baltimore's lack of interest in correcting errors in the paper. She concluded that believing in self-regulating science is counterproductive, because adherence to it allows scientists to disregard their own errors and leave them, even if discovered, for others to correct. Real individuals, and not some disembodied hand, are required to engage the gears of self-regulation. Rather than the expected disinterested search for truth, this disregard of error appeared to congressional investigators to be conveniently myopic self-interest, if not blind ambition.

A third argument that Dingell deployed suggests the marketplace of scientific ideas has big players who can use reputational power to squeeze out little players – that an uneven initial distribution of resources among scientists can lead to an unfair outcome, or even a substantively incorrect one, even under fair rules of exchange. O'Toole testified that after she had approached Baltimore with her concerns, he challenged her to publish them in a letter to the journal, promising that he, too, would write a letter. With both letters published, scientific peers would adjudicate their competing claims (U.S. House 1988b). Who would the peers believe? Dr. David Baltimore, Nobel laureate and director of the Whitehead Institute for Biomedical Research? Or Margot O'Toole, post doc? Where power and institutional authority are implicit in merit, the management of allegations of error or misconduct does not appear to be democratic.

Dingell also refused to accept the premise that an alleged social contract for scientists justified a social contract for science. After taking a good deal of criticism in the wake of his first hearing, Dingell retaliated:

> Other critics have claimed that the Congress is not capable of understanding science, or even raising questions about science. However, no one questions the ability of the Congress to deal with these issues when . . . enormous sums of money are requested for enormous particle accelerator programs in budgets which we are now contemplating (U.S. House 1989: 2).

According to Dingell, congressional scrutiny is symmetric: if members know enough to authorize and appropriate for scientific projects, and if scientists seek such projects, then scientists must bear the scrutiny of oversight. Staffers added, "What would happen to tax revenues if the IRS worked like NIH? It's the same tax dollars." By accepting federal funds, scientists also tacitly accept congressional oversight, in the same way that travelers tacitly accept the sovereign's laws when walking on public roads. Such a response to science's claim to a status exempt from scrutiny could easily have been addressed to Major Powell a century earlier.

Yet in leveling this criticism, Dingell did not necessarily become "anti-science." Staff, in fact, believed they were defending the scientific community by depriving the real enemies of research and peer review of ammunition. In 1991, Representative Roy Rowland (D-GA), a member of Dingell's subcommittee and a physician, expressed just this sentiment at a hearing on financial misconduct in the NIH laboratory of AIDS researcher Dr. Robert Gallo. Evoking Turner's solution to the problem of asymmetric information, Rowland argued that if a researcher were dishonest in his or her personal or financial life, then the researcher might be dishonest in his or her research life (U.S. House 1991). Given that Gallo's AIDS lab was the largest and arguably the most important lab in the NIH intramural system, and that AIDS research funding had increased rapidly from 1987 to 1991 despite great political contention, Rowland hit the mark.[13]

The congressional inquiries, through design or accident, provided a systematic and, to members of Congress, convincing critique of scientific self-regulation. As Bimber and Guston (1995: 567) conclude, these critiques led to "the recognition that the . . . normative structure [of science] is incomplete and that the market of ideas needs regulation." How that regulation would be institutionalized would be determined by both strategy and fortune.[14]

The Preemptive Strike[15]

After these inquiries, the Office of Inspector General (OIG) of HHS issued a report that cast an unflattering light on NIH and the universities in their response to the 1985 legislation.[16] These activities led to public speculation and private consideration of handing the investigation of allegations of misconduct to OIG.

A task force established by Assistant Secretary of Health Robert E. Windom, however, sought a different solution. Chaired by HHS principal deputy general counsel Robert Charrow, the task force included representatives of the department, OIG, and the several PHS agencies. It met three times, twice before May 1988, and it concluded the prevailing organization for managing allegations was untenable. To test the waters in the scientific community for an alternative solution, PHS issued an advanced notice for proposed rulemaking. The notice posed for public comment the question of whether HHS should create "an office of scientific integrity, . . . responsible for receiving all allegations of scientific misconduct . . . , monitoring awardee institutions, conducting investigations where necessary . . . , and determining which allegations appear potentially to have merit" (PHS 1988: 36344–47). It also asked whether that function should instead be vested in OIG.

The responses to the notice disparaged the idea of an "office of scientific integrity" as: "*intrusive, unnecessary, premature, wasteful, inappropriate, impractical, duplicative, costly, ineffective, inefficient, and contrary to the principle that it is the responsibility of the institutions to investigate allegations of misconduct*"(Rhoades 1989: 10; emphasis in the original). Although respondents emphasized the "government should encourage and require the scientific community to police itself," they found an Office of Scientific Integrity "preferable" to OIG because OIG is not "qualified to perform the kind of investigation necessary . . . which requires substantial expertise in the most current research practices and the ability to understand the details of the research" (Rhoades 1989: 10–11).[17]

NIH thought it possessed the requisite scientific expertise, and it merely needed to augment staffing at ILO, which to this point had been managing cases with one and a half full-time equivalent employees. NIH added three staff members, including a financial investigator, to ILO and placed a scientist in charge after the previous institutional liaison officer – a political scientist – resigned.[18] Higher-ups were not convinced, however, that NIH was the right locus because it lacked investigative expertise and was, from their perspective, too close to the scientists. Moreover, NIH manages more than a billion dollars of intramural research, which would place them in the same vulnerable position of investigating their own scientists as universities were. Eventually, the Secretary and the Under Secretary concluded that any investigative office would not be housed in NIH.

By the fall of 1988, as the task force considered its options, Congress gave notice that it would act. Dingell and Waxman proposed an amendment to the NIH reauthorization bill to create an Office of Scientific Investigations, to be housed under the Office of the Secretary of HHS. But in the rush to adjourn before the election, Congress passed the reauthorization without it.[19]

The task force pressed toward a solution similar to the failed amendment. But late in 1988, director Wyngaarden decided to launch a "preemptive strike" against the task force and Dingell. Discovering from a key staff member that Dingell was flexible about the institutional solution, Wyngaarden proposed to the task force a "two-office solution." An office for investigations would be established under the Office of the Director of NIH, and an office to oversee it would be established under the Office of the Assistant Secretary for Health. The task force agreed to Wyngaarden's proposal on the condition that it be cleared through Dingell.[20]

It was, by this time, early January 1989. As a general rule, little of substance happens in Washington in the January following a year divisible by four. No meeting with Dingell to approve the new organization occurred, but the proposal nevertheless went through. On January 17, 1989 Wyngaarden sent a memo to Windom, including a draft *Federal Register* notice. On February 3, Windom, Wyngaarden, and other PHS officials met to discuss the proposal. After more drafts and discussion, and despite the hostile response to the idea in the notice of proposed rulemaking, the statement authorizing the Office of Scientific Integrity (OSI) and the Office of Scientific Integrity Review (OSIR) appeared in the *Federal Register* on March 17.[21] OSI would oversee universities in their management of research integrity, and it would conduct its own investigations when necessary. OSIR would oversee OSI and engage in outreach and educational efforts.

Creating the Office of Research Integrity

Representative Weiss commended NIH on the creation of OSI at the opening of his third hearing. Dingell scarcely acknowledged it at his hearing. Dingell's staff, however, was not oblivious to the congressional inspiration for OSI: "The universities failed to respond, and we need to turn the screws a little, and OSI is our screwdriver."[22]

Dingell held several hearings in the few years after OSI's creation, focusing on the cases OSI pursued and the methods of investigation it employed. OSI was caught in a difficult bind as a proto-boundary organization, attempting to legitimate itself to Dingell, to the scientific community, and to its boss, the new NIH director Bernadine Healy. By the next reauthorization cycle for NIH, Congress intended to protect OSI with the authorization it had not produced in 1988. In June 1991, Waxman introduced the reauthorization, one section of which addressed OSI.[23]

But the fate of OSI hinged on a matter unrelated to scientific integrity – the Reagan administration's controversial ban on fetal tissue research. HHS had issued the ban to placate abortion foes, who argued that permitting research with fetal tissue would encourage abortions (Childress 1991). The reauthorization would overturn the ban and, although both chambers passed the measure, only the Senate achieved a veto-proof majority and the attempt to override President George Bush's veto failed. The authorization for OSI failed along with it.

Meanwhile, the scientific community and NIH director Healy kept up the pressure on OSI. In February 1992, Assistant Secretary of Health James O. Mason forwarded to Secretary Louis Sullivan a plan for reorganization that replaced OSI and OSIR with a new Office of Research Integrity (ORI), consolidated under the Office of the Assistant Secretary (DHHS 1992). The new office consisted of three divisions: Policy and Education, largely what had been OSIR; Research Investigation, largely what had been OSI; and Legal Counsel. After the 1992 election, Congress passed and President Bill Clinton signed The National Institutes of Health Revitalization Act of 1993 (P.L. 103–43), authorizing ORI with this structure.[24]

Procedural Standards and the Boundaries for the Integrity of Science

The primary task of ORI, like OSI before it, has been to oversee the investigations conducted by grantee institutions and, when necessary, to investigate misconduct allegations itself.[25] This function requires an available definition of misconduct and policies and procedures to inquire into allegations of behavior approaching that definition. Both the definition and the policies and procedures have a history dating to about 1980, prior to Gore's initial inquiry. In other work, I have examined the evolution of the definition at PHS, which changed from one in which the government considered research misconduct as just one form of inadequate professional performance, to one in which the government invoked the standards of the scientific community to distinguish research misconduct, now clearly demarcated from other kinds of misconduct (Guston 1999a).[26] Here I focus on the policies and procedures, which have undergone a similar change.

I consider the development of policies and procedures for allegations of research misconduct in five rough historical periods and across three variables. The periods are: 1) "the good old days" – prior to 1980; 2) the debarment standard – 1980–85; 3) the ILO standard – 1980–88; 4) the OSI standard – 1989–92; and 5) the ORI standard – since 1992. The variables are: 1) how allegations are adjudicated; 2) who participates in the process; and 3) what standards of proof and evidence are applied. Each standard, as a composite or repertoire of the variables, implies a different quality and location of the boundary between politics and science.

"The Good Old Days" – Prior to 1980

Little is known about this early period. As Bruce L. R. Smith (1994) relates about the time when the "science-government compact" still held, "[f]raud and misconduct were assumed to be largely nonexistent and in any event were effectively curbed by the informal mechanisms" of science. The epigragh suggests these informal mechanisms were almost personal in manner. Former Stanford University president Donald Kennedy (1997: 219) agrees, recalling episodes in the 1950s when "[i]nformal resolutions of this kind [among colleagues] were standard."

Given the findings of the Gore and Hatch inquiries and the generally shoddy way in which researchers and institutions treated the formal rules after they were initially established, there is little reason to doubt that Riseberg's understanding is roughly accurate. Allegations were not officially adjudicated, but presented to some figure of authority in research or administration for decision. The participants were not predetermined, but were limited as best as possible to those in the know in order to contain the conflict. The standards of proof and evidence were arbitrary. As a system it was, in retrospect, indefensible for any public purpose – assuring the integrity of federally funded research, safeguarding the rights of researchers or whistle-blowers, or providing for the ideological and material support of politics. But it served well the implicitly sharp boundary between politics and science, for it neither admitted the intrusion by an external politics into scientific judgment nor broached appeal by the accused to a broader community.

The Debarment Standard – 1980–85

The 1976 Inspectors General Act created OIGs in all federal departments and major independent agencies. It also set in motion rulemaking at HHS on how to debar poorly performing contractors and grantees from competing for future awards. The final rule on debarment, issued in 1980, treated scientific misconduct as "serious unsatisfactory performance," which was cause for debarment and subject to the same procedures as other causes including, for example, criminal convictions. The rule described debarment actions as "within the discretion of the Secretary and . . . rendered solely in the best interest of the Government;" the rule also specified "serious unsatisfactory performance" as "established by evidence which the Secretary determines to be clear and convincing in nature" (DHHS 1980: 67266).

The rule required HHS to notify the respondent of the planned debarment. It also entitled the respondent to a hearing and representation by counsel, but it was incumbent upon the respondent to request the hearing. The rule charged the Secretary to appoint a hearing officer from within the ranks of HHS to preside over the case and the General Counsel to represent the interests of the department. The rule specified that formal rules of evidence, as in courts of law, would not be applicable, and that the hearing officer would present the determination to the Secretary, whose decision would be final. These procedures, which treated misconduct in research along with financial misconduct and other material failures to perform, implied a boundary almost entirely permeable to politics. Indeed, because of the lack of demarcation between misconduct in research and "serious unsatisfactory performance" in financial management, administration, or other domains, NIH director Fredrickson found the procedures faulty and sought to change them.

ILO Standard – 1980–88[27]

As best as can be determined, no case of scientific misconduct was handled under the 1980 debarment rule, and the various institutes handled cases that came to their attention in an ad hoc manner. But the 1981 hearings made clear to ILO the need for greater centralization. Within a year, PHS designated the associate director for extramural research to coordinate this activity, but it continued to delegate cases to the institutes. PHS outlined its expectations that the "scientific community is . . . to make every effort to prevent misconduct" and that "for every incident of alleged or apparent misconduct which is judged to warrant investigation by an awardee institution, that institution is . . . to report on the matter to head of the appropriate PHS agency" (Brandt 1983).[28] PHS also delegated to the heads of its agencies and offices the responsibilities to implement policies and procedures to handle allegations, to make decisions regarding sanctions, and to delegate to yet another official the responsibility of coordinating with OIG and the Office of General Counsel.

This delegation meant that cases were handled in a variety of ways, although their coordination allowed for some learning through experience with cases. NIH or FDA staff performed the fact finding in cases until the Darsee case surfaced in 1981 and 1982, when the National Heart, Lung, and Blood Institute (NHLBI) created a scientific panel to advise the investigators.[29] Other institutes then applied NHLBI's model to some, but not all, investigations. ILO patterned its investigations after the peer review of grant applications. Its misconduct investigations solicited the opinions of scientific review panels. Accordingly, it was difficult for staffers to have any impact on the panel's decisions unless the decisions were absolutely wrong, in which case staff could attempt to recommend and justify a better result to the ultimate decision maker.

As described above, NIH's 1985 reauthorization required assurances from all institutions applying for NIH funding that they have in place administrative processes for managing allegations of misconduct, and that such processes conform to guidelines the department would issue. In partial response to the legislation, PHS issued interim policies and procedures (NIH 1986: 8).[30]

These interim policies and procedures detailed the responsibilities of misconduct policy officers (MPOs) in each agency and one central MPO to coordinate their activities at the PHS level.[31] The document directed agencies to consider three elements in all cases: the confidential treatment of allegations to protect the rights of the affected parties; the privacy of informants; and the interests of the government. The interim policies required PHS to give notice of investigations to the affected parties, but they authorized PHS to take administrative actions to safeguard the investigation, human or animal subjects, or the government interest.[32] The policies specified certain PHS officials could be informed of current cases, but grant committees could not normally be told of allegations or ongoing investigations.

The policies and procedures directed the MPO in charge of an investigation to give the affected parties every opportunity to respond not only after completed investigations but also during ongoing investigations.[33] Such investigations actually had two stages: an inquiry to determine the warrant for a full scale investigation and an actual investigation. The agency MPO (in consultation with the cognizant agency director and the PHS MPO) conducted the inquiry, based on the accuracy and reliability of sources; the seriousness, scope, and context of the alleged misconduct; and any response provided by the affected parties.

The policies and procedures held that investigations should begin with notice to individuals and institutions under investigation and the entering of the individual into the ALERT system. "Outside consultants," in other words, scientific advisors, could be invited to participate in an investigation (and could be given legal protections available to federal employees). The agency MPO and the director of the cognizant agency were to review the findings of an investigation. If the investigation found no misconduct, there were various provisions for notice and undoing what actions might have been done; otherwise, there were provisions for notice and sanction. Sanctions required the participation of administrative personnel beyond those conducting the investigation. The policies and procedures authorized the agency head to determine whether debarment, or other lesser sanctions, would be sought.

ILO's use of peer review as a model for investigating research misconduct contrasted directly with the debarment standard. It created a demographic boundary between politics and science, arrogating to scientific peers the task of determining misconduct and excluding the staff unless the peers made an egregious error. This model began to formalize the concept of scientific self-regulation inherent in the earlier period and, by formalizing it attempted to delegitimate any political intrusion. These interim policies and procedures held sway until the creation of OSI in the spring of 1989 and the publication of the final rule in August 1989.

OSI Standard[34]

In the mind of NIH director Wyngaarden, who conceived OSI as a means of limiting congressional intervention and preserving the social contract for science, OSI was "self-regulatory in the sense that we put the primary responsibility for investigating allegations of scientific misconduct on people with scientific knowledge."[35] That is, Wyngaarden attempted to preserve the privileged participation of scientists. By crude credentialism, OSI achieved this identity. OSI professionals all had Ph.D.s or M.D.s., and their vitae showed service at NIH and universities. In his initial staffing decisions for OSI, Wyngaarden "look[ed] for people who had a good understanding of science generally, and the processes of science, [and] a high sense of personal integrity."[36] Brian Kimes, the initial acting director of OSI, made every attempt to rotate scientists from elsewhere in NIH into the office.

More important than the credentials of the personnel, however, was how these scientifically trained professionals viewed their jobs and what model of operation they implemented. OSI professionals viewed their jobs with some ambivalence. Kimes was under no illusion that he was doing science at OSI. He was "doing his job," and it was not science because "science is creating. . . . Science is the creation of new information."[37] Kimes believed that science is, for the most part, self-regulating, but that OSI was not "self." Kimes' successor as director of OSI, Jules Hallum, on the other hand, "like[d] to consider [him]self a scientist" and he joked that his friends were the ones who still considered him a scientist even after he joined OSI. Other OSI professionals noted specific characteristics of their work that emphasized its scientific character, including: its heavy reliance on scientific networks and experts to acquire information; its requirement of skills in reading data notebooks, engaging in fact-finding, and using a technical vocabulary; its encouragement of some areas of independent research, such as statistical forensics; and its required, fraternal understanding of scientists and the culture of universities and NIH.

OSI also developed a finely tuned rhetoric about its modus operandi. ILO initiated and OSI implemented a model that sought to reinforce peer review. Suzanne Hadley, the deputy director of OSI, described the approach similarly: "It's an extension of the peer review model. It's an extension of when a study section reviews a grant application, sometimes they'll go back to the scientists and say, we would like to see your data."[38]

Acting director Kimes was first responsible for implementing OSI's policies and procedures. In describing the crux of misconduct cases, Kimes maintained that "data should be able to answer the question" of whether or not misconduct had occurred. OSI's procedures were not oriented toward legalistic interpretations of due process but instead trying to "arrive at the scientific truth as quickly as possible."

Jules Hallum had a similar view. Hallum believed that "OSI was formed within the NIH in a manner similar to the establishment of the Office for Protection from Research Risks or the Office for Recombinant DNA Technology [sic]. These offices have succeeded in their mission because they are part of the scientific community, and therefore, they include an emphasis on review of scientific issues" (PHS 1991: 136). When Hallum became director of OSI in the spring of 1990, people at OSI started speaking of the "scientific dialogue method" of investigating scientific misconduct. Procedures did not change with Hallum's arrival, but this new name for their operation was an attempt to persuade the scientific community that OSI was part of it and had its best interests at heart. It may have also been an attempt to insulate itself from the scrutiny of Dingell's subcommittee, which threatened to reduce its perceived independence vis-a-vis the scientific community by conducting parallel investigations of misconduct allegations.[39]

The scientific dialogue method was an interpretation of normal scientific decision making in which, according to Hallum, the burden of proof rests on the claimant to produce data and sway the audience. This model

> functions in much the same spirit as does an editor of a scientific journal in dealing with problems in a submitted manuscript. Theoretically, if an author makes a claim unsubstantiated by presentation of data, the editor can demand that those data be adduced or the paper will not be published. It is obvious to scientists, though perhaps not to laymen, that in this scientific dialogue, that the burden of proof must always fall on the person who makes claims about his or her data. . . . This does not mean that the burden of proving there is no misconduct falls on the accused. The absence of supporting data would not, standing alone, support a finding of misconduct (Hallum and Hadley 1990: 650).

Thus, the scientific dialogue was interested in "the reliability of data, not the reliability of witnesses." OSI's use of scientific advisory committees was supposed to allow disinterested and skeptical investigations "to convert these [accusations] into the issues of science [and] investigate [them] on the basis of data, not the [basis of] personality" (PHS 1991: 174).

This attitude about the active nature of data – that "the data should be able to answer the question" and the reliability of data being of greater interest than the reliability of witnesses – has consequences for policies and procedures. If a misconduct investigation is framed in terms of disinterested and skeptical scientific claims, for example, then otherwise crucial elements of criminal due process such as confronting and cross-examining witnesses are unnecessary because the process itself is considered the disinterested and skeptical pursuit of truth. The data are the witnesses, and objective scientific data are unbiased witnesses.

Hallum contrasted the scientific dialogue model with a "legal-adversarial model" – implicitly the debarment standard – which "clearly offers the most visible and obvious due process protections. In this courtlike process, with its origins in Anglo-Saxon jurisprudence, the accused receives specific 'charges' in writing, can be represented by counsel, can face and cross-examine all witnesses, and can introduce evidence on his or her own behalf" (Hallum and Hadley 1990: 650). The primary procedural difference between the two models was that, in the former, the accused did not have the opportunity to confront or cross-examine witnesses. For Hallum, the choice between the two models involved enormous stakes: "the role of scientists in such [legal-adversarial] proceedings is likely to be minimized to that of 'expert witnesses' [rather than scientific peers]. This would represent a serious loss to the interests of science, because the issues are resolved on the basis of civil law or administrative law and not principally on scientific evidence" (Hallum and Hadley 1990: 650). "If we want to govern ourselves, we had better use this scientific dialogue."[40]

OSI attempted to recreate the separation of science and politics in its work. Like the boundary imposed by the ILO standard and borrowed from the peer review of grant proposals, OSI's boundary relied on scientific peers and additionally added the fortification of neutral and active scientific data. One might have expected the scientific community to support OSI in its attempt to implement a scientific dialogue method, to maintain self-governance, and to distinguish its investigations from congressional hearings, in order to preserve the interests of science. However, many members of the scientific community instead attacked OSI and its scientific dialogue method for not allowing due process.

Interlude: Challenges to OSI

APA and Due Process. A federal suit filed by James Abbs, a neurologist at the University of Wisconsin and the subject of an investigation by OSI, formally challenged the scientific dialogue model. Abbs charged that OSI failed to provide due process and to promulgate its procedures under the requirements of the Administrative Procedures Act (APA).[41] PHS had attempted to implement the interim rules as regulations, but the Office of Management and Budget blocked this effort as unnecessary. After PHS created OSI in the spring of 1989, it published in the *Federal Register* the final rule derived from the mandate expressed in the Health

Research Extension Act of 1985. The rule specified the responsibilities of PHS applicant institutions, but it did not specify the internal policies and procedures OSI would use to review a university's investigations or to conduct its own. PHS developed OSI's internal policies and procedures without the public comment envisioned by APA and published them in *NIH Guide for Grants and Contracts*.

Abbs argued that he had a property stake in his grant, his academic position, and his reputation, and that OSI had deprived him of this property without due process of law under the fifth and fourteenth amendments to the Constitution. HHS argued that no such property rights exist and, even if they did, that OSI provided due process. HHS also argued that OSI was not required to fulfill any requirements of public notice for its internal procedures, but that it had published them in *NIH Guide* to demonstrate its openness to the scientific community.

The district judge decided the APA claim in Abbs' favor, invalidating OSI's internal policies and procedures in the jurisdiction of the Western District of Wisconsin. The judge decided the due process claim, however, in favor of PHS, declaring the invalid procedures did, in fact, provide sufficient due process. The judge rejected Abbs' claim for a property right, writing that the "grant awards made to the Board of Regents [of the University of Wisconsin for James Abbs] are not made for [the researcher's benefit], but for the benefit of the public that may enjoy the fruits of his research." Both parties appealed the split decision. The Seventh Circuit Court vacated the district court's ruling, validating OSI's APA claim as well as its due process claim.

Abbs initially focused a great deal of scrutiny on OSI, and many commentators misinterpreted the district court's opinion as substantively critical of OSI. Researchers in other federal court districts filed suit, citing *Abbs*, to invalidate OSI procedures, but the circuit court's ruling removed this challenge to OSI. Nevertheless, various aspects of policies and procedures continued to be litigated, including the entry of names into the ALERT system.[42] In all cases to date, the courts have ultimately upheld the government's policies and procedures for managing the integrity of science, although not necessarily specific findings.

Bureaucratic Challenges. Coincident with the district court's split decision in *Abbs*, OSI also came under scrutiny by the new NIH director, Bernadine Healy.[43] Although Healy had stated in a press conference in April 1991 that she did not expect to make any significant changes at OSI (Myers 1991: A23), by August she was embroiled in controversy and testifying before Dingell about her handling of the office. In part because of a "scientific backlash" (Hamilton 1991: 1084) that criticized

OSI as too "zealous" (Davis 1991: 12) and staffed by investigators reminiscent of the "Keystone Cops" (Wheeler 1991: A5), Dingell's subcommittee saw its efforts coming apart. Since OSI was Dingell's tool to "turn the screws" on misconduct, there was great consternation about the challenges to OSI, and Dingell charged that Healy had "made a mockery of the OSI's alleged independence in dealing with misconduct allegations" (Greenberg 1991: 5).

At the hearing, Healy expressed her doubts about "due process, confidentiality, fairness and objectivity" at OSI. She also tried to deflate the "either science or law" rhetoric of OSI by describing:

> [t]he process we have [now as] clearly adversarial, whether one admits it or not. But there are other models of quasi-judicial procedures which are derived from the judicial process, but which do not involve a courtroom battle with teams of lawyers on either side. They include some of the things we have in the Grants Appeals Board, some of the administrative law judge activities. *There are models which are somewhere in between.* When somebody has been accused of some horrible act that is going to deprive them of their livelihood, of their standing in society, you should give them justice. And in our country, the way we give justice is through time-honored judicial proceedings (Greenberg 1991: 5; emphasis added).

The PHS Advisory Committee on Scientific Integrity, which first met a few weeks prior to Healy's testimony before Dingell, shared her concern about finding an appropriate model for due process in misconduct investigations. Committee chairman Nicholas Steneck spoke of how:

> [t]he pursuit of science and the monitoring of integrity no longer takes [sic] place in contained social settings as they did when science was privately funded and of concern primarily only to other scientists. Today scientists must operate in many spheres, from their own laboratories, to programs, departments, institutes, universities, agencies and in public settings. Unfortunately, from the standpoint of consistent policies, the standards for fair or appropriate behavior, such as due process and burden of proof can change dramatically from sphere to sphere (PHS 1991: 35–36).

Steneck hints at the dynamic at work here: scientists like Abbs can appeal to the process in a different "sphere" when they do not like the outcome in their original one. It again recalls E. E. Schattschneider (1960), but this time with respect to his vision of conflict: a potential loser will attempt to expand the scope of conflict in the hopes of winning in a broader battle. Such a dynamic, in which members appeal to authorities outside of science when internal processes run counter to their interests, can hardly be a mark of a separate community, yet alone a self-regulating one.[44] The scientific sphere is embedded in a political one, and members of the narrower sphere also have membership – and rights and responsibilities – in the larger one.

ORI Standard – 1992–Present

Despite the favorable circuit court ruling, PHS revised the scientific dialogue method and reorganized the scientific integrity program. Assistant Secretary Mason forwarded to Secretary Louis Sullivan a reorganization plan for scientific integrity in February 1992. ORI, located within the Office of the Assistant Secretary, replaced OSI and OSIR. In 1995, ORI was again booted upstairs, this time to the Office of the Secretary of HHS.

Inasmuch as OSI had attempted to maintain the primacy of the pursuit of scientific truth to questions of misconduct, ORI acknowledged the importance of more traditional legal concerns. The new structure demonstrated this new concern, as ORI included not only the former OSIR and OSI, but also the Division of Legal Counsel from the Office of the General Counsel. This structural marriage of scientists, investigators, and lawyers represents a greater conceptual unity of functions as well. Indeed, ORI refers to its primary professional staff as "scientist-investigators."[45]

In November 1992, PHS issued notice of an interim procedure in which individuals found by ORI to have committed misconduct could request an administrative hearing before the Research Integrity Adjudications Panel (RIAP) of the Departmental Appeals Board (DAB; PHS 1992).[46] During such hearings, respondents could be represented by counsel, question evidence and cross-examine witnesses, and present rebuttal evidence and witnesses. Despite these enhanced procedural aspects, however, no formal rules of evidence pertain at DAB hearings. The first such hearing occurred in June 1993.

Generally, DAB has been a defender of PHS action on misconduct, all the way back to the 1980 debarment rules. In response to appeals made before it, DAB has confirmed the authority of HHS dating prior to the 1985 authorization and the 1989 rule, to investigate allegations of misconduct involving federal funds and impose administrative sanctions when misconduct has been found. DAB draws this authority from the nature of the grants process, which as the *Abbs* court held is discretionary to the Secretary of HHS. DAB concluded that previous attempts to deal with misconduct, including the 1980 debarment rules and the 1986 policies and procedures, were appropriate expressions of this discretion.

DAB also ruled HHS may place conditions of the future awarding of grants and other aspects of a researcher's involvement with HHS programs (OASH 1994: 6).

One difficulty, however, has been DAB's interpretation of the relationship between the definition of misconduct and its adjudication, especially regarding the burden and standard of proof, standards of conduct, and intent. DAB's ruling on the burden and standard of proof required for a finding of misconduct is rather straightforward: the burden rests on ORI to demonstrate misconduct by a preponderance of the evidence, which is the normal standard in civil cases but even lower than the standard of clear and convincing evidence in the 1980 debarment rule. With respect to standards of conduct, however, DAB has held that ORI must demonstrate the respondent's actions violated standards in effect at the time of the conduct – standards derived either from the relevant scientific community or from federal requirements of conduct. Finally, ORI must also demonstrate the violation of standards was intentional, that is, any reasonable researcher in the respondent's position would have understood the actions as constituting misconduct (ORI 1993; OASH 1994).[47] The introduction of the intent standard by DAB led ORI to drop charges against Robert Gallo in November 1993. DAB also overturned ORI's finding of misconduct in the high profile case against Thereza Imanishi-Kari.[48] Despite these rebuffs by DAB on cases with high profiles, ORI has improved its record. The original findings of misconduct in both of these cases were made under the OSI's repertoire of policies and procedures. DAB has reversed none of the forty-four findings from 1992 to 1996 of misconduct made under ORI's procedures (ORI 1997).

In June 1994, the Office of the Secretary of HHS issued notice that ORI had revised its guidelines for such hearings (DHHS 1994). One of the revisions relates to the inclusion of a scientist or other expert on the RIAP: in the original procedure, a scientist would be included at the discretion of the panel chair; in the revised procedures, a scientist could be included at the request of either HHS or the respondent. These new guidelines, with the inclusion of both explicit legal protections and the optional participation of scientists, appears to have found the ground sought by former NIH director Healy "somewhere in between" the scientific dialogue model and the legal-adversarial model. The guidelines fixed the boundary between politics and science in ORI and in policies and procedures that allow nonscientists and scientists to collaborate in the determination of research misconduct.

ORI as a Boundary Organization

The current process for assuring the integrity of federally sponsored biomedical research thus has the following elements: one reflective of the tradition of Price's "new kind of federalism" in the research system in which grantee institutions have the primary responsibility for investigating allegations of misconduct, under policies and procedures minimally defined by ORI; one of oversight by ORI, which determines the adequacy of institutional investigations post hoc; one of original jurisdiction, in which ORI investigates misconduct allegations regarding intramural research at PHS and can investigate allegations in extramural research either subsequent to or preemptive of institutional investigations; and a triallike one, in which RIAP/DAB provides a more robust interpretation of due process for decisions by ORI that are contested.[49] The status of ORI in between independent grantee institutions on one hand and the legalistic DAB on the other is apparent.

But as described in Chapter 1, a boundary organization is more specifically identified because it provides space that legitimates the creation and use of boundary objects and standardized packages; involves the participation of principals and agents, as well as specialized mediators; and exists on the frontier of two relatively distinct social worlds with definite lines of accountability to each. ORI's character as a boundary organization is clear against these three criteria.

Prior to the creation of ORI, and its predecessor OSI, the system for handling misconduct in science was informal and varied from case to case and institution to institution. There was no consistent definition or notice of what constituted misconduct, no regular procedures for making or adjudicating allegations of misconduct, and no specified sanctions for findings of misconduct. Conceived of as entirely within the domain of science, these functions required specificity only to the extent their participants needed to legitimate them to themselves.

In a relatively homogeneous social world, this ambiguity sufficed. But as the federal government and individual scientists began to assert their interests, the need to satisfy them in these newly diversified social worlds led to the creation of OSI and ORI and their attempt to forge regular mechanisms for managing misconduct – that is, to design boundary objects and standardized packages usable by both the social worlds of science and politics.[50] The definition of misconduct, the procedures used by ORI and by universities to file and adjudicate allegations of misconduct – especially the model policy designed by ORI for emulation, the specific determinations of such adjudicatory mechanisms, and the sanctions they might impose – are all boundary objects in Star and Griesemer's (1989) meaning of the term.[51] To the extent that legitimate and forceful policies and procedures change the behavior of the scientists who may be subject to them, institutions who may implement them, or politicians who may be placated by them, they are standardized packages in Fujimura's meaning (1992).

In order to produce these boundary objects and standardized packages, ORI has relied in several ways on both the principals and the agents of the original relationship. After instigating NIH director Wyngaarden's creation of OSI, Congress sought to authorize it and define the misconduct that would be its purview. Congress eventually authorized ORI and delegated the formulation of a definition, among other tasks, to a department-level commission comprised of a membership, including lawyers and ethicists, outlined by Congress. At the same time, scientists operated OSI and ORI and crafted the interim procedures to appeal to a scientific audience. Of the twelve members of the congressionally chartered commission, the chairman and seven others were esteemed academic physicians or biomedical researchers. The commission solicited the research community by conducting four regional meetings on university campuses (DHHS 1995), and ORI continues to conduct educational and outreach programs on a regional basis. In its report, the commission articulated the principle that "federal investigation and oversight require . . . a mixed expertise in investigative staffing" and therefore directed HHS to "ensure that legal, law-enforcement, and scientist-investigator staff participate in each federally conducted investigation and ensure that scientists participate in hearings and appeals procedures" (DHHS 1995: 27, 28).

ORI, however, does not exist comfortably between politics and science, and its lines of accountability to either community were not clear at the beginning, as the experience of its predecessor OSI demonstrates. Viewed as a congressional tool to "turn the screws" on the scientific community – not just by satisfied members of Dingell's staff but by defensive scientists as well – OSI took great pains to represent itself as "scientific." This strategy proved untenable, but in an ironic way: the scientific community would have none of it. In an argument with overtones of John Edsall's against the hunt for communists, scientists maintained not that OSI was ignorant or unknowledgeable, but that it offered insuffficent due process to researchers accused of misconduct. The procedures for adjudicating misconduct subsequently moved from a situation in which OSI, part of the research establishment at NIH, walked the scientific walk by allowing only researchers to sit in judgment of researchers, to a situation in which ORI, now part of the HHS bureaucracy, offers administrative hearings and appeals that involve scientists only upon the special request of one or the other party.

But ORI's relationship is not just with individual scientists over an investigation of misconduct. ORI also provides important services to – that is, is an agent of – grantee institutions whose competence to manage the integrity of science Congress had refused to continue to accept. ORI educates officials from these institutions, validates their policies for investigating misconduct and their findings in specific cases such that they can continue to apply for federal funding, and bolsters their legitimacy to maintain some degree of control over the integrity of science. Perhaps more importantly, the Commission on Research Integrity has studied whistleblowing and promoted both "responsible whistle-blowing" and a "whistleblower's bill of rights" (DHHS 1995: 21–24). ORI has articulated a "conditional privilege" for whistle-blowers to report allegations of misconduct in good faith, and it has drafted guidelines for universities to apply in a voluntary way to protect whistle-blowers, as well as a sample arbitration agreement for universities to apply in case of retaliation against whistle-blowers.[52] ORI has also studied the impact of misconduct proceedings against scientists who have been cleared of charges.[53] ORI is thus an important agent to universities and to individual scientists who may find themselves in the unfortunate position of blowing the whistle on research misconduct. Integrity is thus a collaborative enterprise and ORI is squarely in the middle, helping the scientific community demonstrate its integrity and helping the political community assure it.

Conclusion

Stanford president Kennedy (1997: 217–18) asserts it is crucial for universities to deal forthrightly with cases of research misconduct because "[t]hey create a rupture in faith in a realm in which there is no alternative to trust." That rupture has already occurred, and it is irreparable for the immediate future. The time when the public patrons of research will assume integrity is an automatic function is over, and it has been since the congressional inquiries into misconduct in science in 1981.

But as the principal-agent structure suggests, there is an alternative to trust. It is collaboration on a regime of formal rules and monitoring to assure the integrity of research. The transition from trust to collaboration was a tortuous one in which attempts by Congress to provide statutory direction to the scientific community and formal authorization to a new institution were delayed by unrelated matters, and in which attempts by some members of the scientific community to preserve what they thought to be the greatest share of self-regulation fell before the attempts of other members of the community to ensure the best treatment of scientists as citizens under the due process of law. After Congress had deconstructed scientific self-regulation, both it as patron and the scientific community as its agent needed a way to assure the integrity of science for their continued mutual benefit. The evolution of the contested OSI into ORI served these joint interests.

Accepting the new role for science policy in assuring the integrity of science, however, required relocating the boundary between politics and science. Whereas earlier politics and science had been starkly divided – to the extent that the scientific process operated invisibly and the political process, even when it existed in formal rules, operated not at all – they are now much more intimate and, indeed, collaborative. The current structure now seems well-fortified, having survived court challenges, bureaucratic maneuvering, and partisan shifts in Congress and the administration.

But now, the line between politics and science is not drawn on either side of ORI. Rather, the boundary organization straddles that blurred and permeable border. My dissection of the boundary organization's innards shows how its skeletal structure provides both political and scientific legitimacy and guides and constrains the case-by-case determination of the boundary with respect to integrity. The demarcation will follow the rough guidance of the model policies and procedures developed by ORI for grantee institutions, and it will follow a definition of misconduct articulated by the government. It will also follow adjudication of allegations of misconduct conducted by independent grantee institutions, but under close oversight by ORI and DAB.

5

Assuring the Productivity of Research

It became apparent that the strong U.S. policy emphasis on R.&D., even now still only slightly less than one half of the world's total, had not produced the results its earlier proponents had proclaimed. . . . [This is] a lesson that is by now well-learned, as a result of mistakenly equat[ing] R.&D. with innovation. . . . We have not appreciated the complexity of the process.

– J. Herbert Hollomon, former Assistant Secretary of Commerce (U.S. Senate 1979b: 20).

Introduction

During the Kennedy administration, Herbert Hollomon had conducted an extensive review of the federal role in technological innovation. Despite the review, as he told Congress a decade and a half later, it was "other nations [that] began to understand and appreciate the importance of innovation and to perceive R.&D. as only one part of the complex process required to bring the new into practical and widespread use" (U.S. Senate 1979b: 19). Hollomon believed the United States had failed to adopt this attitude because of its hegemonic postwar position, which by the time of his testimony it had begun to lose to the aggressiveness of these foreign nations.[1]

As policy scholar Harvey Averch (1985: 43) has argued, "The framers of the post-World War II 'contract' between the federal government and the scientific and technical community felt little concern about an innovation problem."[2] Complacency about the productivity of science was akin to that about the integrity of science – it was assumed to be an automatic function. Such complacency did not mean the framers of the social contract for science completely ignored the complexities of the process. One of the most important issues for Vannevar Bush, the Truman administration, and the congressional debate that followed *Science:*

The Endless Frontier was the disposition of inventions created under government sponsorship. But this issue was also among the most vexing. The wartime policy granted title of inventions to the performers of research and allowed the government to license them. Bush favored extending this liberal policy but many, including Senator Harley Kilgore, found it inappropriate for peacetime. The five-year delay in creating the National Science Foundation enabled a plurality of government agencies' sponsoring research and thus a plurality of patent policies, which precluded any rule about intellectual property from being part of the science policy regime. In this sense, the assumption of automatically productive research was made by default.

Two rationales attempted to explain the connection between the new, government-sponsored research and the economy: The "linear" or "pipeline" model purported to describe how the government's support of basic research, particularly in universities, at one end of the line would promote economically important innovation at the other end. The related "spin-off" model purported to describe how the government's support of mission R&D, particularly in government-owned laboratories, would promote economically important innovations in a tangential fashion. These models had an overt correspondence to experience and, perhaps more importantly, they assuaged mainstream fears of an intrusive industrial policy.

Although scholars critiqued the relationship between research and innovation implicit in these models even as they became ascendant, the models succeeded in patterning the design of policy because, as Hollomon had suggested, of the unique postwar situation of the United States. The American economy, particularly in high-technology sectors, succeeded spectacularly. "The important point" about the assumption of automaticity "was not that it was a half-truth at best, but that the unusual circumstances of the postwar world did not force Americans to question it" (Alic et al. 1992: 10). Scientific triumph conspired with general prosperity to place American policy makers in the position of Stephen Turner's patrons described in the first chapter – complacently relying on a trusted agent and assuming the productivity of research.

With the contributions of scientists during the war fresh in the public mind, this trust was seemingly well placed. The war had been won as much in research laboratories as on the beaches of Normandy or in the sands of Iwo Jima. MIT's Radiation Laboratory delivered radar, Los Alamos delivered the bomb, and laboratories of the Public Health Service (PHS) laboratories delivered penicillin and blood plasma. As long as the federal government maintained the headwaters of research, and as long as "scientists are free to pursue the truth wherever it may lead, there will be a flow of new knowledge to those who can apply it to practical problems in Government, in industry, or elsewhere" (Bush [1945] 1960: 12). The primary way to grow the economy was "through the constant advancement of scientific knowledge and the consequent steady improvement in our technology" (Steelman 1947a: 3–4). The productive consequences of research would take care of themselves.

But economic conditions changed radically in the 1970s, and so did the political principals' satisfaction at assuming the productivity of research was automatic. They began to wonder how to assure themselves the agent was contributing to the economic goal. They began to ask researchers to demonstrate that they were being productive. And in searching for the answers to these questions, they concluded the pipeline model itself was faulty.

This chapter begins with a more in-depth discussion of the assumption that the productivity of research is an automatic function. Parallel to Chapter 4, which showed how Congress discovered for itself that science was not satisfactorily self-regulating, this chapter shows how Congress came to the conclusion that productivity was not unproblematic. Such critical scrutiny led Congress to alter the simplicity of the linear model and spinoff with a series of laws establishing a new national policy for technology transfer. As in the case of scientific integrity, the technology transfer legislation implemented solutions to the principal-agent problem of science policy that the consensus had ignored.

Congress passed legislation to create incentives for researchers and to charter specialized organizations to perform technology transfer. Operating at the boundary of science and politics, such organizations are responsible for demonstrating – to politicians and for scientists – the productivity of science. The chapter concludes with a case study of the boundary work performed by one such organization, the Office of Technology Transfer (OTT) at the National Institutes of Health. OTT is responsible for implementing the incentives for technology transfer by assisting researchers in patenting and marketing innovations. But more than this, it is a boundary organization – like the Office of Research Integrity – that promotes collaboration between nonscientists and scientists over the assurance of the productivity of research.

The Linear Model and Spinoff

A number of colorful metaphors attempt to capture the complacency of U.S. innovation policy, as well as a number of alternatives some scholars have offered.[3] There are two crucial points to make about the old model, founded in the postwar vision: first, it specified a clear boundary between politics and science; second, it was not the practical truth in any event.

Representative George E. Brown, Jr. (D-CA), former chairman of the House Science, Space, and Technology Committee, has argued that in the old model, "federal support for basic research is the only independent variable in the equation. Increases in research funding should automatically lead to new technologies and economic strength" (Brown 1991: 26). By conceptually constraining intervention to the single variable of funding, the linear model helped enforce the separation of science and politics inherent in the social contract for science. Scientists would perform the basic research. Scientists would make the discoveries. The scientific literature would disseminate these discoveries. Industrial scientists and engineers would apply them. And industrial engineers and managers would develop and market them. The early part of the process would be mediated only by scientists and technical workers. It would be fired by scientific curiosity, fueled by the reward system internal to science, and damped by the credibility cycle.

In an early critique of what he called the "linear sequence" model, the Australian chemist J. A. Allen (1967: 23) wrote, "the flow [of innovations] may be increased either by increasing the driving pressure of the left hand end [of basic research], or by applying suction to the right hand end. In practical terms, the latter represents the finding or creating of a market for the product." But this right-hand end was taboo for American economic policy, at least for the civilian sector at that time. The model thus assuaged fears of industrial policy by keeping research "safely separated from the free market" (Alic et al. 1992: 25) as Bush and Steelman had hoped.[4] As such, science-based innovation "was viewed as more or less automatic – unmanaged and cost-free" (Alic et al. 1992: 10). It was unmanaged because innovation occurred in a domain exclusively populated by scientists and technologists and did not require any deliberate, coordinating activities. It was free of costs because research was the only necessary public input, as scientists performed the anticipated tasks with motivations unrelated to any incentives the political community could provide, and as private firms bore the cost of acquisition, development, and marketing of new technologies.

This epiphenomenal aspect to innovation is also known as "spinoff."[5] Similar in its shared assumption of "automatic" technology transfer, the spinoff model is associated with mission agencies, especially the Department of Defense (DOD) and the National Aeronautics and Space Administration (NASA), whereas the linear model is associated with university research. In theory, R&D in pursuit of missions like defense and space exploration would spin products, like computer and aircraft technology, off to the commercial sector. Since intramural research at NIH was not connected directly to the delivery of health care, the spinoff model applies there as well (although the more academic quality of its research makes the proximity of spinoff and the linear model apparent). The idea of spinoff served the interests of both scientists and politicians. With it, scientists justified the grants of resources and autonomy they received from the federal government and convinced skeptical politicians to appropriate money to the agencies sponsoring their research programs (Doctors 1969). Spinoff offered politicians a way to "sugar-coat" expenditures for wary taxpayers (Alic et al. 1992: 60).

Spinoff was a surrogate for an explicit technology policy. Given the failure of national health insurance, for example, biomedical research and its promise of spinoff was a surrogate health policy (Sapolsky 1975). As an intellectual model, spinoff fit some of the prominent examples of science-based innovations that fostered entire industries, but it did not incorporate the great deal of innovation that is process-oriented – a category that became more evident to economists in the early 1960s as they realized "the full importance of competition through new products and processes rather than through direct price competition" (Mansfield 1968: 18). The boundary for science policy was funding the front end of both spinoff and the linear model.

The details of many policy initiatives, however, did not necessarily correspond to the limits implied by the model. Spinoff from research programs at DOD "typically required substantial additional attention and investment," rather than being free and automatic (Alic et al. 1992: 9). The most commercially successful research programs, agriculture and biomedicine, have been concentrated in professional schools, rather than in colleges of arts and sciences, where the connection between research and its application is mediated by other professional roles and consumer demands (Nelson 1982: 464). Even NASA's Technology Utilization Program (TUP) was more than an enterprise to simply share information (Doctors 1969). Thus the model not only failed to describe accurately the process of innovation, but it also failed to describe accurately some of the tasks actually assumed by government. Despite these contradictions, the unusual postwar situation of the United States vis-a-vis potential technological competitors – an unscathed infrastructure, a primed economy, and a fresh pool of highly trained personnel – meant that even a partially accurate and partially implemented model was never consciously challenged as a matter of policy or an article of faith.

Just as scholars critiqued the claims of a unique sociological underpinning for science prior to the discovery of a similar perspective by members of Congress like Dingell and Weiss, scholars also critiqued the relationship between science and technology implicit in the linear and spinoff models. Historians like Derek de Solla Price suggested science and technology have been so intertwined historically that to place science temporally and causally before technology is at best arbitrary and at worst backward.[6] Although they had been gathering evidence of the incapacity of the linear model almost since its genesis, historians did not hold the "funeral" for the old model until the 1972 meeting of the Society for the History of Technology (Wise 1986: 236).[7] But the persistence of the inappropriate model of innovation, however, resulted in inappropriate policies (Cozzens 1988; Sultan 1988). Policy makers finally dispatched the linear model for themselves in 1980, and in doing so established a new boundary between politics and science.

Technology Transfer Policy

An Errant Path

The legislation described below constitutes a discrete and broad-based technology policy, even if only "a tentative first step."[8] It is discrete because it is a piece of and not the accident of other policies, for example, procurement. It is broad-based because it spans agencies and technologies rather than focusing on a single one. Only with the demise of the social contract for science is such a policy, focusing on the elements of the innovation process other than research inputs, possible. Ironically, the Carter and Reagan presidencies, despite their predilection for deregulation and market solutions, wrote this preface for technology policy. Although a major theme of technology transfer policy is the leveraging of federal investments in basic research by coupling them more closely to market incentives – in effect privatizing some aspects of previously public functions – the incomplete nature of this privatization results in a public-private relationship that is often unseemly to liberals and conservatives alike.[9]

Biomedical research provided an errant but ultimately successful path to the part of this new technology policy that emphasized the role of intellectual property in innovation. After World War II, PHS, then under the aegis of the Federal Security Agency (FSA), adopted a system of public ownership. FSA, "as a matter of policy, [took] the position that the results of research supported by grants of public moneys should be utilized in the manner which best serves the public interest [which generally occurs] if inventive advances resulting therefrom are made freely available to the Government, to science, to industry, and to the general public." FSA ([1952] 1978: 1) recognized, however, that under such conditions as joint sponsorship or "in order to foster an adequate commercial development to make a new invention more widely available," title might be granted to performers.

This recognition led to the Institutional Patent Agreement (IPA), codified by the 1953 reorganization of FSA into the Department of Health, Education, and Welfare (DHEW) (U.S. Senate 1978b: 58). PHS negotiated IPAs to allow nonprofit organizations to own the patents on inventions derived from sponsored research, if the recipient's patent policies were consistent with DHEW's goals and the public interest (U.S. Senate 1979a: 57). PHS negotiated eighteen IPAs in the first few years of their availability, but the system then fell into a long period of disuse.[10]

In 1968, the General Accounting Office (GAO) documented barriers to the commercial testing of potential therapeutics under NIH grants in medicinal chemistry. Grant recipients described problems obtaining testing services without patent policies that enabled the commercial testing services to acquire exclusive licenses. Some researchers even directed their work away from testable products to avoid the cul-de-sac of having a product but being unable to test it (GAO 1968: 16). In response, DHEW reestablished the IPA system and created a standard or model IPA, resulting in increased commercial activity.[11] Nevertheless, in November 1977 DHEW undertook a review of IPAs, expressing concern that their use "encourages exclusive licensing and thereby sacrifices the agency's broad objective of influencing the availability and cost of [D]HEW-supported inventions [and that] the use of IPAs is conceptually inconsistent with any objective other than rapid commercialization" (U.S. Senate 1979a: 48).

Technology Innovation Act of 1980

Except in this piecemeal fashion, "the nature of the innovation process . . . received little attention" until President Jimmy Carter's Domestic Policy Review (U.S. Senate 1979b: 18–19).[12] One hour after the President's October 31, 1979 message to Congress on industrial innovation, Senator Gaylord Nelson (D-WI) presided over a joint hearing of the science committees and small business committees of both chambers. Nelson pointed to social realities uncharted by the old map of science policy – a set of "unprecedented economic problems: inflation, energy, and declines in productivity and economic growth." He proposed that "our best hope for resolving these problems is to speed up the process of innovation that has been the trademark of this country since its beginnings." Citing the discrepancy between the acquisition of Nobel prizes by the United States and its failure to promote economic and productivity growth, Nelson argued that "there is a serious imbalance in terms of economic returns" to the nation's investment in R&D (U.S. Senate 1979c: 1–2).[13]

A number of indicators pointed toward what the Congress identified as the diminishing U.S. lead in technology innovation, including declines in real R&D spending since the mid-1960s; the rate of patents of domestic origin; productivity gains compared to foreign competitors; and the trade balance in R&D-intensive products (U.S. House 1980d: 3). By some measures, the industrial support of academic research had declined substantially, and some even attributed this decoupling of universities and industry to the federal government's squeezing out private investment (U.S. House 1980e: viii).[14] The committee recognized technology transfer must consist of direct, person-to-person assistance in addition to more general information dissemination strategies to be effective (U.S. House 1980d: 35). The committee also understood that because technology transfer was not part of the mission of research agencies (except NASA), "work performed in this capacity is not often relevant to professional promotion within the organization" (U.S. House 1980d: 33). There was thus no one responsible and rewarded for engaging in technology transfer.

To leverage the declining spending on R&D and speed innovation for economic growth, Congress sought ways to employ universities and the federal laboratories as resources for state and local government and private industry.[15] Adlai E. Stevenson (D-IL), chairman of the Senate Commerce, Science, and Transportation Committee, introduced S. 1250. With the sponsorship of Representative John Wydler (R-NY) in the House, the bill became known as Stevenson-Wydler.[16]

Although the House and Senate moved the bill back and forth over specific amendments, both chambers passed the bill with broad bipartisan support.[17] Stevenson-Wydler (P.L. 96–480) marked the beginning of the end of the technology clause of social contract for science. The act took a few short but direct steps along the principal-agent dynamic to reduce the moral hazard of funding unproductive research. It outlined new technology transfer missions for the federal laboratories in an effort to align the incentives of delegation with its authority. It required the major federal labs to establish their own Offices of Research and Technology Applications (ORTAs) to license government-owned technologies that were languishing without private interest. The professionals in these ORTAs would be in a position to enhance the productivity of scientific programs by acting from the outside. It established the Center for the Utilization of Federal Technology, in the National Technical Information

Service, to serve as "a one-stop shopping center" for information about federal technologies.[18] It also required the President to award a National Technology Medal for "outstanding contributions to the promotion of technology . . . for the improvement of the economic, environmental, or social well-being of the United States" (94 Stat. 2319), thus making a tiny but remarkable intrusion into the reward system of science.

Patent and Trademark Amendments Act of 1980

Known as the Bayh-Dole Act for its Senate sponsors, Birch Bayh (D-IN) and Bob Dole (R-KS), the Patent and Trademark Amendments Act overhauled the checkerboard federal patent system to provide specific incentives for federally funded scientists and engineers to engage in technological innovation.[19] Influential hearings on patent reform had begun in 1976 before the House Subcommittee on Domestic and International Scientific Planning and Analysis. Howard I. Forman, Deputy Assistant Secretary of Commerce for Product Standards, set the tone by presenting chairman Ray Thornton (D-AK) with a medal from the National Inventors Hall of Fame. The obverse of the medal bears the passage from Article 1, section 8 of the Constitution, describing the authority of Congress to grant patents. The reverse bears Abraham Lincoln's dictum, "The patent system added the fuel of interest to the fire of genius." Forman waxed eloquent. His testimony likened an innovation to the baby King Solomon had ordered divided between two petitioning mothers. Like the baby, Forman argued, proprietorship cannot be divided productively; like Solomon, the government should grant exclusive ownership. Forman even accused the government of suppressing innovation, as populists have often accused large corporations of doing. The government held title to some 28,000 patents and its licensing terms resulted in no more than five percent of these patents' commercialization (U.S. House 1976a: 4–11).

Another witness, Norman J. Latker, patent counsel to DHEW, criticized the status quo for having left "the closing of the enormous gap between the new fields of knowledge . . . and their practical implementation by industry . . . to random and haphazard execution" (U.S. House 1976a: 556).[20] Latker testified the goverment needed to "persuade universities to provide a management capability . . . for identification, receipt, and prompt protection of the invention results of university research for later dissemination to industrial concerns" (U.S. House 1976a: 647). He defined this new role contrary to Bush's idea that the government would provide money and no other interference in university affairs. Indeed, one of the criteria for negotiating the IPAs at HEW was assuring that the university had an adequate capacity to engage in technology transfer.

Members of Congress took such testimony to heart. Senator Bayh interpreted the weak licensing performance of federal patents as indicating "very little return on the billions of dollars we spend every year" on R&D (U.S. Senate 1979a: 1–2). Likewise, Robert W. Kastenmeier (D-WI) of the House Judiciary Committee expressed almost single-minded faith that manipulating the patent system would translate into productivity: "At the heart of the American economy's ability to overcome this [grim economic] situation is our patent system" (U.S. House 1980c: 1).

Through the act, the House Science Committee hoped to unify some twenty-six different patent policies. Because NASA – created in 1958 with a mission including technology transfer – already had a liberal policy, the legislation sought to liberalize other policies to its standard.[21] Bayh-Dole proposed to spur even greater commercialization by allowing small businesses as well as nonprofit organizations such as universities to obtain title to federally sponsored inventions with relative ease. Although the goal of stimulating innovation was widely shared, however, there was significant opposition to manipulating patent law to achieve it. "The general feeling in Washington was that if the government was paying for it, the government should own it."[22]

Jack Brooks (D-TX) of the House Judiciary Committee shared this feeling. The populist Brooks believed that Bayh-Dole would violate "a basic provision of the unwritten contract between the citizens of this country and this government." He educed three arguments: first, no organizations were turning down federal funds because of extant patent policies;[23] second, supporting technology transfer by granting exclusive licenses could restrict competition by restricting the number of producers and marketers of technology;[24] third, leveraging public funds could further decrease private R&D (U.S. House 1980a: 29).[25] Brooks predicted the proposal would change the emphasis of federal R&D from "innovation for the general welfare of the people to [innovation for] commercialization in the marketplace" and, in a metaphor with resonance to populist critics of technology policy some two decades later, would create "another welfare fund for private business" (U.S. House 1980a: 30–31).

Nevertheless, Bayh-Dole (P.L. 96–517) passed resoundingly and created incentives for federally funded scientists to perform more productive science, where productivity would be measured in commercial terms. Bayh-Dole allowed federal agencies, including the government-owned, government-operated (government) laboratories at NIH, to grant exclusive licenses. The legislation also required the organizations granted title to these inventions to share royalties with individual inventors and to use the remaining funds to support additional research, education, and the legal costs of patenting and licensing. By allowing universities, other nonprofits, and small businesses to obtain title, and by requiring them to use a portion of any subsequent licensing revenue to reward inventors, Bayh-Dole applied explicit incentives like those suggested by principal-agent theory. Whereas the prior social contract for science simply assumed technological benefit, the new, more explicit arrangement encouraged some measure of actual performance, albeit a voluntary one based strictly in the marketplace.

Executive Activity

Technology transfer policy continued to gain momentum in the Reagan administration. In 1982, President Ronald Reagan signed the Small Business Innovation Development Act (P.L. 97–219), establishing the Small Business Innovation Research (SBIR) program to require agencies to set aside extramural funding for small businesses.[26] In 1983, Reagan signed a memorandum directing federal agencies to extend to all contractors the rights to claim title to inventions Bayh-Dole had granted to nonprofits and small businesses.

That same year, Reagan's Office of Science and Technology Policy (OSTP) issued a report by its Federal Laboratory Review Panel. "[T]he Panel found that the Federal laboratories have several serious deficiencies, and consequently, a number of laboratories do not meet the quality and productivity standards that can be expected of them" (OSTP 1983: v). The Packard report, after its chairman David Packard, recommended encouraging the laboratories to interact more with industry and universities, and permitting them greater freedom from agency heads in Washington.[27]

Based in part on these findings, the Trademark Clarification Act of 1984 (P.L. 98–620) amended Bayh-Dole to permit the directors of government-owned, contractor-operated (contractor) laboratories to award exclusive licenses. Seeking to turn the federal laboratories into engines of regional economic development akin to Boston's Route 128 (U.S. Senate 1984), the act allowed contractor labs run by universities and nonprofits to retain title to inventions, much as Bayh-Dole had allowed universities and small businesses to do.[28] The act also codified Reagan's extension of Bayh-Dole to large businesses. The Cooperative Research Act (P.L. 98–462) eliminated some antitrust implications for companies wishing to engage in joint, precompetitive R&D and established a number of public-private consortia, most prominently the Semiconductor Research Corporation.[29]

The Federal Technology Transfer Act of 1986

In 1971, a small group of DOD laboratories interested in innovation formed a partnership that, in 1974, expanded to include civilian laboratories and dubbed itself the Federal Laboratory Consortium for Technology Transfer (FLC). By 1984, FLC had attracted more than 300 of the labs as members (U.S. House 1985b: 5).[30] In October 1984, FLC invited a staff member from the House Science, Space, and Technology Committee to a meeting in Seattle to discuss problems with the implementation of Stevenson-Wydler, including the lack of career paths at ORTAs and the continuing inapplicability of technology transfer activities to personnel decisions for researchers. The staff member transformed the discussion into a questionnaire and surveyed 75 laboratories and organizations. The results confirmed FLC's claims, and the staff member began crafting legislation.[31]

This effort led to H.R. 3773, the Federal Technology Transfer Act, to amend Stevenson-Wydler to allow government laboratories to enter into cooperative research and development agreements (CRADAs) with nonfederal organizations and mandate that federal employees receive a portion of the royalties from licenses of their patented inventions. The bill would also establish FLC as a federal agency.[32]

Congressional committees heard testimony about ongoing, anemic economic performance. Senator Slade Gorton (R-WA) cited a finding by the Presidential Commission on Industrial Competitiveness that U.S. industry had lost market share in seven of ten high-technology sectors studied (U.S. Senate 1985: 1). Representative Doug Walgren (D-PA) lamented the expansion of the trade deficit into high-technology areas, especially a $6.8 billion deficit in electronics in 1984 (U.S. House 1985b: 4). Eugene E. Stark, Jr., FLC's chairman, testified that technology transfer under Stevenson-Wydler was operating at "less than 50 percent effectiveness" (U.S. Senate 1985: 3–4).[33]

Partisanship and divided government played a significant role in the politics of FTTA's passage. House Democrats and Senate Republicans bickered for six months over the appropriate rewards for federal employees whose inventions are licensed. Democratic staffers saw linking the laboratories to industrial interests as a way of protecting them against budgetary stringency by increasing their value to a wider constituency.[34] Although the Reagan administration's own Packard report and Commission on Industrial Competitiveness had stoked congressional activity, conservatives suspected FTTA predicated a fuller industrial policy and Reagan threatened to veto it. But Bob Michel (R-IA), the House minority leader, thought that FTTA would play well in Peoria – his home district where the Department of Agriculture had its Northern Regional Research Center – and he failed to circulate the veto threat to his colleagues in time to influence their votes.[35]

Extending Bayh-Dole's principle of payments for performance, FTTA established the sharing of royalties with federally employed inventors at a minimum of 15 percent of royalty income. FTTA capped the payment at $100,000 per year for all inventions, unless the President makes an exception in the form of a presidential award. Members of Congress realized that successfully commercializing a discovery requires contributions from people other than just the inventors (U.S. House 1986a), so the act provided cash awards to others intimately involved with technology transfer. FTTA required laboratories to "ensure that efforts to transfer technology are considered positively in laboratory job descriptions, employee promotion policies, and evaluation in the job performance of scientists and engineers" (100 Stat. 1790 §4(a)(3)).[36] Congress extended the authority to enter into CRADAs to contractor laboratories in the National Competitiveness Technology Transfer Act of 1989 (P.L. 101–189). It further augmented the financial incentives for federal employees and the intellectual property protections available to nonfederal partners in the National Technology Transfer Act (NTTA) of 1995 (P.L. 104–113). Passed after the historic Republican takeover of the Congress following the elections of 1994, NTTA also consolidated the bipartisan status of technology transfer policy.

Technology Transfer Legislation and Principal-Agent Theory

When economist Gordon Tullock wrote *The Organization of Inquiry* (1966), he lamented the scarcity of prizes relative to grants for the support of R&D, because prizes can help "induce" curiosity about specific questions and concerns of interest to the prize giver, and they need to be given only when the criteria of success as designated by the prize giver have been met to his or her satisfaction. Although the legislation discussed here did not change the balance between grants and prizes, it did introduce and begin to institutionalize the logic of prizes.

Congress intended this legislation to provide explicit inducements or incentives to researchers to encourage their active role in assuring the productivity of sponsored research. As a former senior staff member involved in much of this legislation told me, the impetus was "to get the fruits of the federal dollars harvested by the private sector." As the logic of principal-agent theory suggests, he saw the scientists as "the tool to try to get the job done." Congressional patrons saw no reason why the federally funded scientists should not be "keeping one eye cocked toward plying the research they were working on."

Another former senior staff member suggested that redistributing the residuals of commercially successful research back to the laboratories and the inventors was a way of formalizing "bootstrapping," which – part of the moral hazard of sponsoring research – is the practice of diverting funds from an applied research project to a more basic one. Congress would not subject the revenues derived from royalties to the same strict requirements of use and oversight as appropriated funds, as there is "nothing more dear to a lab director's heart than having a pot of unlabeled money – nothing."

Congress thus cast technology transfer policy in terms of the principal-agent relationship. It created new structures and incentives to enhance the pursuit of the old, but previously implicit, goal of productivity and the new goal of technology transfer itself. These new incentives comport with Niskanen's (1971) idea that the principal should redistribute a portion of the residual to agents who cut down on waste and inefficiency to control the moral hazard problem. In this case, researchers whose efforts lead to commercial products are cutting down on waste – operationally defined as research that is not commercialized – and sharing in the profits of patents and licenses. The legislation provided "a way of thinking; it doesn't mean it's [necessarily] a way of doing." It is not a negative sanction against "wasteful" researchers, but a positive one for productive agents to encourage the pursuit of research with a commercial impact. Said a senior staffer, there was "some skewing [of research] that we wanted to happen."

Technology Transfer and Boundaries for the Productivity of Science[37]

Technology Transfer at NIH[38]

In the remainder of this chapter, I provide a detailed study of the implementation of technology transfer policy at the intramural laboratories of the National Institutes of Health (NIH) and the boundary work that goes on there. These laboratories, located on the NIH campus in Bethesda, Maryland, constitute the world's largest biomedical research facility. NIH received an appropriation for intramural R&D of about $1.5 billion in FY 1999, or just over 20% of all federal spending for intramural civilian R&D (AAAS 1998). NIH consists of more than two dozen separate institutes, centers, or divisions (institutes), most dedicated to research directed at specific disorders (e.g., National Cancer Institute) or to specific organs or systems (e.g., National Heart, Lung and Blood Institute). Most institutes maintain both an extramural or grant program and a smaller intramural research program.

As the implementation makes clear, the principal-agent story is not the only story of technology transfer. In order to apply the incentives and generate the patents and other indicators of the productivity of research, the process of implementation also had to confront the boundary of science policy by incorporating the efforts of researchers into technology transfer. No such effort on the part of researchers was anticipated under the social contract for science. The new legislation encouraged it.

Historical Microcosm: Consensus Conferences

Boundaries were an important consideration at NIH even prior to the technology transfer legislation of the 1980s. Donald S. Fredrickson, director of NIH from 1975 to 1981, recognized the boundary work required for NIH to fulfill its mission:

> [W]hen I first became director, even before I was sworn in, I was met by [Senators] Ted Kennedy and Jake Javitz, who at that time were on this technology transfer kick. . . . And I thought about what they said and. . . . I sat down and actually wrote a paper. I was going to write a series of papers to lay out NIH policy, and I never completed but one.[39]

In the paper he did complete, "On the Translation Gap," Fredrickson (1975: 2) wrote of his "own perceptions of where action is particularly needed includ[ing] (1) realistic assessment of the boundaries between biomedical research and health care, with particular attention to the necessary extensions of the research continuum in the direction of clinical investigation without imperiling the research that must precede it." Fredrickson (1975: 6) contemplated how NIH might "extend the continuum of biomedical research across preceivable [sic] gaps in translation."

Fredrickson's gap was a space between the laboratory bench and the examination table that could neither be easily nor, given the dangerous politics of health care in the United States, safely traversed. But Fredrickson received an opportunity to explore this forbidding terrain in 1977 when a mammography program, run under government contract by the American Cancer Society, attracted criticism for safety concerns. Fredrickson suspended the program until he could organize a conference to assess the criticism and have the relevant actors come to some agreement. This consensus development conference was the first of scores of such meetings that NIH uses to assess medical technologies and to disseminate information about them to practitioners. Organized under the Office of Medical Applications of Research (OMAR) in 1978, these consensus development conferences were the focus of technology transfer at NIH into the early 1980s (OTA 1982).

In their study of nearly the first decade of consensus development conferences, Markle and Chubin conclude that the conferences inappropriately excluded discussions about the economic, social, and ethical questions related to new medical technologies. This exclusion occurred because the conferences were "designed around an inadequate model of science [that] assumes that a strict separation of factual from value issues is possible, and further, that objective evidence compels experts to converge on the 'correct' decision" (Markle and Chubin 1987: 20). The Institute of Medicine (IOM 1990) concurred, recommending that conferences should include economic, social, and ethical issues. Fredrickson relates that he has "gotten to a point in [his] dotage" where he advocates the inclusion of economic analysis "because that's also become a new science." The current policy seems to split the difference:

> Although many aspects of a technology under review may be discussed – economic, sociologic, legal, and ethical – the primary purpose of a [consensus development conference] is to provide scientific evaluation. To this end, the statements in general and the recommendations issued in particular should focus on medical safety and efficacy, although they may refer to other issues in passing (OMAR 1993).

Fredrickson's early experience with technology transfer at NIH shows something of a microcosm of my argument. The overall structure of the principal-agent relationship appears in his responsiveness to prompting from Senators Kennedy and Javitz. But the institutional result of their direction was crafted largely through Fredrickson's personal vision and molded by the particular circumstances of the mammography program, thus demonstrating that the principal-agent relationship is a "two-way street" with some very contingent traffic patterns (Moe 1987: 481). Fredrickson also hints at the solution of the boundary organization by following the necessity of satisfying both political demands, by extending the applicability of research, and scientific demands, by protecting the category of research. The result – the consensus development conferences and OMAR – then became the site of continued negotiation about the boundary between politics and science. Within the relative safety of such an organization, scientists like Fredrickson could rationalize the intrusion of more politically relevant criteria like economics by labelling them "science" before admitting them, and in practice such new criteria could be admitted in an informal or voluntary fashion.

Implementing FTTA

Thanks to Fredrickson, OMAR already existed when Congress passed Stevenson-Wydler in 1980 and required the government laboratories to establish Offices of Research and Technology Applications. OMAR became NIH's ORTA. But NIH did not move from a model of technology transfer based on consensus development conferences to a more commercial model in response to congressional action. Rather, the eruption of the biotechnology industry following the patents granted to the inventors of recombinant DNA techniques triggered NIH's transformation from cool quiescence toward industry into mutual, hot pursuit.

Subsequent to FTTA – but consequent to the biotechnology industry's becoming more important as the customer of technology transfer than the practitioner community – NIH created a new Office of Invention Development (OID) to replace OMAR as the designated ORTA (GAO 1989). OID quickly grew into the Office of Technology Transfer (OTT), which became the lead organization for technology transfer not only for NIH but for the Centers for Disease Control and the Food and Drug Administration as well. OTT manages a network of Technology Development Coordinators (TDCs) in each institute. While OTT concentrates on the legal and marketing issues involved with technology transfer, the TDCs interact more closely with the researchers. Much of this interaction involves collaboration in the creation of boundary objects and standardized packages. Although the researchers are ostensibly the agents manipulated by the technology transfer legislation, it is actually the professionals at OTT and the TDCs whose jobs are dependent upon the success of technology transfer.

TDCs and Researchers. The role of the TDCs varies according to the size and activity of the institutes in which they work. Some have left the lab bench to work full time on technology transfer and manage staffs of modest size. Others spend but a fraction of their time on technology transfer and are active researchers the rest of the time. One primary function of TDCs is to educate researchers about opportunities under FTTA. Some TDCs send newsletters out to their scientists and encourage them to attend training sessions. Says one TDC,

> We've had seminars, where we'd teach them. We've brought in patent attorneys to tell what is a patent, *so you know when you're working at the lab, when you've discovered something, and when you should be aware to file a patent application.* We've had seminars on CRADAs: When do you get into a CRADA? Why do you get in a CRADA? So we try to help them

> along the way and advise them, you know, so that they know when they should be involved in tech transfer and encourage them to do so (emphasis added).

Although researchers may believe that knowing when to report an invention is part of professional judgment, they may have problems actually identifying a discovery, especially when it is unexpected (Edge and Mulkay 1976). The need to understand the legal criteria for a discovery is especially acute among foreign researchers, who may be familiar with different requirements for patent protection from their home countries. TDCs remind scientists not to publish their work before filing an invention report, and some institutes screen papers for unreported inventions prior to allowing researchers to publish them. The invention disclosures are thus boundary objects that the researchers and technology transfer specialists have collaborated to create.

TDCs recognize they "can't turn everybody into lawyers;" neither can they turn everybody into participants in technology transfer. But scientists at NIH have their own interests in technology transfer activities. Patents can help secure the priority and integrity of a discovery and can facilitate the reduction of such discoveries to clinical practice. CRADAs can yield increased access to money, expertise, and biological materials for research. The scientists, however, have divergent opinions about technology transfer for commercial purposes, and CRADAs in particular. For some, it seems to be an ideological position about the proper role of publicly supported research. They believe either that publicly funded research should remain public, or commercial interests are necessary for technology transfer. For others, it seems to be a consequence of age and socialization. Older scientists were socialized when biology and commerce were more distant and in opposition, while younger scientists were socialized with the tools of molecular biology and the influence of the biotechnology industry. In any event, the TDCs "don't say [to the researchers], 'go out and find an industrial partner!' " Instead, they match congressional expectations of providing a way of thinking rather than mandating a way of doing.

Assessing and Evaluating Inventions. The process of assessing and evaluating new inventions is also a collaborative one, at times leading to the creation of the boundary object of the patent application. After the TDCs and scientists collaborate on the invention disclosures, a decision must be made about whether to seek patent protection. The process for applying for a patent is time consuming and costly, to the point where OTT has consciously cut back on its patenting activities: Table 3 shows the decline in NIH's patent applications, as well as other indicators of

Table 3 *NIH Technology Transfers Activities, Fiscal Years 1993–1998*

Activity	FY 93	FY 94	FY 95	FY 96	FY 97	FY 98
Invention disclosures	232	259	271	196	268	287
Patent applications*	161	143	147	136	148	132
Issued patents	103	103	100	127	152	171
Executed licenses	75	125	160	184	208	215
Executed CRADAs, total	41	31	32	87	153	166
Standard	41	31	32	44	32	49
Materials	NA	NA	NA	43	121	117

*Numbers for FY 97 and FY 98 include only new U.S. filings.

technology transfer activities.[40] OTT and the institutes cooperate to assess and evaluate on which inventions they will file patent applications. Some of the more active institutes have technical evaluation advisory committees. Says one TDC about his advisory committee,

> It's . . . made up of four extramural scientists, and four intramural scientists, [and] the deputy director of the institute. [W]e have . . . one representative from OTT in licensing and one representative from another institute. . . . And we established that [committee to] have a . . . body of scientists [who] started to understand tech transfer. . . . [W]e hoped that it would serve two purposes. One is that it would help us evaluate inventions to figure out when are they good, when do they have potential, when should we invest federal funds for this. . . . And [two,] to teach some scientists about tech transfer, so that if they go back in their lab, they are familiar with it, they understand it, they can maybe do some positive discussions with their peers. And we have one scientist who absolutely hates any kind of committee work, absolutely detests it. [He] called me up and asked to be removed from one committee and to be put on this committee because he thought it was . . . one of the few worthwhile committees in the government. So that was when I felt we really reached a peak. . . . A scientist asking to be on a committee!

During its first year, OTT created Technology Management Teams (TMTs) to facilitate the collaboration among those involved in technology transfer and evaluate technologies. Each TMT consisted of the inventor, the TDC, a patent specialist and a marketing specialist from OTT, a licensing specialist from the National Technical Information Service, and other relevant program personnel. Together, they would devise a strategy of patent prosecution and licensing. The TMT also served an educative function, communicating the details of the process to the scientists and bringing some of them who previously had bad experiences with technology transfer back into the fold.

Originally, OTT established a TMT for each new invention. This coverage was necessary because the TMT was a "problem-solving routine" and, early on, patent applications were generally of low quality and each new invention would "open a new can of worms." But as OTT began receiving twenty or thirty new inventions each month, and as staff and scientists became more experienced, OTT began to use TMTs only when problems arose.

Pressured by the costs of patenting, in 1992 OTT reinstituted something similar to the TMTs. Under the "cross-function team concept," patenting and licensing personnel work together to make a "business decision" about which patents to pursue. The cross-function team assesses the technology for a potential market in order to set priorities. If the team gives a technology a low priority score, the inventor can revise the invention report or, if OTT rejects the technology, the inventor can seek title on his or her own.

Licensing. OTT attempts to license inventions, whether they have been patented or not. Licensing is streamlined if the invention derives from a CRADA. In the absence of a CRADA, OTT uses several techniques. One is like a scientific meeting but with a marketing twist: the PHS Technology Transfer Forum and the NIH/PMA Technology Transfer Conference.[41] OTT invites potential licensees to these fora, at which scientists who have available technologies or who would like to enter into CRADAs present their research in poster format. Another technique is to secure listings for available NIH technology in private databases, trade journals, and on the Internet.

The third technique is for OTT licensing specialists to do legwork. On one side, they maintain close contact with the scientists who perform research in their portfolio area, for example, cancer or AIDS. The licensing specialist may meet with laboratory chiefs to review their technologies and inquire if any companies have contacted the scientists directly (rather than through OTT). The specialist may also walk through laboratories to identify potentially valuable technologies at an early stage. On the other side, licensing specialists attempt to be proactive in marketing inventions. They identify potential market segments, write letters to potential licensees, and work the telephones. Once a potential licensee is identified, the party files a license application and the licensing specialist evaluates the application.

CRADAs. The invention disclosure, patenting, and licensing processes provide a formalized and interactive version of the traditional process of scientific discovery and communication. In a similar way, CRADAs formalize the traditional process of scientific collaboration. One TDC described the creation of the first CRADA under the authority of FTTA:

> I got involved then because I was one person who could actually act as a facilitator to pull together general counsel, our attorneys, the attorneys for the company – at that time it was . . . Genetic Therapy, Inc., GTI . . . – and Dr. Anderson. And we all sat down in a room together, all the attorneys from the company . . . attorneys from General Counsel, Phil Chen, myself, Dr. French Anderson. And we pretty much spent the whole day in the conference room from maybe 8:30 in the morning till, I don't know, 4:30, 5:00 in the afternoon, banging out the very first collaborative [sic] research and development agreement.

Just as collaboration among the various scientific and nonscientific parties in TMTs could not occur for every technology to license, so too could this "banging out" of the terms not occur for every CRADA. NIH created a model CRADA, boilerplate language with which cooperating researchers and firms could agree or work toward more specialized agreements. CRADAs are thus a kind of standardized package.

But even completing the model CRADA is not a carefree process:

> [S]omebody will come and say, "I have this research project and I've talked to a couple of people. We're trying to get here. What do we do?" *And we basically tell them what to do – tell them how to set up a research plan. [We help] them structure a research plan. . . .* We send it to the company, talk to the company, explain the boilerplate to them, ask them to describe what they're going to contribute to the research plan, reevaluate it. . . . *So . . . we're like taxi cab drivers, essentially. Somebody says, " 'want to go to 45th and 2nd Avenue." No problem! We know the directions. We can get you there. . . .* We try to facilitate the process (emphasis added).

Formulating the research plan for CRADAs is crucial because NIH policy is to reject any proposed cooperative agreement not essential for achieving a scientific objective (as opposed to one that might be useful simply for funding laboratories, obtaining equipment, or other financial reasons).

Materials, Royalties, and Motivations. In FY 1996, OTT introduced the new materials transfer agreement CRADA (MTA CRADA), which researchers pursue when they require a proprietary research material (e.g., a compound, reagent, cell line, etc.) from an outside source such as a pharmaceutical company. In the first year of the availability of MTA

CRADAs, NIH researchers engaged in 44 traditional CRADAs and 43 of the new variety. The use of MTA CRADAs is significant because it provides evidence of the motives and interests of researchers engaged in technology transfer. MTA CRADAs suggest that NIH researchers often require the instruments of technology transfer, and the assistance of the technology transfer specialists, in order to accomplish their own research goals and not just commercial goals of the congressional principal.

Further evidence of the insufficiency of the commercial motive of NIH researchers is the poverty of the financial incentives. If a new invention is licensed, researchers are entitled by law to a share of the proceeds from the license. NIH provides a more generous incentive than FTTA requires – 25% of the first $50,000 of income, 20% of the next $50,000, and 15% of income over $100,000 (GAO 1992: 45). According to scientists, technology transfer specialists, and GAO, the monetary incentives provided by royalty sharing are not effective in changing behavior. The benefits are often "illusory" as researchers discount potential royalties because they usually will not materialize until after the lengthy and expensive process of regulatory approval for the product. Furthermore, only a small share of licenses ever bear royalties and the annual cap of $100,000 limits the potential gain. Finally, reasons one TDC, if the scientists "were motivated by personal income, they wouldn't be working in government."

Rather, the scientists seem to view the royalties as compensation for going out of their way, as one OTT professional said, "Nobody likes the patent application, but the royalties help kill the pain." And as one scientist said, "you hope for a home run." By the accounts of participants, the motivation to engage in technology transfer activities comes not from financial incentives but rather from the opportunity to help move one's research beyond the laboratory. Some researchers have understood the best way for their research to have the impact on health care that they hope for is through intellectual property. They understand research papers may not change medicine the way patents do. Despite initial fears (on the part of traditional scientists) or intentions (on the part of policy makers) that royalties would cause scientists to change the orientation of their research, technology transfer "isn't changing science in the sense that it's changing research," in the words of one TDC. Rather, technology transfer is changing the ability of scientists and non-scientists to collaborate for mutually satisfying ends.

Indicators. That the new technology transfer policy has coaxed researchers into producing invention disclosures, patent applications, and CRADAs is only one aspect of the two-way street of the principal-agent problem. These boundary objects and standardized packages are also indicators by which researchers and their advocates communicate the productivity of their enterprise to their political principals. One TDC, for example, acknowledges that when the economy is bad, research cannot be taken for granted as a good thing: "basic science for basic science is just not going to work. . . . You look to the tangible. CRADAs are tangible. . . . It suggests value . . . in a lot of different arenas. It responds to the demand, 'show us what you've done.' " Although they are not the sine qua non of technology transfer, indicators of the creation of intellectual property and its sequelae of licenses and royalties are regularly offered by OTT and research advocates and received by Congress and GAO as evidence of the productivity of research (Guston 1998). Without the opportunity to collaborate with the technology transfer specialists to create these indicators, researchers would have a more difficult task convincing congressional patrons of their productivity.

OTT as a Boundary Organization

As one TDC put it to me, technology transfer is "highly interactive." But to call it interactive is not to fully explicate its importance. There are additional and crucial inferences to draw from these observations.

The first inference is the answer to the question, over what does the interaction take place? It takes place over the process of discovery, which has been opened up to include technology transfer specialists as well as laboratory scientists. It takes place over the process of cooperative research, which has likewise been opened up to include, for example, the assistance of technology transfer specialists in identifying, negotiating, and planning with research partners. Antiparallel to this movement of the technology transfer specialists into tasks previously dominated by scientists is the influence of scientists on the decisions to pursue patent protection and to market technologies.

In other words, it takes place over the boundary work being performed. It takes place over the creation of the boundary objects and standardized packages of patents and licenses, research plans and marketing plans, and CRADAs and materials transfer agreements. It takes place over the distinction between science and nonscience that was, prior to the change in technology transfer policy, far less complicated. With the legitimacy of boundary work within OTT – the first criterion of the boundary organization – the boundary between nonscience and science has become more permeable. In one direction it has become permeable to legislation that tweaks the sensitivities of researchers, and to technology transfer specialists who assist in the formalizing of research and discoveries. In the other direction, it has become permeable to scientists who want patents and royalties in addition to papers, and to new knowledge and its embodiment in technologies headed toward the Patent and Trademark Office and, ultimately, the market.

The second inference is that something, perhaps unexpected, has happened to the principal-agent relationship. Although both technology transfer specialists and researchers recognize that a collaborative process is now in place, they both also agree to maintain a division of labor to keep the former doing the paperwork and the latter doing the laboratory work. This division is not an essentialist one because, as described earlier for example, licensing experts may intrude upon the laboratory to look for technologies or may help draw up research plans with private sector partners. The collaborative task makes use of the expertise of both parties and often serves to educate them both. The rules for participation in these decisions do not seem to be based on any necessary or transcendent conception of what makes a task scientific. Rather, they are pragmatic rules about the distribution of resources and the ability of participants to learn and perform.[42]

Within this division of labor, like the "taxi driver" metaphor earlier, the technology transfer specialists have become the agents of the researchers, just as the researchers are the agents of the policy makers. Researchers have goals – in gaining access to external materials and expertise, in establishing their discoveries, in protecting and marketing them, and in seeing they have an impact – that they cannot accomplish without the technology transfer specialists. This flexibility of the principal-agent perspective becomes even more readily apparent if the application of the financial incentives to the researchers for their technology transfer activities is as modestly useful as the researchers, the technology transfer specialists, and GAO all suggest.

All this collaborative boundary work is directed at the purpose of demonstrating the productivity of science to the principals and for the agents. Without this effort, the principals would be as uncertain or ignorant about the economic impact of their investment in R&D as they were in the late 1970s and early 1980s, and the scientists would be as vulnerable to accusations of lack of productivity. The professionals in OTT are therefore tied to the interests of both the original principals and the original agents. In the boundary organization, performing the boundary work, they are agents of each. It is in their interest to transgress the boundary between science and politics modestly in each direction – a little visit to the laboratory over here, a little marketing survey over there – to produce the indicators of their job performance, but also the indicators of the productivity of science that all the parties have a stake in.

Conclusion

The productivity of research is a crucial aspect of science policy, but the time when the public patrons of research will assume that productivity is an automatic function is over, and has been as a matter of policy since 1980. The ease of reliance on the simple abstractions of the linear model and spinoff has, for the last generation, been yielding to a more nuanced model. The new model not only attempts, as did the efforts at programmatic direction discussed in Chapter 3, to get more innovative bang for the research buck, but it also takes advantage of new types of funding mechanisms to provide researchers with the appropriate incentives to engage in innovative behavior.

Confirming and supporting the assurance of the productivity of research meant relocating the boundary between politics and science. The linear model and spinoff legitimated the privileged isolation of research in the innovation process, whether or not policy actually achieved this isolation in all cases. Overcoming isolation by linking research in universities and federal laboratories explicitly to commercial goals through technology transfer has opened a door to the possibility of not just a more complete technology policy that would enhance and not just leverage private R&D, but even to the possibility of an industrial policy. The mixing of public and private facilitated by technology transfer policy was a clear goal of administrations and Congresses of both political parties. Yet none are absolutely certain on where the new boundary should be drawn, as the ongoing debate over what, if any, technology policy programs constitute "corporate welfare" demonstrates. What continued intrusion of politics and the market into research will occur and can be countenanced? Where will the line be drawn?

The case of technology transfer suggests no definitive answer to the first question, although if it continues to succeed as it has, what intrusion that has occurred will be reinterpreted as a welcomed Anschluss. But technology transfer does suggest where the line will be drawn. Rather than being drawn analytically between one kind of research and another, or between one institution or even one sector and another, it will be drawn by the practices within a boundary organization. The new boundary between politics and science will exist in different places for different projects, negotiated from pragmatism and professionalism within the context of an organization whose goal is essential for all involved.

6

Between Politics and Science

It is no longer enough to regard research grants as entitlements. . . . [T]he public supports research, but it is also demanding accountability. The "trust us, we're smart" approach no longer works. . . . A fine line exists between the role of Congress as stewards of the public purse and the micromanagement of the programs we fund. On the one hand we want to ensure that the departments and agencies that propose and manage science programs are held to high standards; on the other hand we don't want to create a situation in which Members of Congress are telling scientists how to do their research.

– Representative Robert S. Walker (R-PA, retired), former chairperson of the House Science Committee (Walker 1997: 6).

Introduction

In this intensively technological age, politicians rely on science for both material and ideological support. The material contributions of science to politics depend in part on sound judgments and conclusions. A hypothetical AIDS vaccine is equally useless for easing human suffering and for settling policy conflicts if clinical data supporting its safety and efficacy have been falsified. Ideological support for politics also rests on the integrity of scientists. A community of white-coated rascals cannot be the model of the nonviolent formation of consensus that legitimates democratic politics. If the scientific community cannot regulate the conduct of its members, the support it provides to politics can evaporate and, with it, the reciprocal support politics provides for science.

Similarly, research investments may be difficult to sustain if technological benefits are not continually and visibly forthcoming. If science promises the knowledge it generates will lead to technological innovation and economic productivity, and innovation and productivity sag while Nobel production remains high, then research appears to be a selfish enterprise. Convincing patrons to forego other goods in its favor becomes ever more difficult. Politicians will be tempted to emphasize projects with more visible, measurable returns than basic research. Vannevar Bush understood this tendency when he articulated his "perverse law" governing basic research. John Steelman likewise understood it, seeking to "segregate" basic research. Segregation has proven impossible and unwise, however, and its perversity notwithstanding, the law is the law.

Nevertheless, this logic also suggests that politicians will not let the relationship fail precisely because of their material and ideological stake in the integrity and productivity of science. Under the social contract for science, politicians relied on the scientists themselves as the most efficient way of creating a responsible, productive science. Wanting to maintain integrity and productivity after the social contract for science, politicians and scientists have started to cooperate in assuring integrity and productivity, taking on new tasks and setting new boundaries for science policy.

In the epigragh, former Representative Walker describes the difficult problems these tasks pose for members of Congress. First, they must translate the public's newly and intensely articulated demand for accountability, beyond scientific quality, into policy. Second, once they have decided to assure high standards of research integrity and productivity, they must toe the line between stewardship and micromanagement. But delegation, neglect, and self-promotional hearings are more familiar congressional behaviors than stewardship (Fiorina [1976] 1989), and micromanagement not only promises an enormous sink of time and resources but also threatens the very value of the delegation of research. The challenge of this balancing act led Congress to instigate the creation of the boundary organizations that manage the integrity and productivity of science.

Chapter 6 will review and extend the major themes of this book. First, it will complete my argument about a periodization of science policy based on how policy makers and scientists deal with the difficulties inherent in the delegatory nature of research. While in some ways similar to other schemes that have attempted to periodize the postwar era, my argument avoids ad hoc explanations by linking the periodization to an analytical framework and joins two significant areas of science policy, integrity and productivity, within that framework.

Second, the chapter will review the importance of the principal-agent approach to science policy and elaborate the logic of boundary organizations. These organizations, impossible under the old consensus, have garnered wide bipartisan support and, as sites of the collaboration by nonscientists and scientists over the satisfaction of mutual interests, they help stabilize the boundary between politics and science. Although sharing the characteristics of boundary organizations, the Office of Research

Integrity (ORI) and the Office of Technology Transfer (OTT) are not identical, and this chapter discusses differences between them.

The chapter continues with a discussion of the limits of these boundary organizations. Their measurement of the integrity and productivity of science is not without ambiguity, and the boundaries of science policy are not definitively prescribed by their findings. Moreover, neither presents a complete view of policy. Chapter 6 considers other aspects of government policy toward the integrity and productivity of science. Finally, the chapter concludes with an extension of the recurrent analogy between economics and science that hints at a future dynamic between politics and science.

Periods of Science Policy

The history of the twentieth century hinged on World War II, as did the history of science policy. Despite the argument of political scientist Harvey Sapolsky (1975) that the war was not a significant turning point, the war was a "watershed" event for science policy (Brooks 1996: 18), and its aftermath consolidated a new faith in science and technology and reified it in new mechanisms and new agencies for the support of research. With their recognition of a mutual responsibility or exchange between government and science, and their common assumption of the automatic nature of the integrity and productivity of science, the policy makers and scientists of the immediate postwar period constructed the ideology of the social contract for science. As Chapter 2 elaborated, scholars and policy makers rightfully share a vision of science policy as grounded at that time and in this way, although to identify it with the work of Vannevar Bush alone is inappropriate.

The greater difficulty for scholars has been delineating any further periods of science policy in the postwar period. It is useful to examine the variety of other periodizations of science policy, and I base my account on the able summary by the Sweden-based team of Aant Elzinga and Andrew Jamison (1995). Table 4 characterizes a few of the schemes they summarize, with several additions.

Two schemes – Devine, Thomas, and Adams (1987) and Freeman (1987; 1988) – identify a policy change concerned explicitly with innovation in the late 1950s for the former authors and half a decade later for the latter. Although I do not dispute that some change occurred at this early time, as does Stokes (1997) and to some extent Smith (1994), I maintain the social contract for science encompasses the two early periods, rather than decomposes into them. For example, the dissemination model of the second period of Devine et al. remains predicated on

Table 4 *Periodization Schemes for Science Policy*

	1945 1950 1955 1960 1965 1970 1975 1980 1985 1990 1995			
Divine et al.	Appropriability	Dissemination	Knowledge Utilization	
Freeman	Supply Side	Demand Side	Dual Strategies	
Brooks	Cold War	Social Priorities	Innovation Policy	
Smith	Compact	Breakdown	Partial Renewal	
Stokes	Compact	Breakdown	Partial Renewal	Collapse
Elzinga & Jamison	Institutionalization	Articulation	Relevance	Orchestration
Guston	Social Contract for Science	Collaborative Assurance		

the univariate nature of the appropriability model of the first period. That is, the linear model is still in effect in both periods. Only the knowledge utilization model of the current period allows a greater array of points of intervention – including intervention in the reward system of science and the interposition of nonscientists into the process – that pinpoints the end of the social contract for science.

Other analysts identify a turning point in the mid-1960s. Harvey Brooks (1986) offers a periodization based on a dominant policy priority of the era, for example, the Cold War in the early 1960s and the social relevance of the late 1960s and early 1970s. Although it is critical to recognize the new demands for relevance the public and its representatives articulated in the 1960s, it makes little sense, first, to deny the Cold War its place in the setting of priorities as the Apollo project accelerated toward completion and, second, to ignore its resurgence in the early 1980s. Furthermore, it is clear from other writing by Brooks (1990a) that he believes claims about the end of the social contract for science, at least in periods prior to 1986, are misguided.[1]

Bruce L. R. Smith argues, to some extent like Brooks, that the "science-government compact" ended in cultural upheaval, demands for relevance, and declining federal funds in the late 1960s. But, as I demonstrated in Chapter 3, the demands for relevance and changes in funding have little or nothing to do with the social contract for science. Although the cultural changes may have institutionalized scrutiny of science and technology in such mandates as the National Environmental Policy Act and organizations such as the congressional Office of Technology Assessment, they failed to alter the social contract in a way similar to how the programmatic demands for relevance failed: they both occurred outside of the reward system of science. The demands for relevance influenced the funding entering the system, and technological and environmental assessment applied to the innovations emerging from the system, but neither positioned any mechanisms for accountability, incentives, or control within the system itself.

After arguing that the compact dissolved in the mid-1960s, Smith argues it was reconstituted in the late 1970s and early 1980s, as the Cold War and conservative hostility to civilian technology development increased federal expenditures and altered their composition, shifting relative priorities from applied to basic and from civilian to military. But the same arguments apply. Neither funding nor the transient ideological disposition of a congressional majority or presidential administration can alter the social contract for science, which is much more constitutional. It was the agreement resting beneath the contention. Indeed, Smith (1994: 40) acknowledges this fact in his characterization of the immediate postwar period, emphasizing, as I have, the agreement and not the disputes between Bush and Senator Kilgore.

One scholar, the late political scientist Donald E. Stokes (1997: 91), argues that "[a]lthough the postwar compact rested on weakened foundations and the limits of its underlying paradigm of basic science and technological innovation became increasingly clear, it has crumbled only in the 1990s."[2] Drawing on Smith's periodization, Stokes downplays the 1960s departure that Smith adopts in favor of his own assessment of the current period of fundamental change, which is characterized by extreme confusion about the role of basic research in innovation. Although I am in full agreement with Stokes about the importance of the demise of the linear model, as argued in Chapter 5, the technology transfer legislation of the 1980s dispelled its spectre. Stokes (1997: 2) writes that since the "compact . . . has come unstuck, . . . the scientific and political communities are actively canvassing for the terms of a fresh agreement." But the terms of such an agreement have already been struck. The political community and the scientific community will collaborate at the boundary of politics and science over the integrity and productivity of research, and this collaboration will involve monitoring and incentives that reach, however subtly, into the reward system of science. What remains is for the full extent of that collaboration to be set, and for both the political and scientific communities to come to grips with it.

The key to recognizing that Stokes has overshot his mark by a decade or so is examining his three reasons for why jettisoning the linear model will improve government-science relations. First, he states, "The inspiration that basic research can draw from societal need strengthens its claim on public support in the policy community and from the public to which it responds" (Stokes 1997: 99). Already, the technology transfer legislation of the 1980s constitutes "societal need" as appropriable, commercial innovation and strengthens the political position of research at federal laboratories and universities by helping it to build broader constituencies and become measurably relevant. Stokes' (1997: 104) second reason is that "[t]he societal value of use-inspired basic research within a scientific field strengthens the case for supporting the pure research on which the development of the field partially depends." In a similar way, the success of technology transfer – which has been an option for researchers since 1980 but not a mandate – strengthens the claims of their colleagues because of the overall, demonstrable relevance of the enterprise. It has become an indicator of the productivity of research and a political resource of research institutions. Finally, "The uncertainty as to who will capture the benefit in technology from new scientific knowledge is lessened when basic research is directly influenced by potential use" (Stokes 1997: 106). Reduction of this uncertainty is, of course, what the provisions for intellectual property rights in the technology transfer legislation address.

To be fair, Stokes envisions a connection to societal needs that goes beyond the narrow commercial goals articulated by the technology transfer legislation. Particularly for biomedical research, in which the mission of public health may not in all cases be consonant with the goal of commercialization, realizing Stokes' vision is critical. But the change in policy – the end of the social contract for science in this regard – occurred at the beginning of the 1980s, and the unease Stokes diagnosed is its sequelae and not its indicia of onset. We do not need to devise policies to implement in the wake of the linear model. We need to evaluate the policies we have implemented that killed the linear model in the early 1980s.[3]

Elzinga and Jamison (1995) argue that the different cultural orientations of the authors they survey account for their different periodizations of science policy, and they offer their own periodization based primarily on the science policy doctrine of the Organization for Economic Cooperation and Development. I do not claim my periodization of science policy is in some way transcendent of culture, although the phenomena I discuss do have cross-cultural elements.[4] Rather, I claim it is based on clearer and more appropriate criteria of change than heretofore articulated. Furthermore, I have provided a periodization that makes sense not only for considerations of the productivity of science, but also for the integrity of science – with similar political dynamics, criteria of change, and timing. The reason for this consistency across two crucial domains of science policy is the compelling vision of delegation as the problem of science policy and its underlying principal-agent framework. Not only do policies for the assurance of integrity and productivity change in similar ways in this periodization, but also the criteria to define the beginning of the current period of collaborative assurance are those of monitoring and the application of incentives prescribed by principal-agent theory.

Accepting that science policy has passed from the social contract for science to a new policy regime, which might be called "collaborative assurance," settles the thematic issue of consensus and change raised in Chapter 2. We might wonder, however, if this change has altered in any way the other themes or *obbligati* of the social contract for science, which were provocative but incomplete expressions in that regime. These themes were: 1) the social contract for scientists; 2) science as a public good; and 3) generational equity.

The new regime of collaborative assurance rejects the idea that a social contract for scientists can rationalize a social contract for science, largely because it has rejected the claim that a social contract for scientists can regulate the conduct of its members "in an effective, democratic and self-correcting mode" without assistance (and because it recognized scientists, like O'Toole and Abbs, who made similar claims). The new regime formalizes responsibilities at grantee institutions, legitimates institutions that oversee the performance of these responsibilities and that conduct investigations if necessary, and empowers whistle-blowers who can publicize information about failures of scientific integrity.

The new regime recognizes, as the old one did, the nature of research as a public good, but it takes some explicit steps to address the fact that it is not a free good. It legitimates new mechanisms of technology transfer, assisting research planning, brokering research partnerships, collaborating on identifying new discoveries, and providing incentives for the development of commercializable innovations. At the same time, the new regime seeks the cooperation of scientists in emphasizing the productive rather than consumptive aspect of research as a public good. This cooperation is voluntary and is rewarded, but only marginally. Also unlike the old regime, collaborative assurance does have a normative posture about the distribution of benefits. Efficient commercialization dominates all other goals, from the cost of new medicines to the political consequences of collaborative research.

In seeking collaborative assurance for the integrity and productivity of research, the new regime takes a more "presentist" view of the question of generational equity than did the social contract for science. It responds to the demands of researchers today that justice be done in cases of misconduct, rather than awaiting some hazy future when the truth will out. It encourages researchers to commercialize yesterday's research findings today, rather than waiting for some invisible hand to carry them to market. In these functions, the new regime seeks to formalize – through model investigatory procedures and model collaborative agreements – and thereby to accelerate what had been considered the automatic aspects of the integrity and productivity of research. But this acceleration is targeted only at unusual circumstances – serious cases of alleged misconduct and not the day-to-day conduct of research, and the voluntary episodes of technology transfer and not enforced commercial potential. The alterations to these themes provide corroborating evidence that widespread and significant but subtle changes have occurred in the relationship between politics and science.

Structure and the New Boundary Organizations

The Spectrum from Truth to Power, Revisited

This book began with the premise that more intellectual space between politics and science needs to be sought for science policy. A critique of Don Price's spectrum from truth to power, which found some space in the administrative and professional estates, provided three additional areas to search: the problems of boundaries, mutuality, and stability.

Redressing the problem of boundaries has meant attending to the transactions between politics and science, and administration and the professions, rather than to the functions of these domains. It has meant attempting to abide by the constructivist prescription that the researcher should only observe and not participate in the negotiation of these boundaries. And it has led to the study of boundary organizations, situated between politics and science, which legitimate and protect those boundary negotiations in pursuit of their particular missions.

These boundary organizations represent the mutual interest of politics and science in the integrity and the productivity overlooked by Price's "two-fold principle of freedom and responsibility." As the case studies of the Office of Research Integrity (ORI) and the Office of Technology Transfer (OTT) showed, these boundary organizations produce boundary objects and standardized packages that are useful to politicians and researchers alike. Both parties are better off if ORI and OTT perform their jobs well and can demonstrate that research has integrity and is productive.

This structural position of the boundary organization – existing between politics and science, housing the negotiations of the politics/science boundary, and creating objects of mutual interest to both sides – leads to a perspective for the stability of these organizations that at least supplements, if not supplants, Price's reliance on the traditions of pluralism and federalism to stabilize his system of estates. The next section elaborates this perspective.

The Importance of Principal-Agent Theory

This book has proposed that principal-agent theory is a useful way of structuring the analysis of science policy. Its utility comes from a variety of sources. First, principal-agent theory unifies and formalizes a variety of approaches to science policy, from the intuitive if congratulatory approach of Major Powell to Stephen Turner's literary elaboration of it, and from the actual practice of grants and contracts to the revealing, if often unreflective, rhetoric of the social contract for science. Second, principal-agent theory articulates a set of regular problems exemplified in the behavior of real-world actors. Members of Congress from the Allison Commission to Representatives Dingell and Walker confront the moral hazards of research, and scientists from the nineteenth-century surveys to the intramural laboratories at NIH struggle to demonstrate their integrity and productivity to their patrons. Third, principal-agent theory suggests a regular set of solutions to the problems of agency that also find elaboration, from using financial performance as a metonym for research performance, to developing an ideology of the automatic and costless provision of integrity and productivity, to the application of monitoring and incentives to assure integrity and productivity. The change among these strategies also grounds the novel periodization of science policy, with the movement from the blunt elements of political control attempted under the regime of the social contract for science to the more refined attempts to monitor the integrity and productivity of research and interpose incentives in the reward system of science under the new regime of collaborative assurance.

Further contributions from the principal-agent perspective are possible. Continuing concern about the integrity of research could focus on additional ways to liberate and clarify information from within research laboratories. Unable and unwilling to tread into the labs, concerned politicians and administrators are encouraging and protecting whistle-blowers in their efforts to carry information about possible misconduct out of the labs. Whistle-blowers who cannot get official attention can, if they succeed in demonstrating that the government has been defrauded, be rewarded with substantial damages.

Other creative applications of incentives could encourage greater research productivity. More generous amounts of discretionary funds for laboratory directors can be used to encourage creative research that falls between the cracks of more clearly defined research programs. Additional incentives could be provided for cooperative research projects that involve important goals in addition to commercial potential, for example, better terms of agreement for projects between federal researchers and nonprofit or other governmental research partners. At the intersection of integrity and productivity, the need for definitive record keeping in an environment more concerned with establishing proprietary claims could also have a beneficial impact on integrity by reducing the possibility for disputes based on sloppiness.[5]

Additional research inspired by the principal-agent perspective could focus on departures from the bilateral monopoly argued here. The example of loyalty from Chapter 3 suggests one such instance of the impact of breaking the monopoly, in which conflict between NSF and NIH over the question of how to monitor and enforce the loyalty of researchers resulted in public scrutiny of the practice and a change in the policy at NIH. Then again, this change only brought NIH's requirements into accord with those of NSF, reestablishing the monopoly at least as a matter of policy. The same seems to be the case with the definition of research misconduct, which continues to vary among agencies pending the expected government-wide definition. The question of multiple principals could also be applied to the behavior of scientists who seek funding from multiple sponsors and the quality of the resulting research.[6]

These suggestions for further research have dealt only with the aspect of principal-agent theory implicated in the moral hazard of research. Clearly, investigations into the problem of adverse selection – for example, the study of peer review from the principal-agent perspective – could be fruitful as well.[7]

Despite these contributions from principal-agent theory, its application is not a complete method for the analysis of science policy. One weakness is that, upon initial inspection, the principal-agent interpretation of science policy appears to essentialize the difference between science and politics, participating in their demarcation rather than following the constructivist prescription to observe how others demarcate them. The pattern of principal and agent mirrors the division between political and scientific actors, and the distinguishing characteristic of the asymmetric information seems to reinforce the belief of realists in science's claim to the consensual production of falsifiable knowledge under unique normative arrangements. For this reason, the complementarity of constructivist boundary work is crucial to demonstrate the contingencies and nuance of these distinctions.

But upon deeper scrutiny, this apparent cleavage of politicians and scientists into two distinct camps becomes more complicated, as does the link between principal and agent. The easy, two-party relationship dissolves into a complex one in which the patron is principal to a new set of actors, who themselves perform as agents to the researchers. Figure 4 illustrates the position of the dual agency of the boundary organizations of ORI and OTT.

The politicians, concerned about misconduct in science and no longer willing to rely on the alleged self-regulating mechanisms of science, instigated the creation of ORI to monitor and, where necessary, investigate scientific integrity. Similarly, politicians who are unable to promote economically important innovation without scientists created incentives for them to engage in commercial innovation and created OTT to assist them. Congress called on the professionals within ORI and OTT to report on the integrity of science and the effectiveness of the technology transfer, respectively, and their jobs are directly dependent on their performance of this duty.

As Chapters 4 and 5 showed, the researchers are not fully competent to do what the policy makers have asked them to do about assuring the integrity and productivity of research. The inquiries by Dingell and Weiss demonstrated self-regulation could amount to the naked application of power. The scientific community could no longer plausibly claim it managed misconduct effectively and democratically. As the innovation hearings demonstrated, policies oriented by the linear model failed to maximize the commercial impact of research spending. Researchers do not know, at least initially or autonomously, what constitutes a patentable discovery, or how to identify a CRADA partner or market a new technology. Researchers need agents of their own to help them produce these useful things, which can then be offered to the policy makers as evidence of fulfilled obligations. Through the creation of what other scholars have identified as boundary objects and standardized packages, these dual agents demonstrate to the original principals that science can have integrity and be productive in measurable ways, and they help the

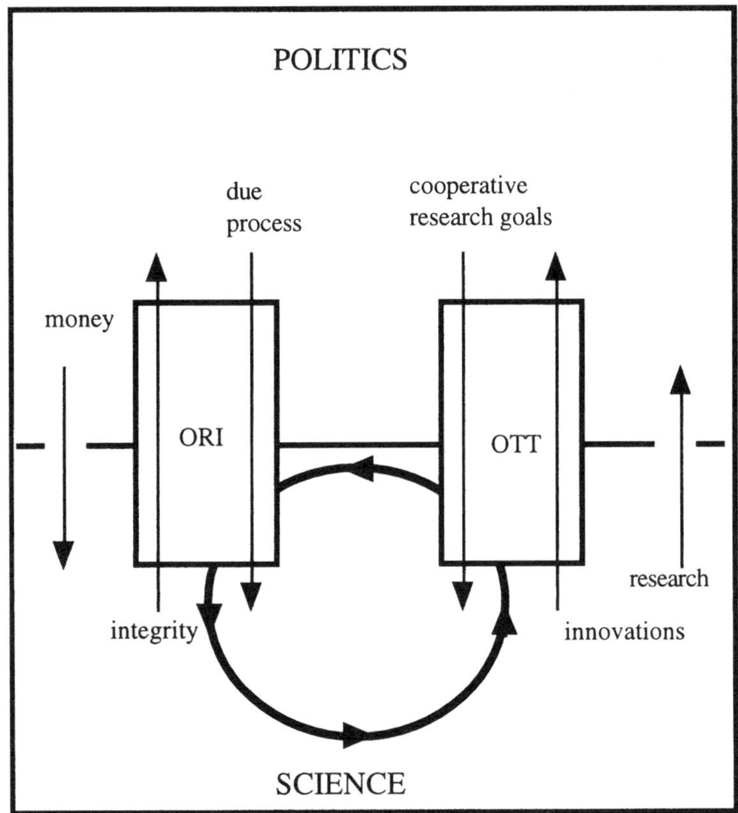

Figure 4 The Position of the Boundary Organization

original agents in achieving and communicating their own goals for integrity and productivity.[8]

It is this dual agency I call a boundary organization. It is a site of what Sheila Jasanoff (1996: 397), following Bruno Latour, has labelled "co-production" – the simultaneous production of knowledge and social order. Boundary organizations are involved in co-production in two ways. They facilitate collaboration between scientists and nonscientists; and they create a combined "scientific and social order." At ORI, researchers, investigators, and adjudicators collaborate to co-produce the integrity of science – a good that is consumed by the scientific community for self-protection and self-promotion and by the political community for accountability and authority. At OTT, researchers, marketers, and patent attorneys collaborate to co-produce the productivity of science – a good that is consumed by the relevant communities for the same reasons. Co-production could not happen under the social contract for science because of the implicit automaticity of integrity and productivity, and the consequent separation of science and politics. Here then is a fourth contribution of principal-agent theory: the insight regarding the logic of stability of boundary organizations, situated as they are at the beckon of two principals and providing assurance to both that the integrity and productivity of research are apparent.

The Logic of Boundary Organizations

As boundary organizations, ORI and OTT inhabit a previously unfortified frontier where the interactions between politics and science over the questions of integrity and productivity had been problematic. Indeed, the border itself – seemingly long dominated by scientists in what policy makers ultimately perceived as unconstructive disengagement – was being contested. Politicians contemplated or engaged in more radical incursions, like the actual investigation by Congress of misconduct allegations or the wholesale privatization of national laboratories. The new outposts did not destabilize the frontier, not only because they were not as provocative as other alternatives, but more importantly because the professionals there became agents of the researchers on the other side as well. The flexible negotiation of the boundary between politics and science continues, but for every inquiry or project, at the level of personal interaction and internalized by the boundary organization. A regular process in grantee institutions and at ORI determines which misconduct investigations will be contained, relatively privately, at the grantee institutions and which will be brought before political principals. A regular process in the intramural laboratories at NIH and at OTT determines which research projects will remain exclusively public and which will be partially privatized through technology transfer activities.

The logic of the boundary organization's stability is akin to the logic, for example, that Bimber (1996) uses to describe the situation of the congressional Office of Technology Assessment (OTA). Prior to its elimination by the new Republican Congress in 1995 – primarily as a sacrifice to the agenda of fiscal discipline – OTA had established itself as a respected and politically neutral institution for the analysis of policy problems with high technical content. Wondering why OTA did not suffer the same fate of politicization over time as other organizations for policy analysis, Bimber points to the dual accountability of OTA to both

Democrats and Republicans on OTA's governing board as well as in OTA's congressional audience. Enhanced further by its clientele in many congressional committees with overlapping or competing jurisdictions, the decentralized demands on OTA elicited a strategy of neutrality that channeled its pursuit of policy analysis. The need to respond to two (or more) principals prescribed a balanced and, with respect to the role of politics and science in the performance of analysis, stable approach to OTA's mission. As a politically neutral organization, OTA did not teeter atop a narrow divide between Democrats and Republicans, but it internalized partisan differences, negotiated them for each study, and produced a boundary object or standardized package that either party could use for its own purposes.

With a similar logic, Jasanoff (1990: 209–16) describes how the Health Effects Institute (HEI) can bring stability to the deconstructive tendencies of an adversary approach to regulatory science through a "public-private partnership for science." In an environment in which government scientists and industry scientists are often on opposing sides of interpreting evidence about environmental health and safety, HEI's experience suggests the benefits of constructing dual agency. Because both government and industry fund HEI, neither party could productively accuse it of being captive to the other. Supplemented by two peer review committees, one of which reviewed research proposals and the other which reviewed research results, HEI has been relatively successful in constructing a reputation for objectivity.

Like Latour's (1987) Janusian visage of science itself, the boundary organization speaks differently to different audiences. Latour's science is able to project authority by appealing to either face in a strategic fashion – for example, by claiming science is a messy, creative process and also by claiming it is a neat, rational process.[9] Similarly, the boundary organization is able to project authority by showing its responsive face to either audience. To the political principal, it says, "I will do your bidding by assuring researchers have integrity and are productive, thus enabling you to better achieve the political goals you have for sponsoring research." To the scientific principal, it says, "I will do your bidding by demonstrating to the politicians you have integrity and are productive, and I will help protect you and facilitate some research goals besides." The boundary organization thus gives both policy makers and scientists an opportunity to construct the boundary between their enterprises in a way favorable to their own perspectives. This solution is almost Madisonian in its use of a balancing of interests to reduce the threat that either side will find the boundary organization inimicable, because it will actually pursue the interests of both parties. The ultimate success of this technique, however, will likely depend not just on a balanced institutional design, but also on such contingencies as leadership and the characteristics of cases of misconduct or technology transfer.

Price (1954) argued against the old idea of unitary sovereignty and in favor of the innovation of a new kind of federalism in the sponsorship of academic research. Likewise, I have argued against the old idea that politics and science should be neatly cleaved and in favor of the innovation of boundary organizations that mix the interests of both. It should not be worrisome that the implementing of boundary organizations is characterized by a political intrusion into the reward system of science, largely because there is a reciprocal intrusion of science into politics. This reciprocation, the struggle to define tacit obligations and authorities, is an aspect of the mutually disjoint constitution of science policy. The politicization of science is undoubtedly a slippery slope. But so is the scientization of politics. The boundary organization does not slide down either slope because it is tethered to both, suspended by the coproduction of mutual interests over the chasm of ruin into which imbalance would slide.

What instead may be worrisome is boundary work performed without the shelter of a boundary organization. Such confrontations happened historically, for example, between the Allison Commission and Major Powell. They happened with respect to the integrity of research between Representative Dingell and David Baltimore, as well as in any allegations of misconduct that universities mishandled. They happen in a recurring fashion with respect to productivity when members of Congress select individual research projects to decry the lack of relevance of an agency's research program (e.g., Senator William Proxmire's "Golden Fleece" awards), or when researchers and private firms strike bargains that exclude legitimate institutional and public concerns. In such circumstances, there is nothing to prevent the boundary work, necessarily laden with interests, from being self-serving in the extreme. Outside of boundary organizations, outcomes are therefore more likely to be determined by the exercise of power, the result that critics of the constructivist approach to science, as well as the politicization of science seemingly represented by the boundary organizations, truly fear.

This role of the boundary organization is compatible with the extensions of boundary work described at the end of Chapter 1. These extensions generally see an importance to maintaining contact with both sides of the boundary, but they fail to anchor that contact into a relationship of accountability to the goals of both principals. The cases elaborated the creation of model policies and procedures for misconduct adjudication and of model CRADAs for cooperative research. These models are essentially standardized packages that are no longer susceptible to the whim of local participants but instead are both more resistant and still consensual. They set a level to which local participants must rise, but more stringent or specific than which they may be – mimicking Price's model of federalism. Such models allow the boundary organization to perform its job with greater efficiency and less conflict, values important to both principals.

Because congressional action created these boundary organizations, it is important to acknowledge that in both cases their creation and implementation has had bipartisan support. Although Dingell's hearings may have been political in the worst connotation of the word, the Republican side of the aisle supported them. There was no partisan opposition to the initial authorizing legislation for the Office of Scientific Integrity and later for ORI, and neither has there been any difficulty in appropriating funds for ORI, even after the Republican Congress imposed a more strict and often ideological test to appropriations. Similarly, the technology transfer legislation of the 1980s and early 1990s was an overwhelmingly bipartisan affair in Congress, and Presidents Carter, Reagan, Bush, and Clinton all signed relevant bills into law. Even the conservative and, over technology policy, confrontational 104th Congress passed the National Technology Transfer and Advancement Act of 1995, which reasserted the goals and fine-tuned the mechanisms of the Federal Technology Transfer Act of 1986. This strong bipartisanship around the boundary organizations is further corroboration of the fundamental change they represent.

Despite their similarities as boundary organizations, ORI and OTT are clearly not identical. Their creation does share the idea that the end of the social contract for science is predicated upon questioning and discovering that science did not seem to be living up to its promises of integrity and productivity. Congress was remarkably effective in critiquing the self-regulatory and linear models, which had undergirded policy toward integrity and productivity. Moreover, ORI and OTT are both predicated on the idea that collaboration between politics and science can enhance integrity and productivity. But the collaboration over integrity is predicated on the revelation that science is not sociologically special in controlling its own integrity, whereas the collaboration over productivity is predicated on the faith that science can be economically special.[10]

To the extent that ORI can measure the integrity of science, it measures such things as investigations and findings of misconduct that are indicators with extremely negative connotations. Furthermore, to create any of these measures, ORI must often engage in an adversary relationship in which the interests of a particular researcher diverge from the interests of both the scientific community and the government. For ORI to stay in business, it must continue to oversee cases of misconduct at grantee institutions and investigate cases at the intramural laboratories. An area of strategic cooperation that ORI seems to have identified, however, is the protection of whistle-blowers. By studying the experiences of the whistle-blowers in allegations of research misconduct and pushing for guidelines for their protection, ORI serves the interests of both scientists, who might find themselves in the position of whistle-blower and thus in need of these protections, and politicians, who like Dingell can pursue their goals of oversight of research through the information provided by whistle-blowers.

To the extent that OTT can measure the productivity of science, however, it measures things like patents and licenses, which are indicators with positive connotations. To create measures of productivity, OTT must help individual scientists achieve their own goals of finding research partners in the private sector and seeing their research have commercial impacts – goals that serve the interests of the researcher and the public as well as OTT. OTT's success, unlike ORI's, does not require anyone else's failure.

Limits to the New Arrangements

Ambiguities of Measurement

This divergence between ORI and OTT suggests a route to examining the limits of the new collaborative assurance. What stands out is the problem of evaluation: what to do with the measurements the boundary organizations produce? Here is where the question of how much money finally reasserts itself.

For example, should there be any financial consequences to findings regarding integrity? For the researcher, there are potential consequences such as debarment from the opportunity to receive federal funds. Institutions are affected by a researcher's debarment to some extent, as well, because they must either release the researcher or shoulder the burden of an employee who has been found lacking in integrity and who will thus lag in productivity. Despite oversight from ORI, institutions still face perverse incentives when they investigate their own researchers.

There are also questions of whether a "tight money" or a "loose money" policy for funding science encourages the greatest integrity. A tight money policy, in which the patrons of research distributed funds only to those researchers of whose integrity they were most sure, would seem to minimize the possibility that a researcher who could commit misconduct would be funded. But such a policy might not provide enough money for other scientists to identify potential falsifications and fabrications or to provide a credible deterrent to misconduct. It could also reduce the rewards expected by members of the community, increasing competition, and perhaps in the extreme leading to anomie and further deviance (see Merton 1973: chapter 18; Weinstein 1979). A loose money system, with relatively more researchers conducting normal science, might provide more integrity, but it also might fund a greater number of marginally socialized or less qualified researchers and attract persons less committed to the ideals of scientific work to the profession, thus reducing overall integrity.

The problem of productivity suffers from the same ambiguity. At NIH, the various institutes that participate in technology transfer have different rates of success, presumably based on the different character of their research and the potential commercial market, as well as the degree to which their researchers have adopted the mission of technology transfer and the level of talent of the technology transfer professionals with whom they collaborate. Successful institutes may bring in additional funds from CRADAs and royalties – perhaps tens of millions of dollars per year. Should Congress consider such funds in appropriating for the institutes and, if so, in which direction? Many researchers at NIH fear that success in commercializing applications might mean Congress would ask an institute to become more reliant on the revenue stream by reducing its appropriation in proportion to technology transfer activity. Such a policy might increase productivity by putting greater market pressures on researchers, but it also might reduce their participation in technology transfer for fear of creating a zero-sum situation for themselves. Congress, however, might be more likely to increase appropriations in order to reward good performance at particular institutes. This policy might increase productivity by rewarding apparently more productive institutes, but it also might reduce productivity by diverting the goals of researchers who should not be engaged in technology transfer or by creating a Matthew effect in which researchers without commercial ties become increasingly impoverished compared to their colleagues with such ties, regardless of the actual relevance of those ties to their research goals.[11] These ambiguities of measurement and its impact call out for additional research.

Incompleteness of Policy

Despite their marking the end of the social contract for science and the beginning of collaborative assurance, these boundary organizations are not a complete policy for the integrity or productivity of science. Beyond the relatively simple problem of the diversity of agencies in which to be concerned about integrity and productivity, there are other categories of interest as well.

Integrity. The idea of a boundary organization to manage research misconduct is not unique to the Public Health Service (PHS). In the National Science Foundation, for example, the Office of Inspector General (OIG) handles allegations of misconduct, currently applying a different definition and following different procedures than those at ORI, but similarly staffed with scientist-investigators and mixing styles of investigation and adjudication. There now appears to be some significant opportunity for the convergence of the two styles. The White House Office of Science and Technology Policy is expected to release a government-wide definition of research misconduct, which makes eminent sense given that researchers may receive funding from more than one federal agency for the same research program. This process has not been an easy one, and given the experience of defining misconduct in HHS and of creating a uniform rule for research on human subjects, one should not expect it to have been otherwise. But a uniform definition could conceivably lead to uniform standards or models for the policies and procedures that grantee institutions should follow, as well as uniform protocols for the boundary organizations in each agency in the conduct of their oversight and investigatory responsibilities. Already some convergence has occurred with the creation of the Research Integrity Appeals Panel, because the closer PHS comes to reinventing the debarment policies of the early 1980s, the closer it comes to the more legalistic role of OIG at NSF.

Even with such a convergence, the scope of the research enterprise covered by boundary organizations' monitoring and assuring the integrity of research is still relatively narrow. With no good estimates of the frequency of misconduct in science, it is nearly impossible to determine how broad an operation is necessary in part because of the lack of a good and consensual definition of misconduct but also because of severe methodological challenges in measuring deviance. But the political reality of the high expectations of scientific integrity that Representative Weiss described demands some coordinated, collaborative effort. The assurance provided by ORI and its kindred offices in NSF and other agencies seems like prudent insurance against future confrontations similar to those in the late 1980s.[12]

Alas, the moral hazard of the integrity of science is not limited to research misconduct in grantee institutions or government laboratories. It also applies to situations in which scientists render policy recommendations related to their work. The need of congressional principals for scientific advice leads them to delegate the chore of analysis to experts who may be biased or ideologically driven. An example of this phenomenon is the set of hearings into "Scientific integrity and public trust: The science behind federal policies and mandates," conducted by the Subcommittee on Energy and Environment of the House Science Committee during the 104th Congress. Subcommittee chairman Dana Rohrabacher (R-CA) framed these hearings as inquiries into the possible politicization of global climate and ozone research, in which scientists might be speaking more from their political preferences than from their data. In one session, the hearings questioned the conclusions of the Scientific Assessment of Ozone Depletion (SAOD), a multi-national, multi-staged review of research on ozone depletion, by impugning the political motives of the scientists involved in the assessment and by providing a forum for additional testimony from scientists that seemed to undermine the conclusions of SAOD. Representative George Brown (D-CA) responded full barrel to the inquiries, arguing the Republicans and not the climate researchers were politicizing science (Brown 1997). Another example is the requirement, expressed by Congress in a rider to an appropriations bill (P.L. 105-277) passed in 1998, that federally funded researchers make their data publicly available under the Freedom of Information Act (FOIA). This requirement, if fully implemented, would allow anyone to check the integrity of the research, especially if it is the basis of regulatory or policy decisions. Although the Office of Management and Budget (OMB 1999) proposed rules for the availability of data that were less onerous than expected (Kaiser 1999), federally funded researchers will still be subject to ad hoc monitoring through FOIA unless Congress changes the law.

The perspective that my inquiry suggests can be brought to this controversy is that, indeed, Congress is perfectly capable of deconstructing the science behind SAOD or opening up sponsored research to similar scrutiny. But, like the Allison Commission of the 1880s, it is not likely to be productive when politicians and scientists confront each other across the dais in a hearing chamber. What counts as politics and what counts as science cannot be helpfully negotiated in such a context. Unfortunately, a boundary organization appropriate for this collaboration – the Office of Technology Assessment – was dismantled. Further research could focus on how Congress might avoid such confrontations in OTA's absence, and how scientists might construct their assessments and presentations to best fend off hostile political deconstruction.[13]

Productivity. As specified by the Stevenson-Wydler Act, all the major federal agencies performing research have offices of research and technology applications, of which OTT is one. Most major research universities also have offices involved in technology transfer, addressing the opportunities provided by the Bayh-Dole Act. OTT therefore has many counterparts, and the professionals involved have increasingly become a coherent community. In addition to the Federal Laboratory Consortium, which Stevenson-Wydler authorized as a federal agency, the National Technology Transfer Center (NTTC) serves a coordinating function for the more than 700 federal laboratories and their interaction with commercial firms for technology transfer. Three professional organizations, the Technology Transfer Society, the Association of Federal Technology Transfer Executives, and the Association of University Technology Managers, provide opportunities for those engaged in the new boundary work required by technology transfer to share experiences with colleagues and develop professionally. They also allow these professionals to express their interests in policies related to technology transfer as a group. That is, they constitute an interest group for technology transfer.

Despite this increase in the organization and professional infrastructure around technology transfer activities, as of yet the scope of this kind of boundary work is also relatively narrow. Only a small fraction of intramural research at NIH, and likely a smaller fraction of extramural research, has potential for commercial technology transfer as envisioned by the laws of the 1980s. This situation is quite appropriate, however, because the congressional principals intended technology transfer to be a voluntary activity, albeit one that was rewarded well. Although this voluntarism, coupled with the inadequate implementation of significant rewards, limits the scope of technology transfer, it demonstrates Stokes' (1997) claim that there is no necessary conflict between research for the sake of knowledge and research for more productive outputs. The question for the productivity of research is not truth or consequences, but how to get both truth and consequences.

In another sign that science is becoming less special and more like other domains of public policy, research agencies along with all other federal agencies fall under the jurisdiction of the Government Performance and Results Act (GPRA). GPRA, passed by a bipartisan majority in 1993 to restore faith in government by asking it to be more efficient and accountable, mandates strategic planning and performance evaluation for federal agencies.[14] After four years of pilot projects and other preparation, agencies submitted their strategic plans to Congress and their annual performance plans (for FY 1999) to the Office of Management and Budget in September 1997. The President submitted the performance plans along with his FY 1999 budget, and by March 2000 the agencies will have submitted their performance reports – evaluations based on the performance plans – to the President and Congress.[15]

Technology transfer and the productivity of science are part of GPRA. For example, the strategic plan of the Department of Health and Human Services (HHS) states as its sixth goal, "Strengthen the nation's health sciences research enterprise and enhance its productivity."[16] Under this goal, HHS articulates six strategic objectives, the first of which is to "improve the understanding of normal and abnormal biological processes and behaviors." To achieve this objective, HHS will promote technology transfer

> through partnerships with industry that enhance the federal capacity for medical research and facilitate the flow of new technology. (This task will be accomplished through the development and implementation of policies, procedures, and guidelines that facilitate patenting, licensing, and cooperative research.)

HHS thus applies technology transfer as a strategy to achieve a scientific goal, in parallel to other such strategies as "adhering to the investigator-initiated, peer-review model for selecting the highest quality research proposals." HHS will measure the success of this goal by "[t]he body of knowledge that has resulted in an improvement to the understanding of normal/abnormal biological processes and behavior," and it has not articulated any refined measures or contributions for technology transfer.[17] Tellingly, HHS also applies the technology transfer strategy to the objective, "improve the prevention, diagnosis, and treatment of disease and disability,"[18] but not to the objectives "accelerate private-sector development of new drugs, biologic therapies, and medical technology" and "ensure that research results are effectively communicated to the public, practitioners, and the scientific community." HHS thus confirms that technology transfer serves goals its researchers have, and not just the goals their political principals have.

Technology transfer is not the epitome of assuring the productivity of science and, as a technology policy, it is similarly incomplete. For example, in order to take advantage of opportunities to collaborate with researchers in federal laboratories or develop for the market technologies that those researchers initially invented, private firms require some significant research capacity of their own. Technology transfer is thus known as a capacity-leveraging policy, because it allows private firms, as well as the government, to do more with less. But technology policy is incomplete without capacity-building policies that provide firms the opportunity to expand their own ability to conduct research and to take advantage of federally sponsored leveraging opportunities (Branscomb and Keller 1998).

In addition to policies to leverage and build capacity, the end of the social contract for science has also created greater opportunities to consider other aspects of technology and innovation policy, including regulatory policy, antitrust policy, and tort reform. Research into the comparative contributions of each of these aspects of technology and innovation would be helpful to policy makers. The role of research in each of these areas would likely resemble the role of research in support of existing agency missions, meaning there would be an ongoing question of, for example, to what extent regulatory policy should be dominated by considerations of innovation, rather than considerations of equity, fairness, competitiveness, or other concerns. Indeed, the strong track record of political support for research in mission agencies like NIH, undergirded by the prevailing economic exceptionalism of science (Bimber and Guston 1995), suggests these other policies may indeed be dominated by a policy for innovation. Additional research could examine the potential of boundary organizations in the collaboration between politics and science in these other policy domains.

Economics and Science

In various parts of this book, I have alluded to implicit or explicit similarities between science and the market. From Michael Polanyi's Republic of Science, to Latour and Woolgar's credibility cycle, to the mutually disjoint constitution and the privileged position of business, the dynamics of the market and of science as allegedly self-regulating enterprises draw inevitable comparisons.

Another comparison, to synthesize these various allusions, is warranted. In *The Great Transformation*, Karl Polanyi ([1944] 1957), the brother of Michael, wrote about the attempts of nineteenth-century liberalism to foster the self-regulating economic market. In Polanyi's account, the economic market was not self-organizing, but rather required the extreme and directed efforts of central organization and controlled government intervention. Liberalism pursued the market largely because it uncritically anticipated the consequences of economic growth. But the market produced an untoward commodification of land and labor – that is, of nature and human beings – that threatened both society in general and political support for the expansion of the market in particular. The political consequences of this impact on humans and nature meant, in no small irony, that "not human beings and natural resources only but also the organization of capitalistic production itself had to be sheltered from the devastating effects of a self-regulating market" (Polanyi [1944] 1957: 132). Self-regulation proved insufficient for managing both the inputs to market production and the political support necessary for the market to become and remain autonomous in a free society.[19]

The analogy I am after should be apparent. The relations between government and science, as recounted here, are similar to the relations between government and the market in Polanyi's account. Polanyi observed that trade, bartering, and markets exist in many cultures and locales, but that the market really did not exist until government brought it to life. Similarly organized inquiry occurred at a small scale in many places for centuries, but it was not until governmental action, coordination, and funding that a large-scale scientific enterprise capable of aspiring to, and approximating, autonomy could exist. Early on, Congress chartered the principal honorific society for scientists, the National Academy of Sciences. Contracts with federal agencies have since sustained the Academy complex in a variety of science policy making roles. The postwar creation of funding agencies helped institutionalize the Republic of Science by placing researchers in key positions of control over the disbursement of funds (Rip 1994). Indeed, what thin postwar consensus there was treated "science, like the economy . . . as a system that could be managed from the outside through the manipulation of funding; its internal institutions functioned satisfactorily" (Hart 1998: 164). Liberalism pursued such a policy because of its uncritical interpretation of progress or, as discussed in Chapter 2, its "technological enthusiasm."

But the tasks of a self-regulating scientific community are more numerous than disbursing the funds offered by the government, and indeed that is why this book has (perhaps too) assiduously avoided the funding of research to concentrate on the assurance of its integrity and productivity. Just as political realities demand that the economic market not obliterate nature and humanity even as it commodifies them, they also demand that science remain an enterprise with demonstrable integrity and productivity, even as it pursues knowledge for its own sake and according to its own agenda. Just as politics ended up cooperating with the market to preserve the latter's privileged position even while regulating aspects of its operation, the increased role of politics in the boundary organizations to assure the integrity and productivity of science may serve to protect a privileged position of science, even while regulating it.

Over time, this explicit relationship of cooperation could take on the character of the automatic relationship that was rejected. The current situation is much like what President Reagan said of the relationship between the United States and the Soviet Union in the last days of the Cold War, when both nations recognized that each required the other to solve its own problems with arms control: "Trust, but verify." The continued delegation represents some continued degree of trust. The boundary organizations represent the attempt to verify. Just as verification in arms control required each country to relinquish a little bit of something it had considered sovereignty, the boundary organizations require the reciprocal intrusion of politics and science into areas of the other's dominion that had previously been off limits. Despite this loss of sovereignty, boundary organizations are stable because they serve as agents to both politics and science, constructing measurements of mutual interest. The forfeiture of what had been considered sovereignty increased the security of both sides and improved prospects for the future.

The boundary organizations are to science what marketers are to economics. As French social scientist Franck Cochoy (1998: 195) has written about marketing, "Half-way between producers and consumers, half-way between economics and managerial practices, marketing specialists have gradually re-invented the fundamental market actors and processes; they have succeeded in disciplining (mastering/codifying) the market economy." The researcher-investigators at ORI and the technology transfer specialists at OTT engage in the same activities of teaching, learning, and standardizing both practice and knowledge for producers and consumers of research that Cochoy's marketers engage in. The better this marketing is, the more stable and seamless the co-production of integrity and productivity by the boundary organizations, the more successful they will be at training politicians to see science as having integrity and being productive, and the more successful they will be at training scientists to demonstrate their integrity and productivity. The more completely the information gathered from verification corresponds to expections, the easier trust can begin to redevelop. The training of scientists for integrity will become part of a researcher's education, and politicians will recognize scientists as having received instruction in integrity as part of being a scientist. Working for productivity will become part of what researchers do, and politicians will recognize that scientists have goals in productivity. For their part, scientists will also have to recognize the role that politicians must have setting an agenda for the integrity and productivity in research and setting standards for their assurance. Verification will breed trust.

None of this will happen without the boundary organizations, but eventually it may appear to be otherwise. ORI may become just another piece of necessary but rarely obtrusive grants administration, and integrity will once again seem to be an automatic function, although it will not, to strict scrutiny, be self-regulation. OTT may be even more integrated with researchers, and productivity will seem automatic, although it will not be through the linear model.

When this transition occurs, integrity and productivity will have reverted to at least a close approximation, if not the actuality, of automatic function, and politics will have provided for science the mutually felicitous appearance of autonomy.

Conclusion

The study of politics and policy is often the study of interests and power. If, like Hobbes, we believe that in science, truth "crosses no mans ambition, profit, or lust," then our politics and policy will pay little attention to science.

But with Vannevar Bush and John Steelman, we recognized through science, we can advance our collective interests. So we interested ourselves in "science and public policy," as Steelman titled his report. We invented a social contract for science to join these two separate entities and assigned responsibility for the integrity and productivity of science to the scientists themselves.

But our understanding of the relationship between interests and science has gone further than Bush and Steelman allowed, and we now recognize that there are interests within science. This recognition spelled the end for the social contract for science. Collaborative assurance replaces self-regulation and the linear model, and it more closely integrates fundamental research with both the state and the market. Collaborative assurance also brings to the fore new concepts like contingent boundaries between politics and science, derived from scholarship in science and technology studies.[20]

These boundaries are dynamic ones. They clearly change over time, although it is difficult to say at what point the old boundaries have ceased to exist and new ones have coalesced. World War II was such a point and, I have argued, the early 1980s was such a point. By the early 1980s, the United States decided it could no longer rely entirely on the scientific community to have integrity and be productive all on its own. The political patrons found flaws in the premises of the social contract for science. They decided that some monitoring and incentives, in effect collaborations between politics and science, were required.

These collaborations now occur in the context of boundary organizations like the Office of Research Integrity and the Office of Technology Transfer. Inspired by Congress, these boundary organizations are also the agents of researchers in demonstrating their integrity and productivity and in achieving certain scientific goals. In their mundane operations, these dual agents negotiate that subtle boundary between politics and science, demonstrating their service to each. Although the boundary organizations provide a regular, stable existence for the negotiation of the boundary between politics and science, they are not complete policies for the integrity and productivity of science.

The perspective of principal-agent theory in providing structure to the study of science policy has, among other benefits, the consequence of rendering science policy a little more like other more familiar areas of public and private action. Science policy is, from this view, more like arrangements with the providers of other services, from greengrocers to physicians to private detectives. At the climax of *The Maltese Falcon*, the ensemble of Caspar Gutman, Sam Spade, Joel Cairo, and Brigid O'Shaunnessy cluster around a table, scraping with a knife at the black coating on the statuette that Spade's secretary has just delivered. Gutman lets out a full belly laugh as he realizes what has happened. They have all been fooled by the falcon's previous owner who, after Gutman had tipped him off by offering to buy the falcon, substituted a leaden falcon for the original golden one.

Their fate highlights another analogy to delegating for research – none of the parties can ever be certain of the value of the outcome, even if they have structured their relationships properly. Even if the patrons of research have written robust contracts with their agents, and both have collaborated in the practice of boundary organizations to assure the integrity and productivity of the enterprise to their mutual satisfaction, there remains a residual uncertainty that may, like the leaden falcon, come home to roost. Research may or may not prove to be valuable to either or both parties. That uncertainty may allow one party to take certain advantage of the other. It might sway the boundary organization, suspended between politics and science, from time to time in one direction or the other. But this motion is, I suspect, irreducible, and the task is to make sure the moorings of the boundary organizations are as secure as possible.

Notes

Preface

1. Harvey Brooks (1968) is responsible for this useful, if even in his mind not completely satisfactory, parsing of science policy.
2. Aaron Wildavsky (1984) most prominently makes this point.
3. See Guston and Keniston (1994).

Introduction

1. Kuehn and Porter (1981) usefully excerpt Price's book as a chapter in their anthology.
2. Such a criticism is characteristic of a constructivist approach to science and science policy. I will take it up later in the introduction.
3. Elzinga and Jamison (1995) discuss a variety of periodization schemes in the science policy literature, including economic interaction, doctrinal approaches, and civic culture in addition to funding activities. See Chapter 6 for a more complete discussion of periodization of science policy.
4. The catchall term at the time was "scientific fraud," but "research misconduct" is currently used. For a review of the changing definitions, see Guston (1999a). Piltdown man was a fraudulent anthropological artifact that combined a human skull and a jawbone from an ape (Weiner 1955; Spencer 1990). The midwife toad fraud involved the injection of ink into the heels of toads in an attempt to demonstrate a theory of inheritance (Koestler 1971). In the patchwork mouse fraud, a researcher painted a white mouse with black ink, initially fooling a review committee, including Nobel laureate Peter Medawar, into believing the researcher had conducted a successful skin graft (Hixson 1976; Medawar 1979). Burt, a British psychologist, falsely reported observations of identical twins raised separately in research on the heritability of personality and intelligence traits (Hearnshaw 1979; Gieryn and Figert 1986; Fletcher 1991).
5. For an early, popular account of the first congressional investigations, see Broad and Wade (1982). For a more comprehensive treatment, see Gold (1993). The more general output of literature on scientific fraud at the time includes Weinstein (1979), Woolf (1981), Bridgstock (1982), Schmaus (1983), Bechtel and Pearson (1985), Ben-Yehuda (1985), Chubin (1985), Klotz (1985), List (1985), and Kohn (1986).
6. In retrospectives of the high-profile case involving several MIT researchers, some (e.g., Sarasohn 1993) are less critical of the investigators than others (Kennedy 1997; Kevles 1998; Rosenzweig 1998).

7. See, for example, Averch (1985) and Wise (1986), as well as the original sources, Bush ([1945] 1960) and Steelman (1947a-d).
8. Beyond applying these incentives specifically to R&D, the federal government has also begun monitoring the productivity of all agencies, including research agencies, through the Government Performance and Results Act of 1993 (GPRA). Chapter 6 describes GPRA's requirement of strategic planning and program evaluation with respect to the productivity of research.
9. The fraction of total basic research is derived from Tables I-5 and I-6 in AAAS (1999: 65–66).

Chapter 1: Science Policy: Structures and Boundaries

1. A great deal of this chapter is based on Guston (1996b). Other authors dealing with principal-agent relations and science policy, in English, include Braun (1993), Rip (1994; 1995), Turner (1996; 1997), Caswill (1998), and van der Meulen (1998). In April 1998, Chris Caswill of the Economic and Social Research Council of the United Kingdom convened a meeting on "Research Funding, Institutions, Processes and Impacts," focusing on principal-agent analyses and involving the author, Braun, and van der Meulen.
2. President Dwight Eisenhower signed Executive Order 10521 in 1954, implementing ideas from both the Bush and Steelman reports to direct the mission agencies to support basic research that would, in the long run, contribute to mission-related technology development.
3. Elzinga and Jamison (1995: 573) are similarly critical of the "technological determinism and scientific optimism that characterized much of the 'first generation' literature on science policy."
4. See, for example, Greenberg's (1967) account of "the politics of pure science," Boffey's (1975) account of the National Academy of Sciences, and Dickson's (1988) "new politics of science."
5. For the major statement of the constructivist perspective on science and technology, see Jasanoff, Markle, Petersen, and Pinch (1995).
6. As such, principal-agent theory has been an aspect of the so-called "new institutionalism" in both sociology (Powell and DiMaggio 1991) and political science (Alt and Shepsle 1990; Weimer 1995).
7. Principal-agent relations are to some degree transitive, but it is productive to study intermediary organizations because their incentives are not constructed entirely by the legislative principals (Braun 1993; Rip 1994; 1995). I address such intermediary institutions or boundary organizations later in this chapter and in Chapters 4 and 5.
8. It is, at its core, methodologically individualist, but as Moe (1984) makes clear, it derives its power from its attempt to address questions of the costs of information and transactions. Also, see Coleman (1990) and Powell and DiMaggio (1991), as well as the discussion in Chapter 2.
9. For the problem of informing members of Congress in matters of science and technology, see Bryner (1992) and Bimber (1996). For the similar challenge of informing state legislators, see Guston, Jones, and Branscomb (1997a; 1997b).
10. These terms are also known as "hidden information" and "hidden action" problems, respectively. See Arrow (1991: 38).
11. The vast majority of all basic research is conducted in the pursuit of missions. In the FY 2000 budget, which proposes $18.1 billion for basic research, some $15.6 billion or 86% will be spent by mission agencies and the remainder by the National Science

Foundation (see AAAS 1999: Table II-1). Also see Hart (1996), who argues that priorities in research funding should be made within the missions to which research contributes, rather than across some unified research budget.

12. Congress has fretted over the possibility that fraudulent research provided the basis for regulations under the Clean Air Act (U.S. House 1984). Misconduct has been identified in a major clinical study of breast cancer (see Crewdson 1994) and what could be called misconduct in the evaluation of technologies for the Strategic Defense Initiative (see Lardner 1992).
13. Lewis M. Branscomb (1995: 43–44) suggests – from a personal experience attempting to replicate possibly fraudulent research – the wasting of time by scientists attempting to replicate or extend research may be among the most serious consequences of the failure of scientific integrity. In other words, self-regulation is not costless.
14. Niskanen (1971: 4) distinguishes himself from Weber by his own "instrumentalist" view of the state, as opposed to Weber's "organic" view.
15. Competition among bureaucratic performers, as well as the pluralism of funding opportunities for researchers, is a primary argument against a single Department of Science. For discussions of a Department of Science in various periods, see U.S. Congress (1986b), Guston (1994), and Walker (1995). Another example of this competition in action may have been the pressure on the National Science Foundation in the early 1990s to become more programmatic in outlook, like the National Institutes of Health, rather than disciplinary. See Mikulski (1994).
16. Congress passed the Inspectors General Act in 1976 to establish an Office of Inspector General in every cabinet-level department and major agency to report both to the cabinet secretary (or administrator) and Congress on the efficiency and effectiveness of programs. As discussed in Chapter 4, the Public Health Service first promulgated regulations dealing with research misconduct as part of its implementation of this act.
17. It is also the logic behind many of the reforms of the Clinton administration's National Performance Review.
18. For example, see the debate over congressional dominance in the *American Political Science Review* by Cook and Wood (1989).
19. Moe (1987) convincingly argues that the claims for congressional dominance do not prove influence but only the potential for it. For example, budgets are not dependable instruments of control because input is too widely shared among committees and between Congress and the President (see Chapter 3 on this issue). Threats of new legislation are largely empty because of the difficulty of passing a law and the existence of the Presidential veto. The confirmation power is extremely limited in time and reach.
20. A more sociological approach has been taken before with the bureaucracy (Kaufman 1981) and with Congress (Weatherford 1985; Fenno 1990). Although the interview is a research tool shared by most social scientists, I use the interviews I conducted to discover how the subjects interpret and order their environments. Political scientist Richard Fenno (1990: 65) makes the distinction between perceptual questions such as these and behavioral questions more often of concern to political scientists. A compelling aspect of principal-agent theory is that it provides a strategic blueprint for intentional actors to follow. As Fenno (1990: 113) says, "If something is important to them, it is important to you [as a researcher]. Their view of the world is as important as your view of the world." That is, if principals are dissatisfied with the level of control they exert over their agents, then it is logical for them to make the kinds of structural changes and apply the kind of inducements laid out by the theory. This strategy becomes clearer in the following section on boundaries. I have interviewed key actors

on both ends of the principal-agent dipole and supplemented these with documentary evidence, hearing transcripts, and press coverage. I interrogate the actors and the documents about issues derived from principal-agent theory: questions about information, incentives, and institutional innovation.

21. See Jasanoff (1990) and Bimber and Guston (1995) for the deconstruction of science by policy makers in regulatory and legislative settings, respectively.
22. Much of the following section is derived from Guston (1999b).
23. Popper (1959) distinguishes science from nonscience by the former's production of statements thought to be empirically falsifiable. Merton (1973: Chapter 13) maintains that science is a unique enterprise demarcated by the adherence of scientists to a specialized set of norms, originally expressed as communism, the proprietorship of research by the entire scientific community and not any one individual; universalism, the application of impersonal criteria of evaluation; disinterestedness, the motivation of advancing institutionalized goals of science; and organized skepticism, the rejection of dogma and the suspension of judgment until evidence and argument is produced. Kuhn ([1962] 1970) argues that the consensus within a paradigm demarcates mature science from other areas in which first principles are constantly in dispute.
24. Ezrahi (1990) describes how science and liberal democracy have had a mutually reinforcing relationship since their birth in seventeenth-century England. Not only has science provided instrumental support to democratic government by producing useful technologies, but it also has provided ideological support by exemplifying peaceful and progressive conflict resolution and by rendering natural and social scientific causes more transparent, thus enhancing the idea of impersonal authority and accountability.
25. For examples of this fear, see Holton (1993a; 1993b) and Gross, Levitt, and Lewis (1996).
26. For a more popular perspective, see Sagan (1995).
27. Such work includes: Collins and Pinch (1993), Nelkin (1994), Lewenstein (1995), and Irwin and Wynne (1996).
28. For a similar perspective on science and the courts, see Jasanoff (1995).
29. Daniel Lee Kleinman (1995) adopts Paul Hoch's (1988) concept of "intermediate" or "boundary" elites – personages like Vannevar Bush who, with accumulated social capital in both science and politics, readily spanned both realms – to help explain policy outcomes such as the creation of the National Science Foundation. Kleinman's boundary elite perform largely the same bridging function as Moore's public interest organizations, but in making no reference to the constructivist perspective on boundaries Kleinman implicitly accepts there were separate realms of science and politics that needed bridging rather than some other arrangement. Similarly, Hoch describes the mediating role of these elite within the "military-industrial-scientific alliance" with little concern for how the actors involved negotiate the boundaries within the alliance.
30. In some cases, the definitions and explanations are almost functional, elaborated around the ability of the boundary object or standardized package to perform a particular task, rather than explaining that ability.
31. This is not to mention the possibility of instability in a consensual system, in other words, voting instabilities. See Arrow (1951).
32. Braun (personal communication) views "funding organisations [as] the prototype of [the] boundary organisation."
33. The important sources for the Allison Commission are Dupree (1957), Manning (1967; 1988), Kevles (1978), and Guston (1994a). The hearings are published in U.S. Senate ([1886] 1980).

34. The original members of the Allison Commission were Senators Allison, Eugene Hale (R-ME), and George Pendleton (D-OH) and Representatives Hilary Herbert (D-AL), Robert Lowry (D-IN), and Theodore Lyman (I-MA) (who was a geologist and a member of the National Academy of Science).

Chapter 2: Understanding the Social Contract for Science

1. The philosopher Michael Sandel (1982) implies this perspective on the realism of the initial situation when he criticizes Rawls' social contract as being doubly hypothetical, in that it is a contract that never happened among beings that could never exist.
2. In an example of the delegation of parental authority to public schools as a disjoint constitution, Coleman (1990, 349–52) shows how brief an initial elaboration of the three elements is necessary to begin a useful analysis based on social contract.
3. For a history of NSF and its grants programs, see England (1982) and Wilson (1983), among others. For a history of PHS research and grants programs, particularly those at the National Institutes of Health (NIH), see Harden (1986) for the prewar period, Strickland (1989) for the postwar period, and Fox (1987) and Fredrickson (1993) for the transition. Sapolsky (1990) provides a detailed history of the creation of ONR.
4. Nelkin cites Smith (1965) and Kevles (1977) as describing the creation of "this postwar contract," but I have not found any such language in either source. In a contemporaneous work, Nelkin speaks of "an implicit contract between science and the Congress" that "has been subject recently to erosion precisely at the original point of contention – over the scope of political control of science and the extent to which science must be accountable" (Franklin Institute 1978: 86).
5. This section relies on my interpretation of interviews of sixty-nine current and former bureaucrats and congressional staff during the fall and winter of 1991–92 and during January 1993.
6. Interview with Dr. James B. Wyngaarden, former director, NIH, Washington, DC, December 2, 1991.
7. Although a policy that is often controversial among conservatives, the government support of the arts and humanities operates much the same way, albeit at a vastly smaller scale. Perhaps because of the controversy, there seems to be a stronger sense in the arts than in science that state support threatens integrity and autonomy. There is, however, a less well-developed economic argument for public support of the arts.
8. Organs of the scientific community voice this pragmatic aspect of the social contract for scientists, for example, in a style manual for publishing in biomedical research:

   > Scientists build their concepts and theories with individual bricks of scientifically ascertained facts, found by themselves and their predecessors. Scientists can proceed with confidence only if they can assume that the previously reported facts on which their work is based are indeed correct. Thus all scientists have an unwritten contract with their contemporaries and those whose work will follow to provide observations honestly obtained, recorded, and published (Huth 1983: 1).

9. The specification of patents and copyrights in the U.S. Constitution (article 1, section 8) is an attempt to address this problem by offering protective monopolies to creators and inventors in order for them to realize the returns on their inventiveness more easily. By the 1880s, the difficulty of private support for science became part of the increasingly successful rationale for the expanding federal role in funding science in

both federal bureaus and the nascent research universities (U.S. Senate [1886] 1980; Miller 1970). Although corporations and private philanthropies began to invest larger amounts in scientific research by the turn of the century and particularly after World War I, much of these funds dried up during the Great Depression, reemphasizing the unreliability of private support (Weiner 1970; Kevles 1978).

10. Bimber and Guston (1995) argue that after contentious politics has discredited the special epistemological, normative, and sociological status of science, this "economic exceptionalism" is all that remains.

11. There is a newly expanding engagement between the economic study of science, which had focused on the economic rationale for and consequences of investments in research and development (e.g., Smith and Barfield 1996), and the social studies of science, which had focused more on the internal dynamics of science as a social practice. See, for example, the special issue of *Knowledge and Policy* on "The Economics of Science," edited by economist Arthur M. Diamond, Jr. (1996).

12. The "investment budget," regularly proposed in Congress through the mid-1990s, is a way of clarifying federal expenditures according to their presumed generational impact. For FY 1999, the Clinton Administration proposed a Research Fund for America, similar in concept but that really highlighted presidential priorities in R&D and did not provide a formal way to aggregate R&D spending or trade off among R&D expenditures (AAAS 1998).

13. This method is not unlike Rawls' method of reflective equilibrium, in which he circulates between areas of empirical consensus and those of theoretical concern to build a complete argument. For example, he hones in on what aspects of the human condition are morally relevant with the empirical observation that slavery is now broadly agreed to be morally wrong.

14. Representative George Brown (1991: 26) describes it as a "biblical command for robust, no-strings-attached federal support of scientific research." Former NIH director Donald S. Fredrickson describes the habit of referring to the Bush report in science policy analyses as "a hopeless ritual." (Interview with Donald S. Fredrickson, former director, NIH, Bethesda, MD, January 5, 1993.) Sarewitz (1996) uses the Bush report as the rhetorical template for a number of the myths that pattern a now misdirected U.S. science policy.

15. See Price (1954), Kevles (1977), England (1982), Reingold (1991), Kleinman (1995), and Hart (1998). This conflict parallels in the United States the debate in the United Kingdom between Michael Polanyi and J. D. Bernal. See Turner (1990b) and Brooks (1996). But in this debate, as in politics generally, the United States displayed a relatively constrained spectrum of options compared to its European counterparts. The divide is being repeated to some degree in the recent so-called science wars. See Holton (1993a).

16. Parsons (1946: 9) reported the liberals felt that OSRD "should not serve as a precedent for peace-time conditions." England (1982: 11) found that even OSRD staff believed it "is not democratic enough in organization for peacetime – the director has too much autocratic power."

17. The major sources disagree on the origins of the letter. England and Kevles are unclear whether Bush actually wrote the first draft of the letter, although they support some role for him in its preparation. Zachary (1997) attributes the first draft to Bush himself. Fredrickson (1993) suggests that Bush did not draft the letter, and the original impetus came from individuals such as Mary Lasker, the leader of the disease lobby, who were interested in medical research. Kleinman (1995) assigns the initiative to Oscar Cox, an

attorney in the Roosevelt Administration and counsel to Bush, and attributes the authorship to Cox, Bush, and OSRD staff.

18. Steelman (1947a: ix) avoided addressing the patent issue because the Attorney General had recently reported on government policy.
19. The previous budget director, Harold Smith, warned President Roosevelt about Bush's lax attitude toward political accountability (Zachary 1997).
20. The geographic distribution of research funds was, as it is today, also a conflict between private colleges and universities, which generally oppose formula distribution, and the public universities, which often favor it. Since the 1940s, the issue has evolved into not one of formulae, but one of earmarks by members of Congress for research to be conducted in their districts. Such pork-barrel science increased rapidly through the early 1990s, reaching a high of $763 million in 1993, and then declined to $296 million in 1996, only to increase again to $495 million in 1998. See Cordes (1998) and Savage (1999).
21. According to Parsons' (1946: 7) commentary on the original two bills, "[t]he Magnuson Bill involved no innovations in patent policy, following the practice of OSRD. . . . The Kilgore Bill, on the other hand, provided for rather radical innovations in this field."
22. Hart (1998) studies the variety of options that existed for the design of the relationship among science, technology, and the economy in the New Deal and World War II era. They were not limited to even the ones listed here.
23. Zachary (1997) also notes the similarities between Bush and Kilgore, particularly in contrast to Jewett.
24. For a more complete critical analysis of the impact of the Bush report, see Guston (1997).
25. In 1995, the fiftieth anniversary year of *Science: The Endless Frontier*, there were at least three major convocations on the theme: Sigma Xi's "Vannevar Bush II: Science for the 21st Century" (Sigma Xi 1995); Columbia University's series of public meetings, "Science, The Endless Frontier, 1945–1995: Learning from the Past, Designing for the Future" (see in particular Crow 1998); and a session at the annual meeting of the American Association for the Advancement of Science entitled, "Return to the Frontier: The Vannevar Bush Report, Then and Now" (Guston and Brooks 1995).
26. The entrepreneurial aspect of these policies and their compatibility with Bush's career and vision is stressed in Etzkowitz (1995).
27. The speaker is Christopher Hill, then of the Congressional Research Service. The context is a discussion, "Dialogue on Science and Congress," among political scientists and science policy participants that focused in part on the social contract for science.
28. Of course, there was no complete laissez faire. From the patent section in the Constitution to distribution of scientific patronage to university scientists by John Wesley Powell (Turner 1977) to the National Advisory Committee on Aeronautics (once headed by Bush), the government has interfered with science. Also see Dupree (1957).
29. Bush seems to be making an argument akin to Ken Newton's (1976) argument that the federal government is less movable by special interests compared to state governments. For more on Bush's arguments about states, see Guston (1996a). The history of the development of research institutions at the federal level, however, could scarcely be described as "free from the influence of pressure groups," particularly in biomedical research. See Strickland (1972).
30. It is also possible, however, given the uncertainty in the delegation of research from principal to agent, that applied research will create slack for the conduct of basic

research. This phenomenon, by which scientists conducting very directed research sneak less-directed research onto the same funding, is often known as "bootstrapping." Bush's argument is strikingly reminiscent of Tocqueville's, who, a century earlier, argued that industrialism in American democracy would assure the application of science and therefore "the whole of organized society should be directed to the support of higher studies and the fostering of a passion for pure science" (Tocqueville [1848] 1969: 464). See Guston (1993) for more detail on Tocqueville's view of science. Bush's statement depends on the implicit distinction between basic and applied research, which many in recent times (e.g., Stokes 1997) have rightfully attacked as pernicious. But Bush's law seems ultimately dependent on stringent political oversight that prefers near-term and measurable results to long-term and unmeasurable ones.

Chapter 3: Challenges to the Social Contract for Science

1. Sandel (1982) describes how two related ideals – reciprocity and autonomy – provide two different aspects of the moral force of contracts. Reciprocity highlights fairness and the obligation of parties that already exists, for example, integrity. Autonomy highlights the acceptance of new obligations, for example, productivity.
2. See, for example, Diamond (1996) and the conference, The Need for a New Economics of Science, University of Notre Dame, South Bend, Indiana 13–16 March 1997, organized by Philip Mirowski and Esther-Mirjam Sent.
3. Arie Rip (1988) has expanded the notion of the credibility cycle to account for the entrepreneurial behavior of research councils (corporations) in addition to individual scientists. This not so casual metaphor also evokes the more contemporary relations of scientific research to economic development spurred by the technology policy legislation of the 1980s, for example, Johnston and Edwards (1987) and Slaughter and Leslie (1997).
4. This marketlike perspective on the scientific community is largely similar to the system of competition for recognition from their colleagues described by Hagstrom (1975: 78) or Bourdieu's (1991: pt.1) "economy of linguistic exchanges."
5. The market metaphor need not be a complete model for it to be powerful. Generally missing from the metaphor that would be needed in a robust model would be prices for all the transactions discussed. See Mowery and Rosenberg ([1979] 1982) for a discussion of the shortcomings of market models in discussing technological innovation.
6. Latour and Woolgar (1979: 70) cross this policy question in yet another crucial way, but still manage to avoid it. When the participant-observer in their study is tempted with "going native," the question that returns the anthropologist to his critical equilibrium is, "How can we account for the fact that in any one year, approximately one and a half million dollars is spent to enable twenty-five people to produce forty papers?"
7. Polanyi provides a self-effacing example of his and Bertrand Russell's inability, in January 1945, to predict any "possible technical uses" of the special theory of relativity. Some forty years after the formulation of special relativity and a mere seven months before its manifestation at Hiroshima, Polanyi and Russell did not predict the atomic bomb. Although this claim is rhetorically powerful, if it is not disingenuous it may be just as damaging to their reputations as to the proposition that science can be channeled. Obviously, the scientists who proposed the atomic bomb predicted a technical use of special relativity. It might be Polanyi has missed a step in his argument, one that says something like, "Only scientists very close to the facts and theories can

predict with certainty the next, small incremental step of technical uses." But Frederick Soddy speculated much earlier in the century on the possible destructive forces derived from the energy in atomic nuclei (Sclove 1989), and H.G. Wells (1933) speculated about a powerful weapon based on the atom.

8. Polanyi cites his own work on the relationship between academic and industrial research on this regard, a 1961 article in *J. Inst. Met.*, which I have been unable to locate.
9. NSF still, however, conditioned grants on an individual's not being an avowed Communist or having been determined to be a Communist, or not advocating extra-constitutional means of changing the government (including persons convicted of sabotage).
10. NIH reports its 1951 budget for grants and operations at $46 million and its 1960 budget at $381 million, an increase of more than eight times. See NIH (1997: Chapter 3). Steelman (1947a: 29) had proposed $200 million for NIH for 1957. NIH reports a $170 million for that year, although Greenberg (1967: 272) reports $213 million.
11. For an analysis of the history and activities of the House Government Operations Committee, see Henderson (1970).
12. Fountain used his subcommittee to challenge the appropriations subcommittees on NIH funding. Government Operations could often find itself in this position. (Henderson 1970). Strickland (1972) reports other members of Congress came to Fountain to challenge the appropriations for NIH, because they feared going up against the Appropriations Committee.
13. Wooldridge does not perform a marginal analysis, however. It is possible the quality of the supported work would have improved even more had less money been spent.
14. In particular, he pointed to a five-year "moral commitment" to a block grant to Sloan-Kettering Cancer Institute (Strickland 1972: 219). Beyond the problem of promising funds not yet appropriated, Fountain pointed out the quality of research at Sloan-Kettering did not appear to be "universally high" to warrant the block grant, as twenty of thirty-four individual grant applications submitted over the previous two-and-a-half years had been rejected (Strickland 1972: 220). The notion of such "block grants" is intriguing in the context of Price's description of "a new type of federalism."
15. There is some evidence that real DHEW basic extramural research was the site of larger relative cuts, however. DHEW basic research lost 11% in real terms, the largest percentage of major programs, with NSF second at 6.5%. But this decrease in current dollars was $26 million, or $6 million more than the NIH cut reported by Strickland, which is attributable to other DHEW research agencies that constitute less than one quarter of the DHEW basic research program. Furthermore, DHEW basic intramural research increased in real terms $12 million or 21%, so there was some reprogramming occurring as well. Again, some of this increase was undoubtedly for intramural research other than NIH. Nevertheless, given the larger budgetary climate, this evidence still seems weak to conclude that Fountain signaled a major change.
16. These critiques include Carson (1962) and environmentalism, Nader (1965) and consumerism, and Ellul ([1954] 1964) and Roszak (1969) of technological society more generally.
17. John Fogarty, the health appropriations subcommittee chairman, was a member of the Select Committee as well. Kevles (1978: 413) compares the Elliott Committee, as a "full-scale investigation into federally funded science," to the Allison Commission.
18. The Select Committee compared proposed Joint Committee on Research Policy to the Joint Economic Committee, which was viewed as a counterweight to the Council of Economic Advisors. Compare this institutionally driven innovation with Bimber's

(1996) account of the creation of the congressional Office of Technology Assessment (OTA).

19. The Senate created a new Government Research Subcommittee of the Government Operations Committee to help scrutinize federal programs.
20. COSPUP had been created by the Academy in 1962 as the standing Committee on Government Relations and was renamed COSPUP in 1963. Its creation was intimately associated with OST and the activities of George Kistiakowsky, who became its first chairman (Cochrane 1978). The reports were *Basic Research and National Goals* (1965), *Applied Science and Technological Progress* (1967), and *Technology: Process of Assessment and Choice* (1969).
21. There are many brief secondary accounts of Project Hindsight, including U.S. House (1986b: 59–60) and Mansfield (1968: 177–78). The project issued a interim report in 1966, published an article based on that material (Sherwin and Isenson 1967), and issued a final report in 1969.
22. According to a DOD review, four percent of its 6600 projects would be affected (U.S. House 1986b: 62). See also Smith (1990: 81–82).
23. Robert Ketcham helped draft the Mansfield Amendment. He recalls that scientists were up in arms about it, and their reaction might have indicated it was breaking the social contract for science. (Interview with Robert Ketcham, former general counsel, House Science Committee, Chevy Chase, MD, January 17, 1992.) Former presidential science advisor D. Allan Bromley (1988: 20) speaks of a "Ghost Mansfield Amendment" that, after the original amendment had been watered down, percolated down to DOD program officers and caused them to refrain from funding irrelevant basic research should some future Mansfield Amendment be reinstated.
24. TRACES employed a methodology different from Hindsight, tracing the key innovations from a variety of new civilian technologies back fifty years. These included magnetic ferrites, birth control pills, video recorders, and electron microscopes (U.S. House 1986b: 60).
25. The newly reorganized Office of Management and Budget had a role in the expansion of RANN, as NSF basically exchanged some programmatic control for larger budgets (Wilson 1983: 34–38). Also, see U.S. House (1980f: 500–06) and Smith (1990: 79).
26. The use of contracts rather than grants suggests that NIH, as principal, had some specific programmatic goals to pursue. Some members of the research community found the use of contracts an inappropriate expression of political goals. See, for example, the comments of Mahlon B. Hoagland of the University of Massachusetts Medical School at a 1978 conference jointly sponsored by the Franklin Institute and the congressional Office of Technology Assessment (Franklin Institute 1978).
27. A similar pattern seems to have emerged with funding for the human genome initiative. For a history of the development of the initiative and its funding mechanisms, see Cook-Deegan (1991).
28. Other important views of the period include Goodfield (1977), Rogers (1977), Krimsky (1982), Fredrickson (1991), Wright (1993), and Weiner (1994).
29. In 1947, the war crimes tribunal at Nuremberg established a list of ten precepts governing the use of human subjects. This Nuremberg Code served as the basis for the Declaration of Helsinki of the World Medical Association, published in 1964 (Swazey 1979). In the United States, Senator Walter F. Mondale (D-MN) had been calling for a commission to investigate the use of human subjects in research as early as 1969 (Culliton 1979). These concerns were crystallized by revelations of federally funded research that disregarded imperatives of informed consent (particularly the Tuskeegee

syphilis study), resulting in the creation of the National Commission for the Protection of Human Subjects of Biomedical and Behavioral Research in 1974. This case, akin to programmatic research, was really about regulating inputs to research and not regulating the research process or the rewards system.

30. Many of these concerns were visible a decade earlier (see Weiner 1994) and some, like eugenics, had been of concern for nearly a century (Kevles 1985).
31. The following account relies mainly on Krimsky (1982).
32. Susan Wright (1993) supports this interpretation, suggesting the problem was constructed as a public health problem rather than a moral or ethical problem, and therefore a problem with scientific and not political solutions.
33. The City Council imposed a moratorium on the research, causing worries that patchwork local regulations would complicate research and increasing pressure for some national legislation. Cambridge overturned the moratorium, however, and in doing so relieved some of this pressure.
34. The expectations of the research community that Congress would regulate are expressed in contemporaneous dialogue (Franklin Institute 1978).
35. Congressional inaction, however, was only a penultimate event in the history of recombinant DNA regulation. Under pressure from a research sector represented by increasingly allied academic and industrial scientists, the regulations promulgated by NIH became interpreted as a handicap in a technological race against technological competitors. After using its power to turn back Congress, the research sector was able to redeploy and succeeded in achieving major deregulation in 1978 and 1980 and still further deregulation since then (Wright 1993: 95). In 1996, NIH director Harold Varmus proposed eliminating RAC. Facing significant public opposition, Varmus retained RAC, but reduced its size from twenty-five to fifteen people and made its review of protocols advisory to the Food and Drug Administration, which also must approve the kind of protocols RAC has.
36. Walter Stewart and Ned Feder, two NIH researchers who independently investigated scientific misconduct, appeared before the task force to discuss authorship and publication practices in science and the ability of the peer review system to deter or detect misconduct (U.S. House 1986c). At the group discussion, House Science Committee staffer and task force study director John Holmfeld said of the early 1980s that "[t]here were vague, often unarticulated feelings that the system was not working as it was supposed to. The trigger was concern that came from the emergence of fraud. . . . So some members began raising questions about the scientific community's ability to self-regulate, to work things out on its own" (Hamlett 1990: 38).
37. Personal communication with Patrick Hamlett, one of the organizers of the group.

Chapter 4: Assuring the Integrity of Research

1. Holton (1993b), for example, sees undue attention to misconduct in science as one of a triumvirate of new forces conspiring to threaten the productive relationship between modern science and democracy. Also see Gross, Levitt, and Lewis (1996: 31–38).
2. The exclusivity of this focus is warranted, given that PHS has been the site of the greatest number of cases, as well as the most prominent ones. The reason for this concentration of misconduct in biomedical research is hotly contested (Woolf 1988). It could simply be a function of the dominant share of biomedical research in the federal portfolio, or it could be related to contextual factors particular to biomedical research, for example, extreme competitiveness among researchers, increased commer-

cial interests, proximity of basic research to applications, the presence of M.D.s, etc. But no discipline has been without cases. See NAS (1992: Chapter 4) for additional discussion.

3. Unless otherwise noted, this section is based significantly on privileged interviews conducted between November 1991 and January 1992 by the author with members of the staff of the House Science and Technology Committee and the Senate Labor and Human Resources Committee.
4. The increased role in oversight was itself tied to other secular developments, such as: the congressional challenge of expanding, postwar executive leadership and activity; distrust of the executive branch from experiences with Vietnam and Watergate; increasing professionalization of the Congress, including increased staffing levels; and the decreasing ability and incentive for members of Congress to engage in legislative, rather than oversight, activity due to the constraints of fiscal politics (Aberbach 1990).
5. The 1978 *Science and the Congress* meeting had a substantial discussion of the regulation of science, but the integrity of science did not appear on the agenda (Franklin Institute 1978). The similarly timed *Limits to Scientific Inquiry* volume also made no mention of it (Holton and Morison 1979).
6. Interview by the author with Mary L. Miers, former Institutional Liaison Officer, Office of Extramural Research, NIH, December 6, 1991. This example also demonstrates how the unitary actor implied by the principal-agent framework yields to a multiplicity of perspectives upon closer scrutiny, but still retains the same logic.
7. Such a system in which the federal government explicates responsibilities of the recipients of its funds is an example of the aptness of Price's description of this relationship as a new kind of federalism.
8. Also see Chapter 3 for more on the House Science Policy Task Force.
9. Unless otherwise noted, this section is based significantly on privileged interviews conducted between November 1991 and March 1992 by the author with members of the staff of the House Committee on Energy and Commerce: the House Government Operations Committee, and the House Science, Space, and Technology Committee.
10. Representative Weiss assumed the chair of Intergovernmental Affairs Subcommittee in 1983 after Representative Fountain retired (Foreman 1988).
11. This section relies on Bimber and Guston (1995).
12. Jasanoff (1995) also argues that this political deconstruction of science occurs in the courtroom in addition to the legislative hearing chamber.
13. Dingell's investigation of Sarin came on the heels of the criminal conviction of Dr. Zaki Salahuddin, also from Gallo's lab, on similar charges of financial misconduct, and in the midst of ongoing charges of inappropriate behavior of Gallo and colleague Popovic in the research leading to the discovery of the human immunodeficiency virus (HIV), for which Gallo and Popovic were eventually cleared.
14. At roughly the same time, Representative Dingell also began investigating possible abuses in indirect cost accounting at universities, including Stanford and MIT. Although these investigations contributed to a climate of scrutiny and even condemnation of universities, indirect cost accounting does not implicate the social contract for science for much the same reason the Fountain inquiries did not: because it involves the actual contractual obligations regarding the amount of money flowing from the federal government to the universities. For partial accounts, see Kennedy (1997: 164–75) and Rosenzweig (1998: 68–77; 120–21).
15. Unless otherwise noted, this section is based on interviews with officials in the Office of the Director and the Institutional Liaison Office at NIH.

16. OIG reported that only 22% of NIH grantees had misconduct procedures in place. Criticism of the report focused on its statistical presentations, however, pointing out the institutions that had procedures in place represented 86% of NIH funding. The majority of grantees without procedures in place were small businesses and small colleges. See DHHS (1989).
17. The National Science Foundation's program in scientific integrity is maintained by its OIG, but it has had notably greater support from the scientific community.
18. There were rumors of a new office when the scientist was put in charge of ILO. Janet Newburgh, that scientist, was told when she interviewed for the job (which she began on October 10) that a new office was a long way off.
19. Although the scientific press reported that lobbying from the academic community defeated the amendment on its merits (Mervis 1988), it was rather the give-and-take of a conference committee, pressured by time at the end of session prior to an election, that prevailed. "It was really an issue of time rather than what outside forces were saying." (Interview with former congressional staff member, March 13, 1992.)
20. Wyngaarden based this proposal on his previous success with moving the Office of AIDS Research to the Office of the Director. That move "had quieted the critics, so I thought, 'this has worked once, let's try it again.' And so rather than doing nothing, and let the Inspector General walk off with it, I decided we needed some kind of new organization with visibility and a move that would be interpreted as a reorganization internally."
21. On February 22, the Assistant Secretary received from the Deputy Assistant Secretary for Health Operations a longer memo and a recommendation, including staffing and resources for the new offices. Acting Assistant Secretary Ralph Reed signed off on the Statement of Organization, Functions and Delegations of Authority for OSI and OSIR on March 3.
22. Interview with professional staff members, Energy and Commerce Committee, Washington, DC, November 5, 1991.
23. National Institutes of Health Revitalization Amendments of 1991 (H.R. 5207). Title I, part II, subtitle C discusses scientific integrity and section 151 refers to OSI.
24. The legislation also directed the Secretary to establish a definition of research misconduct, informed by a Commission on Research Integrity to be established by the Secretary as well. Chaired by Harvard physician Kenneth Ryan, the commission met for the first time on June 20, 1994 and reported on November 3, 1995.
25. ORI also conducts other educational and outreach tasks, as had OSIR before it. ORI conducts investigations itself where intramural research is concerned and when grantee institutions cannot conduct a fair investigation.
26. The Office of Science and Technology Policy is expected to release a government-wide definition of research misconduct. See Francis (1999).
27. Unless otherwise noted, this section is informed by interviews with staff members of the Institutional Liaison Office.
28. PHS thus implemented part of the institutional assurances prior to its obligation under the law.
29. John Darsee was a researcher under the mentorship of Harvard Medical School researcher Eugene Braunwald. Colleagues caught Darsee faking research results, and Harvard's subsequent investigation of the matter was widely perceived as flawed. Darsee's large number of publications, many of which were coauthored by his mentor and other prestigious researchers who were thus potentially implicated in Darsee's fraud, attracted the attention of Ned Feder and Walter Stewart, who presented their research on these papers to the House Science Policy Task Force.

30. The policies relegate cases "involving the possible misuse of federal funds" to department audits, OIG, or the General Accounting Office, and cases involving human subjects regulations and animal welfare policy to the Office for Protection from Research Risks (OPRR).
31. The policies and procedures consisted of three documents in addition to internal policies: "general policies and principles" little different but for the definition from the 1983 statement; "summary of procedures affecting regulated research," largely for FDA research, which operates under a strict monitoring program; and "policies and procedures for agencies authorized to conduct research," for grantee institutions to use in conjunction with fulfilling their assurance obligations.
32. Recall how the debarment rule required notice only of a hearing and not of an investigation.
33. Again, recall the contrast with the debarment rule in which response was relegated to the final stage.
34. Unless otherwise noted, this section relies on interviews with officials at OSI.
35. Interview with James Wyngaarden.
36. Interview with James Wyngaarden.
37. Kimes was not clear, however, on why a finding of misconduct or lack of misconduct would not constitute "new information."
38. Kimes also acknowledged that the peer advisory system of grant application review was the main interpretive model for OSI. Wyngaarden, however, said he does not recognize that description.
39. One of the sensitive issues was the confidentiality of ongoing investigations. Scientists accused OSI of breaching confidentiality by leaking case information. OSI denied being the source of such leaks, often responding that the congressional subcommittees to which it was responsible and to which it gave case documents had done the leaking.
40. Further, Hallum believed "the use of normal scientific dialogue in dealing with our very occasional instances of misconduct will best serve the public interest" (PHS 1991: 140). In other words, preserving a social contract for scientists would help preserve the social contract for science.
41. *Abbs v. Sullivan*, U.S. District Court for the Western District of Wisconsin, 90–C-470–C, December 20, 1990.
42. In 1992, PHS altered the ALERT system, so names were entered only after the conclusion of an investigation and a finding of misconduct by an institution or ORI. Of course, this change countered the initial intention of the system.
43. Wyngaarden left the post in the spring of 1989. William Raub became the acting director, but no replacement was found until Healy was formally nominated in January 1991 and sworn in in June 1991.
44. Coleman (1990: 325) describes how the legitimacy of norms may be inferred by members of a community accepting sanctions against them.
45. Nevertheless, ORI continues to emphasize its technical credentials, for example, by listing publications and presentations by its staff members in its annual reports.
46. DAB provides an opportunity for the independent review of disputed decisions across HHS programs. The Board consists of five members and has a staff of approximately 30 additional attorneys. A subcommittee of DAB, together with an outside scientist who may be appointed at the request of either party, constitutes RIAP.
47. The standard of reasonable researcher can emphasize the role of researchers in deciphering intent.
48. Responses to the dropping of charges ranged from Gallo's claims of complete vindication to unease at the case being settled on a technicality. See Recer (1993) and

Greenberg (1994), inter alia. After ORI dropped the case against Gallo, Dingell's committee continued to pursue it. But a report expected from Dingell was cut off by his loss of the chairmanship in the wake of the 1994 elections. Kennedy (1997), Kevles (1998), and Rosenzweig (1998) all interpret DAB's rulings in these cases as rebukes of ORI, but it is neither obvious nor necessary that DAB's standards are more appropriate than ORI's – especially when the *Abbs* court had validated OSI's procedures as adequate due process. Kevles (1998: 290), however, feels that the *Abbs* case was decided on a technicality.

49. There is no such recourse for decisions made solely by grantee institutions not involving federal sanctions.
50. I mean the diversification to encompass only the novel assertion of interests by individual scientists and the federal government. Some explanations of the problem of research integrity have cited the demographic diversification within the scientific community, asserting that the new influx of female and foreign-born students has rendered the old, informal system of transfering norms of conduct among like-socialized, white males more difficult. See, for example, the language in NAS (1992: 69–70).
51. ORI (1997) reports 25 percent of the institutional policies it has received and approved were based on its model policies.
52. For details on whistle-blowers, see ORI (1998).
53. ORI (1997) finds the majority report a neutral overall impact, but a sizable minority report a negative overall impact.

Chapter 5: Assuring the Productivity of Research

1. Hollomon also identified a technological malaise in the United States, linking economic indicators such as declining productivity increases and the trade imbalance to technological failures such as the nuclear accident at Three Mile Island.
2. Averch (1985: 5) analyzes "how we think" about science policy by examining key science policy documents and reducing these to formal propositions about the respective roles of government and the scientific community in science policy. My analysis is somewhat parallel and sympathetic.
3. For Allen (1967), the old and new models are the "linear sequence" and the "wheel, hub and axle," respectively. For Shapley and Roy (1985), they are the "one tree" and "two tree" models. Dorf and Worthingham (1987) contrast the old "relay race" to the new "basketball game," and Gomory (1990) dubs the old model the "ladder" and the new model the "cycle."
4. Ezrahi (1990) calls the insulation of science from political or economic forces the "autonomy of truth," a modernist concept that scientific truth is and should be acontextual adhered to by seminal American thinkers such as Franklin and Jefferson.
5. Other terms of art including "spillover" and "fallout" (Mansfield 1968) emphasize the almost accidental nature of the operation.
6. Significant here is de Solla Price's work on the relationship between citations of papers in science and technology, and most interestingly his statements before congressional committees on the matter. See Cozzens (1988) for a review of his work.
7. See a collection of papers from the conference in *Technology and Culture*, introduced by Thomas P. Hughes (1976)
8. As described by Howard W. Cannon (D-NV), chairman of the Senate Commerce, Science, and Technology Committee (U.S. Senate 1979b: 1).
9. This slippage between public and private is exactly what Price (1965) had suggested science could facilitate.

10. In a 1965 study of patenting, the Federal Council for Science and Technology (FCST) of the White House Office of Science and Technology had pointed favorably to IPAs (U.S. Senate 1978b: 58).
11. The number of IPAs increased to 72 by the end of 1968, facilitating the commercialization of at least 75 medical inventions by 1977 (U.S. Senate 1979a: 57, 48).
12. For more about the relationship between Carter's Domestic Policy Review and technology policy, see Barfield (1982: Chapter 2).
13. The United States had 103 prizes in physics, chemistry, and medicine at the time, compared to Japan's three.
14. Jacob E. Goldman, then senior vice president and chief scientist at Xerox Corporation, testified the ratio of federal support to industrial support of university research increased from approximately 8:1 in 1960 to 30:1 in 1967, and stabilized at about 20:1 in 1975. Lewis M. Branscomb, then vice president and chief scientist at IBM, presented a slightly different view, comparing the ratio of total industrial R&D to federal R&D in 1962 (about 1:2) to that in 1980 (about 1:1). See U.S. Senate (1979b).
15. There are more than 700 federal laboratories, which are often separated into those that are both government owned and government operated (government labs) and those that are government owned but contractor operated (contractor labs). Their effective utilization had been on the agenda at least since hearings by the Research Subcommittee in 1968. For an updated view of their management, see Crow and Bozeman (1998). A 1978 committee print discusses two reports by the Council of State Governments on technology transfer to state and local governments. Technology transfer to industry was a relative newcomer. See the testimony of Albert H. Teich in U.S. House (1979: 3–23).
16. The impetus began in the Senate with the multiple perspectives that Stevenson – who also served on a banking subcommittee dealing with the Export-Import Bank and whose committee had a jurisdiction much broader than science – brought to overseeing the research enterprise.
17. The Senate passed S. 1250 on May 28, 1980. The House passed an amended version on September 8. On September 26, the Senate concurred with some House amendments and disagreed with others, and on October 1, the House finally either concurred in or receded from the remaining amendments.
18. Stevenson-Wydler also proposed the establishment of Centers for Industrial Technology as loci for university-industry cooperation and technology transfer. The centers, however, depended on the changes in patent law that were being contemplated in parallel legislation (U.S. Senate 1979b: 175). Oriented to provide an institutional context aligned with congressional interests in innovation, the centers were not fully implemented by the Reagan administration.
19. For a history of the development of federal R&D patent policies prior to Bayh-Dole, see U.S. House (1976b; 1976c) and Eisenberg (1996).
20. Latker had been the chairman of FCST's ad hoc Subcommittee on University Patent Policy.
21. Representative Toby Moffett (D-CT) opposed the idea of a uniform set of patent policies because the current policies were each based on considered congressional opinion that was more likely to be appropriate for the specific technologies each agency dealt with than a single, uniform standard (U.S. House 1980b: 24). His perspective is similar to that of Branscomb and Keller (1998) that there is no single technology policy for all technologies.
22. Interview with Robert C. Ketcham.

23. Brooks was thus arguing that researchers continued to tacitly assent to the social contract for science.
24. Senator Russell P. Long (D-LA) agreed with Brooks. Long saw "not even a shred of evidence to support" the position that patent policies stifled innovation. Long conjured an old metaphor from Nobel economist Wassily Leontief that granting patent rights to a federal R&D contractor was no more reasonable than allowing a federal road contractor to collect tolls. As the former chairman of the Monopoly Subcommittee of the Small Business Committee, Long had held hearings on federal patent policy as early as 1959 (U.S. Senate 1980: 463–64). For a current skeptical view, see Mowery, Nelson, Sampat, and Ziedonis (forthcoming).
25. Elsewhere, Brooks cited the testimony of Admiral Hyman Rickover that the bill, if enacted, would actually impede industrial innovation (U.S. House 1980b). Analysts continue to advance the argument that the long-term detrimental effects of emphasizing proprietary technology transfer could decrease private R&D spending (Stewart 1987) or impede private innovation (Eisenberg 1989; Cohen and Noll 1995).
26. The Senate had begun working on the Small Business Innovation Act (S. 1860) in 1979, in parallel to Bayh-Dole. SBIR was very controversial, but it is less so now, even though Congress has increased the set-aside amount and expanded the definition of small business. See Anuskiewcz (1992) and Wallsten (1998).
27. The report also raised such age-old questions as multiyear and discretionary funding for laboratories and a separate science and technology personnel system within the civil service. Steelman himself raised these questions in 1947.
28. Luger and Goldstein (1991) suggest such centers of local development are very difficult to duplicate, although studies of individual laboratories confirm their crucial role in the local economy (Markusen, et al. 1995).
29. See Branscomb (1993: Chapter 3).
30. Until then, no HHS or NASA laboratories had participated. By the end of 1986, FLC had 328 member laboratories, including three from HHS and ten from NASA. See FLC (n.d. [1986]).
31. Interview with senior staff member, House Science, Space, and Technology Committee, Washington, DC, January 26, 1992.
32. H.R. 3773 built upon the Uniform Patent Procedures Act (S. 2171), a bill that Senator Dole had introduced in the previous Congress, along with the amendments to the Bayh-Dole Act, which had first suggested the use of "cooperative research and development arrangements" in the government laboratories (see U.S. Senate 1984: 5).
33. Stark did not make clear how effectiveness was measured, however.
34. Interview with senior staff member, House Science, Space, and Technology Committee, Washington, DC, January 26, 1992. Indeed, at this time it became clearer that the defense roles of the national laboratories would shrink in the future. The Department of Energy became particularly aggressive in 1986 and 1987, for example, as its Office of Health and Environmental Research pushed for involvement in a human genome project (OTA 1988; Cook-Deegan 1991).
35. Interview with senior staff member, House Science, Space, and Technology Committee, Washington, DC, January 26, 1992.
36. The drafters of FTTA had concerns about conflicts of interest, but they decided the agencies involved were too different for specific legislative direction. Instead, FTTA required agencies to issue their own regulations as needed (U.S. Senate 1986: 10). The problem they recognized was "the patent without the inventor is useless," so the congressional goal was to get the invention out and rely on the agencies to protect

themselves from conflicts. Nevertheless, Congress recognized "[t]his incentive approach is an innovation in the Federal Government which should be monitored [so that] royalty income over and above a laboratory's normal budget does not adversely affect the laboratory's primary mission" (U.S. Senate 1986: 12).

37. Much of the following is adapted from Guston (1999b).
38. All the major federal agencies that perform R&D engage in technology transfer activities, although these activities are tailored to suit the agency's mission, resources, and potential research partners. There may be reason to think that, given the politics of health care in the United States, the issue of boundaries may be more sensitive and self-conscious at NIH than elsewhere. My claims with respect to principal-agent theory and boundaries will therefore have to be tested for their generalizability, but articulating the argument is my purpose here. Kaghan (1998), however, makes many of the same findings about boundary work with respect to university offices of technology transfer. Likewise, Mowery, Nelson, Sampat, and Ziedonis (forthcoming) find that the Bayh-Dole Act has provided universities with marketing opportunities that many of them have taken advantage of, without having a significant impact on the content of academic research.
39. Interview with Donald S. Fredrickson.
40. Data from OTT (1999).
41. PMA is the Pharmaceutical Manufacturers Association, a trade group, now PhRMA, the Pharmaceutical Research and Manufacturers Association.
42. Gieryn (1995: 411) describes the work of Abbott (1988), who offers a typology for describing how separate professions settle conflict over jurisdiction. The division of labor, in this scheme, means the splitting of tasks between two interdependent professions with roughly equal status and resources. This situation is close to that of "intellectual control" in which the production of abstract knowledge is separately controlled from its applications. Because the technology transfer specialists collaborate with the researchers in identifying discoveries, making research plans, and other tasks to engage in cooperative research and development, and researchers collaborate in licensing and marketing, the jurisdictional settlement is not as neat as intellectual control would suggest and therefore division of labor is appropriate.

Chapter 6: Between Politics and Science

1. The criticism of using priorities to measure changes in the social contract for science would likewise apply to Lubchenco (1998), who as quoted in Chapter 2 argues for a new social contract for science to address new environmental priorities.
2. Stokes attributes the demise of the compact to three developments: the end of the Cold War and thus a major inspiration for the extreme delegation of authority and funds to scientists; the integration of the world economy and thus greater pressure on American firms to increase productivity; and the fiscal difficulties of the federal government and thus greater strains to pay for research. I would emphasize Stokes' third factor over others and add that the scrutiny was facilitated by the improved congressional information sources discussed briefly in Chapter 3. There is no evidence of an erosion of public faith in science or its technological consequences that would support a populist cause for the change. NSF finds public confidence in the scientific community is consistently higher than confidence in other institutions, with the exception of medicine, and was remarkably stable from the late 1970s to the early 1990s (NSB 1991: 483).
3. Indeed, some recent work (e.g., Branscomb and Keller 1998) claims this agenda.

4. A dissertation written in Sweden (Baldursson 1995) describes how a similarly constituted "science-society contract" emerged and changed across a number of national contexts, suggesting some cultural invariance. Similarly, work on research councils by Braun (1993) and Rip (1994) and general work by van der Meulen (1998) suggest similar dynamics of accountability at work in the United States and in Western Europe. Vavakova (1998) also adopts the social contract vocabulary to assess changes in science and the economy in France.
5. The federal government now encourages universities to keep administrative costs down by a new system of managing indirect cost reimbursement that redistributes some of the savings to the universities (Likens and Teich 1994).
6. There are hints that having multiple principals, at least where they are from both government and private sector, may increase the productivity of researchers. See Blumenthal, Cambell, Causino, and Louis (1996).
7. One of the key difficulties identified by participants in the April 1998 meeting on principal-agent theory and research on science policy, organized by Chris Caswill of the Economic and Social Research Council of the United Kingdom, was that an extended research agenda would likely need to focus on quantifying transaction costs in scientific exchanges.
8. It is also interesting to note that both ORI and OTT have incorporated attorneys into their organizations.
9. Science is even more flexible than two-faced Janus – perhaps as flexible as Proteus. Consider that science may be a way of knowing, a body of knowledge, or an enterprise organized for knowing. It may be a variety of styles of research or a more or less inclusive list of disciplines. It may be a set of institutions performing research, or a set of institutions funding it. It may be a set of norms invoked in one set of circumstances, and a set of counternorms invoked in another. The ability of science to appeal credibly to any of these characters – its Protean nature – makes it exceedingly difficult not only to define and describe but also to govern.
10. See Jasanoff (1990; 1995) and Bimber and Guston (1995) for the extent to which political institutions can deconstruct science on their own accord. Also see the latter for more on the erosion of sociological and other kinds of "specialness" of science and remaining privilege of economic specialness.
11. Merton (1973: 445) described how researchers with greater resources and reputations continue to accumulate resources and reputation. He named this "the Matthew effect" after the passage in the Gospel According to St. Matthew, which attests that "For unto every one that hath shall be given, and he shall have abundance: but from him that hath not shall be taken away even that which he hath."
12. Both Kennedy (1997) and Rosenzweig (1998) make the point that the lack of a consensual definition and the subsequent lack of knowledge about the frequency of misconduct makes for troubled policy. NAS (1992) took the view that even without a good measure, the scientific community bore the burden of pursuing the highest level of integrity. One could estimate rates of misconduct from the perceptions of researchers at the bench, as Swazey, Anderson, and Lewis (1993) have attempted. But because misconduct is often a victimless crime, such a method is likely to both miss episodes of misconduct, as well as to double count episodes that are multiply observed and wrongly count episodes of error or other behavior that does not qualify as misconduct. One could also count the real findings of misconduct by these boundary organizations, but this method would, of course, miss all undiscovered episodes and any that might have been wrongly adjudicated or suppressed at lower levels.
13. The 105th Congress required witnesses to reveal the sources of their research funding

with their testimony, ostensibly so members could evaluate any possible link between financial support and research findings.

14. The National Institutes of Health led research agencies by developing a strategic plan under the directorship of Bernadine Healy in 1992, prior to any statutory obligation.
15. Alongside this planning, some agencies will also engage in pilot projects for performance budgeting, but the implementation of performance budgeting requires additional legislation beyond GPRA.
16. All quotes from taken from DHHS (1997).
17. See Guston (1998) for a more complete discussion of indicators for technology transfer.
18. HHS will measure the achievement of this goal with the "[e]mergence of new or improved medical technologies and medical products such as vaccines, diagnostics, and therapeutics."
19. French sociologist Michel Callon (1998: 2) also points to these instructive aspects of Polanyi's work.
20. This passage is inspired by Elzinga and Jamison (1995: 592), although they do not discuss the integrity and the productivity of science explicitly in these terms. The science and technology studies literature, different from the previous work, attends explicitly to interests within science.

References

Abbott, Andrew. 1988. *The system of professions*. Chicago: University of Chicago Press.

Aberbach, Joel D. 1990. *Keeping a watchful eye: The politics of congressional oversight*. Washington, DC: The Brookings Institution.

Aldrich, Howard E. 1979. *Organizations and environments*. Englewood Cliffs, NJ: Prentice-Hall.

Alic, John A., Lewis M. Branscomb, Harvey Brooks, Ashton B. Carter, and Gerald L. Epstein. 1992. *Beyond spinoff: Military and commercial technologies in a changing world*. Boston: Harvard Business School Press.

Allen, J. A. 1967. *Scientific innovation and industrial prosperity*. New York: Elsevier.

Alt, James E., and Kenneth A. Shepsle. 1990. *Perspectives on political economy*. New York: Cambridge University Press.

American Association for the Advancement of Science (AAAS). 1997. *AAAS report XXII: Research & development, FY 1998*. Washington, DC: AAAS.

——. 1998. *AAAS report XXIII: Research & development, FY 1999*. Washington, DC: AAAS.

——. 1999. *AAAS report XXIV: Research & development, FY 2000*. Washington, DC: AAAS.

Anuskiewcz, Todd. 1992. SBIR first decade: Results, benefits, problems from a Michigan perspective. *Journal of Technology Transfer* 17 (1): 8–15.

Arrow, Kenneth J. 1951. *Social choice and individual values*. New York: Wiley.

——. 1991. The economics of agency. In *Principals and agents: The structure of business*. Edited by John W. Pratt and Richard J. Zeckhauser. 37–51. Boston: Harvard Business School Press.

Averch, Harvey A. 1985. *A strategic analysis of science and technology policy*. Baltimore: Johns Hopkins University Press.

Baldursson, Eirikur. 1995. "The elusive frontier: On the emergence and change of a science-society contract." Ph.D. dissertation, Göteborg University, Göteborg, Sweden.

Barfield, Claude. 1982. *Science policy from Ford to Reagan: Change and continuity*. Washington, DC: American Enterprise Institute.

Barke, Richard P. 1990. "Beyond the 'Endless Frontier': Changes in the political context of American science and technology policy." Paper presented at the annual meeting of the Society for Social Studies of Science, Minneapolis, 19 October.

Bayles, Michael D. 1983. *Professional ethics*. Belmont, CA: Wadsworth.

Bechtel, H. Kenneth Jr., and Willie Pearson, Jr. 1985. Deviant scientists and scientific deviance. *Deviant Behavior* 6: 237–52.

Ben-Yehuda, Nachman. 1985. *Deviance and moral boundaries*. Chicago: University of Chicago Press.

Bimber, Bruce. 1996. *The politics of expertise in Congress: The rise and fall of the Office of Technology Assessment*. Albany: State University of New York Press.

Bimber, Bruce, and David H. Guston. 1995. Politics by the same means: Government and science in the United States. In *Handbook of science and technology studies*. Edited by Sheila Jasanoff, Gerald Markle, Trevor Pinch, and James Petersen. 554–71. Beverly Hills: Sage.

Blanpied, William A. 1998. Inventing U.S. science policy. *Physics Today* 51: 34–40.

Blumenthal, David, Eric G. Cambell, Nancyanne Causino, and Karen Seashore Louis. 1996. Participation of life-science faculty in research relationships with industry. *The New England Journal of Medicine* 335: 1734–39.

Boffey, Philip. 1975. *The brain bank of America*. New York: McGraw-Hill.

Bourdieu, Pierre. 1991. *Language and symbolic power*. Edited and with an introduction by John B. Thompson. Translated by Gino Raymond and Matthew Adamson. Cambridge: Harvard University Press.

Bozeman, Barry. 1987. *All organizations are public*. San Francisco: Jossey-Bass.

Brandt, Edward N., Jr. 1983. PHS perspectives on misconduct in science. *Public Health Reports* 98 (March/April): 136–40.

Branscomb, Lewis M., ed. 1993. *Empowering technology: Implementing a U.S. strategy*. Cambridge: MIT Press.

——. 1995. *Confessions of a technophile*. Woodbury, NY: American Institute of Physics Press.

Branscomb, Lewis M., and James Keller, eds. 1998. *Investing in innovation: Creating a research and innovation policy that works*. Cambridge: MIT Press.

Braun, Dietmar. 1993. Who governs intermediary organizations? Principal-agent relations in research policy-making. *Journal of Public Policy* 13 (2): 135–62.

Bridgstock, Martin. 1982. A sociological approach to fraud in science. *Australia and New Zealand Journal of Sociology* 18: 364–83.

Broad, William J., and Nicholas Wade. 1982. *Betrayers of the truth: Fraud and deceit in the halls of science*. New York: Simon and Schuster.

Bromley, D. Allan. 1988. Science advice: Past and present. In *The Presidency and science advising*. Vol. 5. Edited by Kenneth W. Thompson. 1–25. New York: University Press of America.

Brooks, Harvey. 1968. *The government of science*. Cambridge: MIT Press.

——. 1986. National science policy and technological innovation. In *The positive sum strategy: Harnessing technology for economic growth*. Edited by Ralph Landau and Nathan Rosenberg. 119–67. Washington, DC: National Academy Press.

——. 1990a. Can science survive in the modern age? *National Forum* 71 (4): 31–33.

——. 1990b. Lessons of history: Successive challenges to science policy. In *The research system in transition*. NATO ASI Series D, Vol. 57. Edited by Susan E. Cozzens, Peter Healey, Arie Rip, and John Ziman. 11–22. Boston: Kluwer Academic Publishers.

——. 1996. The Evolution of U.S. science policy. In *Technology, R&D and the economy*. Edited by Bruce L.R. Smith and Claude Barfield. 15–40. Washington, DC: The Brookings Institution and American Enterprise Institute.

Brooks, Harvey, and Roland W. Schmitt. 1985. Current science and technology policy issues: Two perspectives. *Occasional Paper No. 1*. Washington, DC: George Washington University.

Brown, George E. Jr. 1991. A perspective on the federal role in science and technology. In *AAAS science and technology policy yearbook, 1991*. Edited by Margaret O. Meredith, Stephen D. Nelson, and Albert H. Teich. 23–33. Washington, DC: American Association for the Advancement of Science.

——. 1992. The objectivity crisis. *American Journal of Physics* 60: 779–81.

——. 1997. Environmental science under seige in the U.S. Congress. *Environment* 39 (2): 12–ff.

Bryner, Gary C., ed. 1992. *Science, technology, and politics: Policy analysis in Congress*. Boulder: Westview Press.

Bunge, Mario. 1996. In praise of intolerance to charlatanism in academia. In *The flight from science and reason*. Edited by Paul Gross, Norm Levitt, and Martin W. Lewis. Annals of the New York Academy of Sciences, Vol. 775. 96–115. New York: NYAS.

Bush, Vannevar. [1945] 1960. *Science: The endless frontier*. Washington, DC: National Science Foundation.

Callon, Michel. 1994. Is science a public good? *Science, Technology, and Human Values* 19 (4): 395–424.

Callon, Michel, ed. 1998. *The laws of the markets*. Malden, MA: Blackwell Publishers/The Sociological Review.

Carson, Rachel. 1962. *Silent spring*. Boston: Houghton Mifflin.

Caswill, Chris. 1998. Social Science Policy: Challenges, interactions, principals and agents. *Science and Public Policy* 25 (5): 286–96.

Childress, James F. 1991. Deliberations of the human fetal tissue transplantation research panel. In *Biomedical politics*. Edited by Kathi E. Hanna. 215–57. Washington, DC: National Academy Press.

Chubin, Daryl E. 1985. Misconduct in research: An issue of science policy and practice. *Minerva* 23 (Summer): 175–202.

Cochoy, Franck. 1998. Another discipline for the economic market: Marketing as a performative knowledge and knowhow for capitalism. In *The laws of the markets*. Edited by Michel Callon. 194–221. Malden, MA: Blackwell Publishers/The Sociological Review.

Cochrane, Rexmond C. 1978. *The National Academy of Sciences: The first hundred years, 1863–1963*. Washington, DC: National Academy Press.

Cohen, Linda, and Roger G. Noll. 1995. Feasibility of effective public-private R&D collaboration: The case of cooperative R&D agreements. *International Journal of the Economics of Business* 2 (2): 223–40.

Coleman, James S. 1990. *Foundations of social theory*. Cambridge: Harvard University Press.

Collins, Harry, and Trevor Pinch. 1993. *The golem: What everyone should know about science*. New York: Cambridge University Press.

Cook, Brian J., and B. Dan Wood. 1989. Principal-agent models of political control of the bureaucracy. *American Political Science Review* 83: 965–78.

Cook-Deegan, Robert Mullan. 1991. The human genome project: The formation of federal policies in the United States, 1986–1990. In *Biomedical politics*. Edited by Kathi E. Hanna. 99–175. Washington, DC: National Academy Press.

Cordes, Colleen. 1998. The academic pork barrel begins to fill up again. *The Chronicle of Higher Education* June 19: A30–31.

Cozzens, Susan. 1988. Derek Price and the paradigm of science policy. *Science, Technology, and Human Values* 13: 361–72.

Cozzens, Susan E., Peter Healey, Arie Rip, and John Ziman, eds. 1990. *The research system in transition*. NATO ASI Series D, Vol. 57. Boston: Kluwer Academic Publishers.

Crewdson, John. 1994. Fraud in breast cancer study: Doctor lied on data for decade. *The Chicago Tribune* March 13: 1.

Crow, Michael M. 1998. Expanding the policy design model for science and technology: Some thoughts regarding the upgrade of the Bush model of American science and technology policy. In *AAAS science and technology policy yearbook, 1998*. Edited by Albert H. Teich, Stephen D. Nelson, and Celia McEnaney. 57–72. Washington, DC: American Association for the Advancement of Science.

Crow, Michael, and Barry Bozeman. 1998. *Limited by design: R&D laboratories in the U.S. national innovation system*. New York: Columbia University Press.

Culliton, Barbara. 1979. Science's restive public. In *Limits of scientific inquiry*. Edited by Gerald Holton and Robert S. Morison. 147–56. New York: W. W. Norton.

Daniels, George H. 1967. The pure-science ideal and democratic culture. *Science* June 30: 1699–1706.

Davis, Bernard. 1991. Is the Office of Scientific Integrity too zealous? *The Scientist* May 13: 12.

Department of Health and Human Services (DHHS). 1980. Debarment and suspension from eligibility for financial assistance. *Federal Register* 45: 67262–69.

——. 1989. *Misconduct in scientific research*. Office of Analysis and Inspections, Office of Inspector General. OAI-88-07-00420. Washington, DC: DHHS.

——. 1992. Statement of organization, functions, and delegations of authority. *Federal Register* 57: 24262–63.

——. 1994. Hearing procedures for scientific misconduct. *Federal Register* 59: 29808–11.

——. 1995. *Integrity and misconduct in research: Report of the Commission on Research Integrity*. Office of the Secretary, Office of Research Integrity. Rockville, MD: DHHS.

——. 1997. Strategic plan. Data base online. Available from aspe.os.dhhs.gov/hhsplan. September 30.

Devine, Michael D., James E. Thomas, Jr., and Timothy I. Adams. 1987. Government supported industry-university research centers: Issues for successful technology transfer. *Journal of Technology Transfer* 12 (1): 27–37.

Diamond, Arthur M., Jr. 1996. Special issue: The economics of science. *Knowledge and Policy* 9 (2/3).

Dickson, David. 1988. *The new politics of science*. Chicago: University of Chicago Press.

Doctors, Samuel I. 1969. *The role of federal agencies in technology transfer*. Cambridge: MIT Press.

Dodd, Lawrence C., and Richard L. Schott. 1986. *Congress and the administrative state*. New York: McMillan.

Dorf, Richard C., and Kirby K. F. Worthingham. 1987. Models for commercialization of technology from universities and research laboratories. *Journal of Technology Transfer* 12 (1): 1–8.

Downs, Anthony. 1957. *An economic theory of democracy*. New York: Harper.

Duderstadt, James. 1996. "Basic research and the American research university." Paper presented at *Science: The endless frontier*, 1945–1995: A policy evaluation and formulation conference series, Columbia University, New York City, September 21.

Dupree, A. Hunter. 1957. *Science in the federal government: A history of policy and activities to 1940*. Cambridge: Harvard University Press.

Edelman, Murray J. 1977. *Political language: Words that succeed and policies that fail*. New York: Academic Press.

Edge, David O., and Michael J. Mulkay. 1976. *Astronomy transformed: The emergence of radio astronomy in Britain*. New York: Wiley.

Edsall, John T. 1988. Government and the freedom of science. In *Science, technology, and society: Emerging relationships*. Edited by Rosemary Chalk. 24–27. Washington, DC: American Association for the Advancement of Science. First published in *Science*, April 29 1955: 615–19.

Eisenberg, Rebecca S. 1989. Patents and the progress of science: Exclusive rights and experimental use. *The University of Chicago Law Review* 56 (3): 1017–86.

——. 1996. Public research and private development. Patents and technology transfer in government-sponsored research. *Virginia Law Review* 82: 1663–1727.

Ellul, Jacques. [1954] 1964. *The technological society*. Translated by John Wilkinson. New York: Vintage Books.

Elzinga, Aant, and Andrew Jamison. 1995. Changing policy agendas in science and technology. In *Handbook of science, technology, and society*. Edited by Sheila Jasanoff, Gerald Markle, Trevor Pinch, and James Petersen. 572–97. Beverly Hills: Sage.

England, J. Merton. 1982. *A patron for pure science*. Washington, DC: National Science Foundation.

Etzkowitz, Henry. 1995. Lost on the endless frontier: Vannevar Bush and the "contract" between science and government. *Technology Access Report*, October: 5–6.

Ezrahi, Yaron. 1980. Science and the problem of authority in democracy. In *Science and social structure: A festschrift for Robert K. Merton*. Transactions of the New York Academy of Sciences, Vol. 39. Edited by Thomas F. Gieryn. 43–60. New York: NYAS.

——. 1990. *The descent of Icarus: Science and the transformation of contemporary democracy*. Cambridge: Harvard University Press.

Federal Laboratory Consortium (FLC). n.d. [1986]. *Report to the federal agencies on the activities of the Federal Laboratory Consortium, September 1984–August 1986*. Prepared by Margaret M. McNamara. New London: Naval Underwater Systems Center.

Federal Security Agency (FSA). [1952] 1978. *Inventions . . . from research grants*. Order 110–1. Reprinted in U.S. Congress. Select Committee on Small Business Subcommittee on Monopoly and Anticompetitive Activities. *Government patent policies: Institutional patent agreements*. 95th Cong., 2d sess.

Fenno, Richard F., Jr. 1990. *Watching politicians: Essays on participant observation*. University of California, Berkeley: IGS Press.

Fiorina, Morris. [1976] 1989. *Congress: Keystone of the Washington establishment*. 2d ed. New Haven: Yale University Press.

Fletcher, Ronald. 1991. *Science, ideology, and the media: The Cyril Burt scandal*. New Brunswick, NJ: Transaction Publishers.

Foreman, Christopher H., Jr. 1988. *Signals from the Hill: Congressional oversight and the challenge of social regulation*. New Haven: Yale University Press.

Fox, Daniel M. 1987. The politics of the NIH extramural program, 1937–1950. *Journal of the History of Medicine and Allied Sciences* 42: 447–66.

Francis, Sybil, 1999. Developing a federal policy on research misconduct, *Science and Engineering Ethics* 5 (2): 261–72.

Franklin Institute. 1978. *Science and the Congress*. The Third Franklin Conference. Philadelphia: The Franklin Institute Press.

Fredrickson, Donald S. 1975. On the translation gap. National Institutes of Health. Mimeographed.

——. 1991. Asilomar and recombinant DNA: The end of the beginning. In *Biomedical politics*. Edited by Kathi E. Hanna. 258–307. Washington, DC: National Academy Press.

——. 1993. Biomedical science and the culture warp. In *Emerging policies for biomedical research*. Edited by William N. Kelley, Marion Osterweis, and Elaine R. Rubin. Health Policy Annual III. 1–42. Washington, DC: Association of Academic Health Centers.

Freeland, Richard M. 1971. *The Truman doctrine and the origins of McCarthyism*. New York: Knopf.

Freeman, Christopher. 1987. *Technology policy and economic performance: Lessons from Japan*. London: Frances Pinter.

——. 1988. Quantitative and qualitative factors in national policies for science and technology. In *From research policy to social intelligence*. Edited by Jan Annerstedt and Andrew Jamison. 114–28. London. MacMillan.

Fujimura, Joan. 1992. Crafting science: Standardized packages, boundary objects, and "translation." In *Science as culture and practice*. Edited by Andrew Pickering. 168–211. Chicago: University of Chicago Press.

Funtowicz, Silvio O., and Jerome R. Ravetz. 1992. Three types of risk assessment and the emergence of post-normal science. In *Social theories of risk*. Edited by Sheldon Krimsky and Dominic Golding. 251–73. London: Praeger.

Geertz, Clifford. 1973. Ideology as a cultural system. In *The interpretation of cultures*. 193–233. New York: Basic Books.

General Accounting Office (GAO). 1968. *Problem areas affecting usefulness of results of government sponsored research in medicinal chemistry*. B-164031(2). Washington, DC: GAO.

——. 1989. *Technology transfer: Implementation status of the Federal Technology Transfer Act of 1986*. RCED-89-154. Washington, DC: GAO.

——. 1992. *Technology transfer: Barriers limit royalty sharing's effectiveness*. RCED-93-6. Washington, DC: GAO.

Gieryn, Thomas F. 1995. Boundaries of science. In *Handbook of science and technology studies*. Edited by Sheila Jasanoff, Gerald Markle, Trevor Pinch, and James Petersen. 393–443. Beverly Hills: Sage.

Gieryn, Thomas F., and Anne Figert. 1986. Scientists protect their cognitive authority: The status degradation ceremony of Sir Cyril Burt. In *The Knowledge Society*. Edited by Gernot Böhme and Nico Stehr. 67–86. Dordrecht: Reidel.

Gold, Barry D. 1993. Congressional activities regarding misconduct and integrity in science. In *Responsible science: Ensuring the integrity of the research process*. Vol. 2. Panel on Scientific Responsibility and the Conduct of Research. 90–115. Washington, DC: National Academy Press.

Gomory, Ralph. 1990. Of ladders, cycles and economic growth. *Scientific American* 262 (June): 140.

Goodfield, June. 1977. *Playing God: Genetic engineering and the manipulation of life*. New York: Random House.

Graham, Loren R. 1979. Concerns about science and attempts to regulate inquiry. In *Limits of scientific inquiry*. Edited by Gerald Holton and Robert S. Morison. 1–22. New York: W. W. Norton.

Greenberg, Daniel S. 1967. *The politics of pure science*. New York: New American Library.

——. 1991. Q&A with NIH director Bernadine Healy. *Science & Government Report*, November 1: 5.

——. 1994. The misconduct follies. *Science & Government Report*, June 15: 1.

Gross, Paul, Norm Levitt, and Martin W. Lewis, eds. 1996. *The flight from science and reason*. Annals of the New York Academy of Sciences, Vol. 775. New York: NYAS.

Guston, David H. 1993. The essential tension in science and democracy. *Social Epistemology* 7: 3–23.

——. 1994a. Congressmen and scientists in the making of science policy: The Allison Commission, 1884–1886. *Minerva* 32 (1): 25–52.

——. 1994b. The demise of the social contract for science: Misconduct in science in the nonmodern world. *Centennial Review* 38 (2): 215–48.

——. 1996a. New technology role for states. *Forum for Applied Research and Public Policy* 11 (3): 38–44.

——. 1996b. Principal-agent theory and the structure of science policy. *Science and Public Policy* 23 (4): 229–40.

——. 1997. Critical appraisal in science and technology policy analysis: The example of *Science: The endless frontier*. *Policy Sciences* 30 (4): 233–57.

——. 1998. Technology transfer and the use of CRADAs at the National Institutes of Health. In *Investing in innovation: Creating a research and innovation policy that works*. Edited by Lewis M. Branscomb and James Keller. 221–49. Cambridge: MIT Press.

——. 1999a. Changing explanatory frameworks in the U.S. government's attempt to define research misconduct. *Science and Engineering Ethics* 5 (2): 137–54.

——. 1999b. Stabilizing the boundary between U.S. politics and science: The role of the Office of Technology Transfer as a boundary organization. *Social Studies of Science* 29 (1): 87–112.

Guston, David H., and Harvey Brooks. 1995. "Return to the frontier: The Vannevar Bush report, then and now. A symposium at the annual meeting of the American Association for the Advancement of Science. Atlanta.

Guston, David H., Megan Jones, and Lewis M. Branscomb. 1997a. The demand for and supply of technical information and analysis in state legislatures. *Policy Studies Journal* 25 (3): 451–69.

——. 1997b. Technology assessment in the U.S. state legislatures. *Technological Forecasting and Social Change* 54 (2/3): 233–50.

Guston, David H., and Kenneth Keniston. 1994. *The fragile contract: University science and the federal government*. Cambridge: MIT Press.

Habermas, Jurgen. 1979. *Communication and the evolution of society*. Translated by Thomas McCarthy. Boston: Beacon Press.

Hackett, Edward J. 1990. Science as a vocation in the 1990s. *Journal of Higher Education* 61: 241–79.

Hagstrom, Warren O. 1975. *The scientific community*. New York: Arcturus Books.

Hallum, Jules V., and Suzanne W. Hadley. 1990. OSI: why, what and how. *ASM News* 56: 647–51.

Hamilton, David P. 1991. Can OSI withstand a scientific backlash? *Science*, September 6: 1084–86.

Hamlett, Patrick W. 1990. Dialogue on science and Congress. In *Science, Technology and Politics, 1990: A Yearbook*. Vol. 4. Edited by Jon Alexander. 23–74. Ottowa: Odda Tala Press.

Hammett, Dashiell. [1929] 1972. *The Maltese Falcon*. New York: Vintage Books.

Harden, Victoria A. 1986. *Inventing the NIH: Federal biomedical research policy, 1887–1937*. Baltimore: Johns Hopkins University Press.

Hart, David M. 1996. "A confusion of means and ends: The debate over the federal role in organizing, managing, and funding the Nation's science and technology." Paper presented at *Science: The endless frontier*, 1945–1995: A policy evaluation and formulation conference series, Columbia University, New York City, September 21.

——. 1998. *Forged consensus: Science, technology, and economic policy in the United States, 1921–1953*. Princeton: Princeton University Press.

Hearnshaw, Leslie Spencer. 1979. *Cyril Burt, psychologist*. Ithaca: Cornell University Press.

Henderson, Thomas A. 1970. *Congressional oversight of executive agencies*. Gainesville: University of Florida Press.

Hixson, Joseph R. 1976. *The patchwork mouse*. Garden City, NY: Anchor Press.

Hobbes, Thomas. [1651] 1983. *Leviathan*. Edited and with an introduction by C. B. MacPherson. New York: Penguin Books.

Hoch, Paul K. 1988. The crystallization of a strategic alliance: The American physics elite and the military in the 1940s. In *Science, technology and the military*. Vol. 12. Edited by Everett Mendelsohn, Merritt Row Smith, and Peter Weingart. 87–116. Dordrecht: Kluwer Academic Publishers.

Holton, Gerald. 1979. From the endless frontier to the ideology of limits. In *Limits of scientific inquiry*. Edited by Gerald Holton and Robert S. Morison. 227–42. New York: W. W. Norton.

——. 1993a. *Science and anti-science*. Cambridge: Harvard University Press.

——. 1993b. The value of science at the "end of the modern era." In *Ethics, values and the promise of science: Forum proceedings*. 115–32. Research Triangle Park: Sigma Xi, The Scientific Research Society.

Holton, Gerald, and Robert S. Morison, eds. 1979. *Limits of scientific inquiry*. New York: W. W. Norton.

Hughes, Thomas P. 1976. The development phase of technological change: Introduction. *Technology and Culture* 17: 423–31.

——. 1989. *American genesis: A century of invention and technological enthusiasm*. New York: Penguin Books.

Huth, Edward J. 1983. Ethical conduct in authorship and publication. *CBE style manual: A guide for authors, editors, and publishers in the biological sciences*. 5th ed. Bethesda, MD: Council of Biology Editors.

Institute of Medicine (IOM). 1990. *Consensus development at the NIH: Improving the program*. Council on Health Care Technology. Washington, DC: National Academy Press.

Irwin, Alan, and Brian Wynne, eds. 1996. *Misunderstanding science: The public reconstruction of science and technology*. New York: Cambridge University Press.

Jasanoff, Sheila. 1987. Contested boundaries in policy-relevant science. *Social Studies of Science* 17: 195–230.

——. 1990. *The fifth branch: Science advisors as policymakers*. Cambridge: Harvard University Press.

——. 1992. What judges should know about the sociology of knowledge. *Jurimetrics Journal* 43: 345–59.

——. 1995. *Science at the bar: Law, science, and technology in America*. Cambridge: Harvard University Press.

——. 1996. Beyond epistemology: Relativism and engagement in the politics of science. *Social Studies of Science* 26: 393–418.

Jasanoff, Sheila, Gerald Markle, Trevor Pinch and James Petersen, eds. 1995. *Handbook of science and technology studies*. Beverly Hills: Sage.

Johnston, Robert F., and Christopher G. Edwards. 1987. *Entrepreneurial science: New links between corporations, universities, and government*. New York: Quorum Books.

Kaghan, William. 1998. "Court and spark: Studies in professional university technology transfer management." Ph.D. dissertation, School of Business Administration, University of Washington.

Kaiser, Jocelyn. 1999. Plan for divulging data eases fears. *Science*, February 12: 914–15.

Kaufman, Herbert. 1981. *The administrative behavior of federal bureau chiefs*. Washington, DC: Brookings Institution.

Kennedy, Donald. 1997. *Academic duty*. Cambridge: Harvard University Press.

Kevles, Daniel J. 1977. The National Science Foundation and the debate over postwar research policy, 1942–1945: A political interpretation of *Science: The endless frontier*. *Isis* 68: 5–26.

——. 1978. *The physicists: The history of a scientific community in modern America*. New York: Knopf.

——. 1985. *In the name of eugenics: Genetics and the uses of human heredity*. New York: Knopf.

——. 1998. *The Baltimore case: A trial of politics, science, and character*. New York: W. W. Norton.

Kleinman, Daniel Lee. 1995. *Politics on the endless frontier: Postwar research policy in the United States*. Durham, NC: Duke University Press.

Klotz, Irving M. 1985. *Diamond dealers and feather merchants: Tales from the sciences*. Boston: Birkhauser.

Koestler, Arthur. 1971. *Case of the midwife toad*. London: Hutchinson.

Kohn, Alexander. 1986. *False prophets: Fraud and error in science and medicine*. New York: Basil Blackwell.

Krimsky, Sheldon. 1982. *Genetic alchemy: The social history of the recombinant DNA controversy*. Cambridge: MIT Press.

Kuehn, Thomas J. and Alan L. Porter, eds. 1981. *Science, technology, and national policy*. Ithaca, NY: Cornell University Press.

Kuhn, Thomas S. [1962] 1970. *The structure of scientific revolutions*. 2d revised ed. Chicago: University of Chicago Press.

Lambright, W. Henry. 1985. *Presidential management of science and technology: The Johnson Presidency*. Austin: University of Texas Press.

Lane, Neal. 1997. A devil's paradox: Great science, greater limitations. In *AAAS science and technology policy yearbook, 1996/97*. Edited by Albert H. Teich, Stephen D. Nelson, and Celia McEnaney. 125–30. Washington, DC: American Association for the Advancement of Science.

Lardner, George, Jr. 1992. Scientist says Army seeks to fire him for criticizing SDI. *The Washington Post*, January 10: A17.

Latour, Bruno. 1987. *Science in action: How to follow scientists and engineers through society*. Cambridge: Harvard University Press.

——. 1988. *The pasteurization of France*. Translated by Alan Sheridan and John Law. Cambridge: Harvard University Press.

——. 1991. The impact of science studies on political philosophy. *Science, Technology, and Human Values* 16: 3–19.

Latour, Bruno and Steve Woolgar. 1979. *Laboratory life: The social construction of scientific facts*. With an introduction by Jonas Salk. Beverly Hills: Sage.

Lederman, Leon. 1991. *Science: The end of the frontier?* Washington, DC: American Association for the Advancement of Science.

Lewenstein, Bruce. 1995. From fax to facts: Communication in the cold fusion saga. *Social Studies of Science* 25: 403–36.

Likins, Peter, and Albert H. Teich. 1994. Indirect costs and the government-university partnership. In *The fragile contract: University science and the federal government*. Edited by David H. Guston and Kenneth Keniston. 177–93. Cambridge: MIT Press.

Lindblom, Charles E. 1977. *Politics and markets: The world's political-economic systems*. New York: Basic Books.

List, C. J. 1985. Scientific fraud: Social deviance or the failure of virtue? *Science, Technology, and Human Values* 10: 27–36.

Locke, John. [1689] 1963. *Two treatises of government*. With an introduction and notes by Peter Laslett. New York: New American Library.

Lowi, Theodore J. 1979. *The end of liberalism: The second republic of the United States*. 2d ed. New York: W. W. Norton.

——. 1995. *The end of the Republican era*. Norman: University of Oklahoma Press.

Lubchenco, Jane. 1998. Entering the century of the environment: A new social contract for science. *Science*, January 23: 491–97.

Luger, Michael I., and Harvey A. Goldstein. 1991. *Technology in the garden: Research parks and regional economic development*. Chapel Hill: University of North Carolina Press.

Manning, Thomas G. 1967. *Government in science: The U.S. Geological Survey, 1867–1894*. Lexington: University of Kentucky Press.

——. 1988. *U.S. Coast Survey vs. Naval Hydrographic Office: A 19th-Century rivalry in science and politics*. Tuscaloosa: University of Alabama Press.

Mansfield, Edwin. 1968. *The economics of technological change*. New York: W. W. Norton.
——. 1991. Academic research and industrial innovation. *Research Policy* 20: 1–12.
Markle, Gerald E., and Daryl E. Chubin. 1987. Consensus development in biomedicine: The liver transplant controversy. *The Milbank Quarterly* 65 (1): 1–24.
Markusen, Ann, James Raffel, Michael Odin, and Marlen Llanes. 1995. "Coming in from the cold: The future of Los Alamos and Sandia national laboratories." Working paper No. 91, Center for Urban Policy Research/Project on Regional and Industrial Economics. New Brunswick, NJ: Rutgers, The State University of New Jersey.
Medawar, Peter B. 1979. *Advice to a young scientist*. New York: Harper and Row.
Merton, Robert K. 1965. *On the shoulders of giants: A Shandean postscript*. New York: Harcourt Brace Jovanovitch.
——. 1973. *The sociology of science: Theoretical and empirical investigations*. Edited and with an introduction by Norman W. Storer. Chicago: University of Chicago Press.
Mervis, Jeffrey. 1988. A threat to monitor science is quashed. *The Scientist*, October 31: 1.
Mikulski, Barbara A. 1994. A congressional view of science in the national interest. In *Science and technology policy yearbook, 1994*. Edited by Albert H. Teich, Steven D. Nelson, and Celia McEnaney. 177–83. Washington, DC: American Association for the Advancement of Science.
Miller, Howard S. 1970. *Dollars for research: Science and its patrons in Nineteenth-Century America*. Seattle: University of Washington Press.
Moe, Terry M. 1984. The new economics of organization. *American Journal of Political Science* 28: 739–77.
——. 1987. An assessment of the positive theory of congressional dominance. *Legislative Studies Quarterly* 12: 475–520.
Moore, Kelly. 1996. Organizing integrity: American science and the creation of public interest organizations, 1955–1975. *American Journal of Sociology* 101 (6): 1592–1627.
Mowery, David, Richard R. Nelson, Bhaven M. Sampat, and Arvids A Ziedonis. The effects of the Bayh-Dole Act on U.S. university research and technology transfer. In *Industrializing Knowledge*. Edited by Lewis M. Branscomb, Fumio Kodama, and Richard Florida, Cambridge: MIT Press. Forthcoming.
Mowery, David, and Nathan Rosenberg. [1979] 1982. The influence of market demand upon innovation: Critical review of some recent empirical studies. In *Inside the black box: Technology and economics*. Edited by Nathan Rosenberg. 193–241. New York: Cambridge University Press.
Mulkay, Michael J. 1975. Norms and ideology in science. *Social Science Information* 4/5: 637–56.
Myers, Christopher. 1991. NIH director plans no big changes in dealing with misconduct. *The Chronicle of Higher Education*, May 1: A23.

Nader, Ralph. 1965. *Unsafe at any speed*. New York: Grossman Publishing.

Narin, Francis, Kimberly S. Hamilton, and Dominic Olivastro. 1997. The increasing linkage between U.S. technology and public science. *Research Policy* 26 (3): 317–30.

National Academy of Sciences (NAS). 1965. *Basic research and national goals*. Committee on Science and Public Policy. Washington, DC: National Academy Press.

——. 1967. *Applied science and technological progress*. Committee on Science and Public Policy. Washington, DC: National Academy Press.

——. 1969. *Technology: Process of assessment and choice*. Committee on Science and Public Policy. Washington, DC: National Academy Press.

——. 1992. *Responsible science: Ensuring the integrity of the research process*. Vol. 1. Panel on Scientific Responsibility and the Conduct of Research. Washington, DC: National Academy Press.

National Institutes of Health (NIH). 1986. Policies and procedures for dealing with possible misconduct in science. *NIH Guide to Grants and Contracts* 15: 1–37.

——. 1997. *National Institutes of Health Almanac, 1997*. Pub. No. 97–5. On Line Information Team. Division of Public Information. Bethesda, MD. Data base online. Available at www.nih.gov/welcome/almanac97/toc.htm#TOP.

National Science Board (NSB). 1973. *Science indicators 1972*. Washington, DC: NSB.

——. 1991. *Science and engineering indicators 1991*. 10th ed. NSB-91–1. Washington, DC: NSB.

Nelkin, Dorothy. 1979. Threats and promises: Negotiating the control of research. In *Limits of scientific inquiry*. Edited by Gerald Holton and Robert S. Morison. 191–211. New York: W. W. Norton.

——. 1994. The public face of science: What can we learn from disputes? In *The fragile contract: University science and the federal government*. Edited by David H. Guston and Kenneth Keniston. 101–17. Cambridge: MIT Press.

Nelson, Richard R. 1982. Public policy and technical progress: A cross-industry analysis. In *Government and technological progress: A cross-industry analysis*. Edited by Richard R. Nelson. 1–9. New York: Pergamon Press.

Newton, Kenneth. 1976. Feeble governments and private power: Urban politics and policies in the U.S. In *The new urban politics*. Edited by Lewis H. Masotti and Robert L. Lineberry. 37–58. Cambridge: Ballinger.

Niskanen, William A., Jr. 1971. *Bureaucracy and representative government*. Chicago: Aldine-Atherton.

Office of the Assistant Secretary of Health (OASH). 1994. *Office of Research Integrity: Annual report, 1993*. Public Health Service. Washington, DC: OASH.

Office of Management and Budget (OMB), 1999. Uniform administrative requirements for grants and agreements with institutions of higher education, hospitals, and other non-profit organizations. *Federal Register* 64: 5684–85.

Office of Medical Applications of Research (OMAR). 1993. Introduction. *Guidelines for the planning and management of consensus development conferences*. Office of the Director. National Institutes of Health. Bethesda, MD. Data base online. Available at odp.od.nih.gov/consensus/about/process.html. Updated March 1995.

Office of Research Integrity (ORI). 1993. DAB confirms HHS authority to investigate scientific misconduct. *ORI Newsletter* 1 (4): 5.

——. 1997. *Annual report, 1996*. Department of Health and Human Services. Bethesda, MD. Data base online. Available at ori.dhhs.gov/annualreports.htm.

——. 1998. Whistleblower issues. Department of Health and Human Services. Bethesda, MD. Data base online. Available at ori.dhhs.gov/whistle.htm.

Office of Science and Technology Policy (OSTP). 1983. *Report of the White House Science Council*. Washington, DC: Executive Office of the President.

Office of Technology Assessment (OTA). 1982. *Technology transfer at the National Institutes of Health*. OTA-TM-H-10. Washington, DC: U.S.G.P.O.

——. 1986. *Research funding as an investment: Can we measure the returns?* OTA-TM-SET-36. Washington, DC: U.S.G.P.O.

——. 1988. *Mapping our genes: The genome projects – how big, how fast?* OTA-BA-373. Washington, DC: U.S.G.P.O.

Office of Technology Transfer (OTT). 1999. NIH technology transfer stats. Data base online. Available at www.nih.gov/od/ott/nih93-98.htm.

Ogul, Morris S., and Burt A. Rockman. 1990. Overseeing oversight: New departures and old problems. *Legislative Studies Quarterly* 15: 5–24.

Parsons, Talcott. 1946. National science legislation. *Bulletin of Atomic Scientists* 2: 7–9.

Polanyi, Karl. [1944] 1957. *The great transformation*. Introduction by R. M. MacIver. Boston: Beacon Press.

Polanyi, Michael. [1946] 1964. *Science, faith and society*. Chicago: University of Chicago Press.

——. 1962. The republic of science: Its political and economic theory. *Minerva* 1: 54–73.

Popper, Karl R. 1959. *The logic of scientific discovery*. New York: Harper.

Powell, Walter W., and Paul J. DiMaggio, eds. 1991. *The new institutionalism in organizational analysis*. Chicago: University of Chicago Press.

Press, Frank. 1988. "The dilemma of the golden age." Address at the 125th annual meeting of the National Academy of Sciences, Washington, DC, April 26.

Price, Don K. 1954. *Government and science: Their dynamic relation in American democracy*. New York: New York University Press.

——. 1961. The scientific establishment. *Science*, October 13: 1039–86.

——. 1965. *The scientific estate*. Cambridge: Harvard University Press.

——. 1979. Endless frontier or bureaucratic morass? In *Limits of scientific inquiry*. Edited by Gerald Holton and Robert S. Morison. 75–92. New York: W. W. Norton.

——. 1981. "The spectrum from truth to power." In *Science, technology, and national policy.* Edited by Thomas J. Kuehn and Alan L. Porter. 95–131. Ithaca, NY: Cornell University Press.

Public Health Service (PHS). 1985. "Policies and procedures for dealing with possible misconduct in science." October 10. Mimeographed.

——. 1988. Announcement of development of regulations protecting against scientific fraud or misconduct; request for comments. *Federal Register* 53: 36344–47.

——. 1991. Transcript. Advisory Committee on Scientific Integrity. July. Bethesda, MD: C.A.S.E.T. Associates.

——. 1992. Opportunity for a hearing on Office of Research Integrity scientific misconduct findings. *Federal Register* 57: 53125–26.

Rawls, John. 1971. *A theory of justice.* Cambridge: Harvard University Press.

Recer, Paul. 1993. U.S. drops charges on AIDS scientist. *The Boston Globe,* November 13: 3.

Reingold, Nathan. 1991. *Science, American style.* New Brunswick, NJ: Rutgers University Press.

Rettig, Richard. 1977. *Cancer crusade: The story of the National Cancer Act of 1971.* Princeton: Princeton University Press.

Rhoades, Lawrence J. 1989. "Analysis of responses to ANPRM on developing regulations protecting against scientific fraud and misconduct." Office of Scientific Integrity Review. Mimeographed.

Rip, Arie. 1988. Contextual transformations in contemporary science. In *Keeping science straight.* Edited by Andrew Jamison. 59–85. Göteborg: University of Göteborg.

——. 1990. An exercise in forethought: The research system in transition – to what? In *The research system in transition.* NATO ASI Series D, Vol. 57. Edited by Susan E. Cozzens, Peter Healey, Arie Rip, and John Ziman. 387–401. Boston: Kluwer Academic Publishers.

——. 1994. The republic of science in the 1990s. *Higher Education* 28: 3–23.

——. 1995. "The Post-Modern Research System." Paper presented at the conference of the Observatiore des Sciences et Techniques, Science Policy Research Unit, and *Nature*, Paris, September 28–29.

Rogers, Michael. 1977. *Biohazard.* New York: Alfred A. Knopf.

Rosenzweig, Robert M. 1998. *The political university: Policy, politics and presidential leadership in the American research university.* Baltimore: Johns Hopkins University Press.

Roszak, Theodore. 1969. *The making of a counter culture: Reflections on the technocratic society and its youthful opposition.* Garden City, NY: Doubleday.

Rottenberg, Simon. 1968. The warrants for basic research. In *Criteria for scientific development: Public policy and national goals.* Edited by Edward Shils. 134–42. Cambridge: MIT Press.

Sagan, Carl. 1995. *The demon-haunted world: Science as a candle in the dark.* New York: Random House.

Sandel, Michael. 1982. *Liberalism and the limits of justice*. New York: Cambridge University Press.

Sapolsky, Harvey M. 1975. Science policy. In *The handbook of political science*. Edited by Fred Greenstein and Norman Polsby. 79–110. Reading, MA: Addison-Wesley.

——. 1990. *Science and the navy: The history of the Office of Naval Research*. Princeton: Princeton University Press.

Sarasohn, Judy. 1993. *Science on trial: The whistleblower, the accused, and the Nobel laureate*. New York: St. Martin's Press.

Sarewitz, Daniel. 1996. *Frontiers of illusion: Science, technology, and the politics of progress*. Philadelphia: Temple University Press.

Savage, James D. 1999. *Funding science in America: Congress, universities and the politics of the academic pork barrel*. New York: Cambridge University Press.

Schattschneider, E. E. 1960. *The semi-sovereign people*. New York: Holt, Rinehart, and Winston.

Schmaus, Warren. 1983. Fraud and the norms of science. *Science, Technology, and Human Values* 8: 12–22.

Sclove, Richard E. 1989. From alchemy to atomic war: Frederick Soddy's "technology assessment" of atomic energy, 1900–1915. *Science, Technology, and Human Values* 14: 163–94.

Shapley, Deborah, and Rustum Roy. 1985. *Lost at the frontier: U.S. science and technology policy adrift*. Philadelphia: Institute for Scientific Information.

Sherwin, Chalmers W., and Raymond S. Isenson. 1967. Project Hindsight. *Science*, June 23: 1571–77.

Sigma Xi. 1995. *Vannevar Bush II: Science for the 21st Century*. Research Triangle Park, NC: Sigma Xi, The Scientific Research Society.

Slaughter, Sheila, and Larry L. Leslie. 1997. *Academic capitalism: Politics, policies, and the entrepreneurial university*. Baltimore: Johns Hopkins University Press.

Smith, Alice Kimball. 1965. *A peril and a hope: The scientists' movement in America, 1945–47*. Chicago: University of Chicago Press.

Smith, Alice Kimball and Charles Weiner, eds. 1980. *Robert Oppenheimer: Letters and recollections*. Cambridge: Harvard University Press.

Smith, Bruce L. R. 1990. *American science policy since World War II*. Washington, DC: The Brookings Institution.

——. 1994. The United States: The formation and breakdown of the postwar government-science compact. In *Scientists and the state: Domestic structures and the international context*. Edited by Etel Solingen. 33–62. Ann Arbor: The University of Michigan Press.

Smith, Bruce L. R., and Claude Barfield, eds. 1996. *Technology, R&D, and the economy*. Washington, DC: The Brookings Institution and the American Enterprise Institute.

Smith, Bruce L. R., and Joseph J. Karlesky. 1977. *The state of academic science: The universities in the nation's research effort*. New York: Change Magazine Press.

Spencer, Frank. 1990. *Piltdown: A scientific forgery*. New York: Oxford University Press.

Star, Susan Leigh and J. R. Griesemer. 1989. Institutional ecology, "translation" and boundary objects: Amateurs and professionals in Berkeley's Museum of Vertebrate Zoology, 1907–39. *Social Studies of Science* 19: 387–420.

Steelman, John R. 1947a. *Science and public policy*. Vol. 1, *A program for the nation*. The President's Scientific Research Board. Washington, DC: U.S.G.P.O.

——. 1947b. *Science and public policy*. Vol. 2, *The federal research program*. The President's Scientific Research Board. Washington, DC: U.S.G.P.O.

——. 1947c. *Science and public policy*. Vol. 3, *Administration for research*. The President's Scientific Research Board. Washington, DC: U.S.G.P.O.

——. 1947d. *Science and public policy*. Vol. 5, *The nation's medical research*. The President's Scientific Research Board. Vol. 5. Washington, DC: U.S.G.P.O.

Stern, Philip. 1969. *The Oppenheimer case: Security on trial*. With the collaboration of Harold P. Green. New York: Harper & Row.

Stewart, Charles T., Jr. 1987. Technology transfer vs. diffusion: A conceptual clarification. *Journal of Technology Transfer* 12 (1): 71–79.

Stewart, Walter and Ned Feder. 1987. The integrity of the scientific literature. *Nature* 325: 207–14.

Stokes, Donald E. 1997. *Pasteur's quadrant: Basic science and technological innovation*. Washington, DC: The Brookings Institution.

Strickland, Stephen P. 1972. *Politics, science and dread disease: A short history of United States medical research policy*. Cambridge: Harvard University Press.

——. 1989. *The story of the NIH grants program*. New York: New York University Press.

Sultan, Paul E. 1988. Passage on the rope bridge between science and technology: Tales of valor with virtue and vanity with vertigo. *Technological Forecasting and Social Change* 34: 213–30.

Swazey, Judith. 1979. Protecting the "animal of necessity": Limits to inquiry in clinical investigation. In *Limits of scientific inquiry*. Edited by Gerald Holton and Robert S. Morison. 129–46. New York: W. W. Norton.

Swazey, Judith P., Melissa S. Anderson, and Karen Seashore Lewis. 1993. Ethical problems in academic research. *American Scientist* 81: 542–53.

Theoharis, Athan G. 1971. *Seeds of repression: Harry S. Truman and the origins of McCarthyism*. Chicago: Quadrangle Books.

Tocqueville, Alexis de. [1848] 1969. *Democracy in America*. Edited by J. P. Mayer and translated by George Lawrence. Garden City, NY: Anchor Books.

Truman, Harry S. 1965. *Public papers of the President, 1950*. Washington, DC: National Archives and Records Administration.

Tullock, Gordon. 1966. *The organization of inquiry*. Durham: Duke University Press.

Turner, Stephen P. 1977. The Survey in Nineteenth-Century American geology: The evolution of a form of patronage. *Minerva* 25 (3): 282–330.

——. 1990a. Forms of patronage. In *Theories of science in society*. Edited by Susan E. Cozzens and Thomas F. Gieryn. 185–211. Bloomington: Indiana University Press.

——. 1990b. "Science as a polity." Paper presented at the annual meeting of the Social Studies of Science, Minneapolis, MN, November.

——. 1996. Directions for future research. *Knowledge and Policy* 9 (2/3): 99–105.

——. 1997. "Scientists as agents and representatives: A Coasian approach." Paper presented at the conference on The Need for a New Economics of Science, Notre Dame University, South Bend, IN, March 15.

U.S. House. 1976a. Committee on Science and Technology. Subcommittee on Domestic and International Scientific Planning and Analysis. *The ownership of inventions resulting from federally funded R&D*. 94th Cong., 2d sess.

——. 1976b. Committee on Science and Technology. *Background materials on government patent policies*. Vol. 1, *The ownership of inventions resulting from federally funded research and development*. 94th Cong., 2d sess.

——. 1979. Committee on Science and Technology. *Role of the federal laboratories in domestic technology transfer*. 96th Cong., 1st sess.

——. 1980a. *Amending the patent and trademark laws*. 96th Cong., 2d sess. H. Rept. 96–1307, pt. I.

——. 1980b. *Amending the patent and trademark laws*. 96th Cong., 2d sess. H. Rept. 96–1307, pt. II.

——. 1980c. Committee on the Judiciary. Subcommittee on Courts, Civil Liberties, and the Administration of Justice. *Industrial innovation and patent and copyright law amendments*. 96th Cong., 2d sess.

——. 1980d. *Stevenson Technology Innovation Act of 1980*. 96th Cong., 2d sess. H. Rept. 96–1199.

——. 1980e. Committee on Science and Technology. Subcommittee on Science, Research, and Technology. *Summary of House and Senate hearings on government-university-industry relations*. 96th Cong., 2d sess.

——. 1980f. *Toward the endless frontier: History of the Committee on Science and Technology, 1959–1979*. 96th Cong., 2d sess.

——. 1981. Committee on Science and Technology. Subcommittee on Investigations and Oversight. *Fraud in biomedical research*. 97th Cong., 1st sess.

——. 1984. Committee on Energy and Commerce. Subcommittee on Oversight and Investigations. *Air quality standards*. 98th Cong., 2nd sess.

——. 1985a. Committee on Science and Technology. Task Force on Science Policy. *Goals and objectives of national science policy*. 99th Cong., 1st sess.

——. 1985b. Committee on Science and Technology. Subcommittee on Science, Research, and Technology. *Technology transfer*. 99th Cong., 1st sess.

——. 1986a. *Federal Technology Transfer Act of 1986*. 99th Cong., 2d sess. H. Conf. Rept. 99–953.

——. 1986b. Committee on Science and Technology. Task Force on Science Policy. *A history of science policy in the United States, 1940–1985*. Background Report No. 1. 99th Cong., 2d sess.

——. 1986c. Committee on Science and Technology. Task Force on Science Policy. *Research and publications practices.* 99th Cong., 2d sess.

——. 1988a. Committee on Government Operations. Subcommitee on Human Resources and Intergovernmental Relations. *Federal response to misconduct in science: Are conflicts of interest hazardous to our health?* 100th Cong., 2d sess.

——. 1988b. Committee on Energy and Commerce. Subcommittee on Oversight and Investigations. *Fraud in NIH grant programs.* 100th Cong., 2d sess.

——. 1989. Committee on Energy and Commerce. Subcommittee on Oversight and Investigations. *Scientific fraud.* 101st Cong., 1st sess.

——. 1991. Committee on Energy and Commerce. Subcommittee on Oversight and Investigations. *Apparent financial wrongdoing by an official in the Laboratory of Tumor Cell Biology of the National Institutes of Health.* 102d Cong., 1st sess.

U.S. Senate. 1978a. Committee on the Judiciary. *The University and Small Business Patent Procedures Act.* 96th Cong., 1st sess.

——. 1978b. Select Committee on Small Business. Subcommittee on Monopoly and Anticompetitive Activities. *Government patent policies: Institutional patent agreements.* 95th Cong., 2d sess.

——. 1979a. Committee on the Judiciary. *University and Small Business Patent Procedures Act.* 96th Cong., 1st sess.

——. 1979b. Committee on Commerce, Science, and Transportation. Subcommittee on Science, Technology, and Space. *National Technology Innovation Act.* 96th Cong., 1st sess.

——. 1979c. Committee on Commerce, Science, and Transportation; Committee on Small Business; House Committee on Science and Technology; and Committee on Small Business. *Industrial innovation, part 1.* 96th Cong., 1st sess.

——. [1886] 1980. *Testimony before the Joint Commission to Consider the Present Organizations of the Signal Service, Geological Survey, Coast and Geodetic Survey and the Hydrographic Office of the Navy Department.* Edited by I. Bernard Cohen. 49th Cong., 1st sess. S. Misc. Doc. 82. New York: Arno.

——. 1980. Committee on Commerce, Science, and Transportation and the Committee on the Judiciary. *Patent policy, part 2.* 96th Cong., 2d sess.

——. 1981. Committee on Labor and Human Resources. *National Cancer Institute contracting and procurement procedures, 1981.* 97th Cong., 1st sess.

——. 1984. *Amending Title 35 of the U.S. Code for the purpose of creating a uniform policy and procedure concerning patent rights in inventions developed with federal assistance.* 98th Cong., 2d sess. S. Rept. 98–662.

——. 1985. Committee on Commerce, Science, and Transportation. Subcommittee on Science, Technology, and Space. *New technologies on economic competitiveness.* 99th Cong., 1st sess.

——. 1986. *Federal Technology Transfer Act of 1986.* 99th Cong., 2d sess. S. Rept. 99–283.

van der Meulen, Barend. 1998. Science policies as principal-agent games: Institutionalization and path dependency in the relation between government and science. *Research Policy* 27 (4): 397–414.

Vavakova, Blanka. 1998. The new social contract between governments, universities and society: Has the old one failed? *Minerva* 36: 209–28.

Wallsten, Scott. 1998. Small Business Innovation Research Act. In *Investing in innovation: Creating a research and innovation policy that works.* Edited by Lewis M. Branscomb and James Keller. 194–220. Cambridge: MIT Press.

Walker, Robert S. 1995. Research and development and the new Congressional leadership. In *AAAS Science and Technology Policy Yearbook, 1995.* Edited by Albert H. Teich, Stephen D. Nelson, and Celia McEnaney. Washington, DC: American Association for the Advancement of Science.

——. 1997. The quest for knowledge versus the quest for votes. *IEEE Technology and Society Magazine* 16 (1): 4–7.

Wang, Jessica. 1992. Science, security, and the Cold War. *Isis* 83: 238–69.

Weatherford, J. McIver. 1985. *Tribes on the Hill.* New York: Bergin and Garvey.

Weber, Max. 1946. Bureaucracy. In *From Max Weber: Essays in sociology.* Edited by H. Gerth and C. Wright Mills. 196–266. New York: Oxford University Press.

Weimer, David L., ed. 1995. *Institutional design.* Boston: Kluwer Academic Publishers.

Weiner, Charles. 1970. Physics in the Great Depression. *Physics Today*, October, 31–37.

——. 1994. Anticipating the consequences of genetic engineering: Past, present and future. In *Are genes us? The social consequences of the new genetics.* Edited by Carl Cranor. 31–51. New Brunswick: Rutgers University Press.

Weiner, J. S. 1955. *The Piltdown forgery.* New York: Oxford University Press.

Weinstein, Deena. 1979. Fraud in science. *Social Science Quarterly* 59: 639–52.

Wells, H. G. 1933. *The shape of things to come.* New York: Macmillan.

Wheeler, David L. 1991. NIH office that investigates scientists' misconduct is target of widespread charges of incompetence. *The Chronicle of Higher Education*, May 15: A5.

Wildavsky, Aaron. 1984. *The politics of the budgetary process.* 4th ed. Boston: Little, Brown and Company.

Wilson, John T. 1983. *Academic science, higher education, and the federal government.* Chicago: University of Chicago Press.

Winner, Langdon. 1977. *Autonomous technology: Technics-out-of-control as a theme in political thought.* Cambridge: MIT Press.

Wise, George. 1986. "Science and technology." In *Historical perspectives on American science: Perspectives and prospects.* Edited by Sally Gregory Kohlstedt and Margaret W. Rossiter. 229–46. Baltimore: Johns Hopkins University Press.

Wolin, Sheldon S. 1989. *The presence of the past: Essays on the state and the Constitution.* Baltimore: Johns Hopkins University Press.

Wooldridge, Dean E. 1965. *Biomedical science and its administration: A study of the National Institutes of Health*. A Report to the President. Washington, DC: The White House.

Woolf, Patricia. 1981. Fraud in science: how much, how serious? *The Hastings Center Report*, October: 9–14.

——. 1988. Deception in scientific research. *Jurimetrics Journal* 29 (Fall): 67–95.

Wright, Susan. 1993. The social warp of science: Writing the history of genetic engineering policy. *Science, Technology, and Human Values* 18: 79–101.

Zachary, G. Pascal. 1997. *Endless frontier: Vannevar Bush, engineer of the American century*. New York: The Free Press.

Zuckerman, Harriet. 1977. Deviant behavior and social control in science. In *Deviance and social change*. Edited by Edward Sagarin. 87–138. Beverly Hills: Sage.

——. 1984. Norms and deviant behavior in science. *Science, Technology, and Human Values* 9: 7–13.

Index